BARRY LONG knew he was dying. He set about writing down his last words on the main themes of his spiritual teaching. He wanted to leave behind a full account of what he considered to be his original contribution to the evolving consciousness on Earth.

No one before him had been able to strip away spiritual traditions to reveal the universal truth with such boldness and practicality; with such contemporary relevance. No other teachers of his generation were quite so willing to take on the unhappiness of the human condition by dealing with personal intimate questions about relationships, and particularly sexual relations – all without losing sight of the divine. No other enlightened teacher or master had seen into the cosmic scheme of things and at the same time been able to bring universal principles down to earth with such power and immediacy.

Between the covers of this book you will find all he wanted us to hear about the human condition, the errors we make in ignorance of the truth of life; about love and its transcendent power to change us; about the dismantling of the selfish body of unhappiness we carry around with us; about the cosmic scheme of all our lives, the purpose of death, the purpose of love, the purpose of life itself.

Also by Barry Long

Meditation: A Foundation Course

Knowing Yourself

Wisdom and Where To Find It

The Origins of Man and the Universe

Making Love

Only Fear Dies

Stillness is the Way

To Woman In Love

To Man In Truth

Raising Children in Love, Justice and Truth

The Way In

Where the Spirit Speaks To Its Own

A Prayer for Life

My Life of Love and Truth

Audio Books

Start Meditating Now

A Journey in Consciousness

Seeing Through Death

Making Love

How to Live Joyously

BARRY LONG

FROM HERE TO
Reality

My Spiritual Teaching

BARRY LONG BOOKS

Published in 2015 by
BARRY LONG BOOKS
BCM Box 876, London WC1N 3XX, England
6230 Wiltshire Blvd – Suite 251, Los Angeles, Ca 90048, USA

'Barry Long Books' is the publishing imprint of
The Barry Long Foundation International

www.barrylongbooks.com
www.barrylong.org

Paperback: ISBN 978-1-899-324-31-6
Ebook: ISBN 978-1-899324-32-3

Cataloguing-In-Publication Data
A catalogue record for this book is available from
The British Library.

Front cover photo © Rita Newman / www.newman.at
Other photos: The Barry Long Foundation International
Cover design: Ginny van Rensen

Digitally printed in the UK, USA and Australia

CONTENTS

Going Deeper

The Bigger Picture

FROM HERE TO REALITY

Author's Note

This book consists of one hundred and eight separate essays on the spiritual life. Beginning with everyday relationships, it takes the reader into the bigger picture of love, life, death, God and recurrence, and culminates in the author's perception of reality. In an attempt to make each item complete in its own context within the overall theme, some necessary repetition or recapping occurs. After an initial reading, this will enable the reader to keep 'dipping into' the text over time and discovering new insights without getting lost. The purpose of the book is to awaken the dormant and powerfully revealing self-knowledge that is in everybody underneath the concerns of the surface mind and emotions.

FROM HERE TO REALITY

Preface

What I've written in this book is from my self-knowledge, from my realisations of what I call God, love, life or truth, as well as from my experience of having lived in the world for nearly eighty years. I don't expect what I say or write to agree with anyone else's knowledge, opinions or beliefs. If anyone disagrees that's okay; I've nothing to prove that I know of. The reader will either enjoy the book, learn from it, find in it affirmations of their own knowledge – or discard it. To me negative reactions are irrelevant but to the reader they are important indications of new areas of self-knowledge yet to be addressed. Nevertheless, it's always pleasing to know someone has enjoyed and gained from what is offered. I'm frequently asked where my knowledge and seeming authority originates. As I've said, the source of all real knowledge is God, the indescribable reality. But there was an overt point in my early mystical life where a divine authority was apparently bestowed on me, although I didn't realise the full significance at the time. It happened in broad daylight in a vision. The Lord or God spoke to me revealing the fundamental truth of everybody's existence. An account of the vision is in the text. I don't ask anyone to believe this. All I can suggest is that you read to the end of the book and form your own conclusion as to whether or not I have the knowledge, the gnosis, to write such a work.

Barry Long, 2003

Relationships

FROM HERE TO REALITY

1

The Trials of Love

To be in relationship with anyone or any thing means you are dependent on that object. Dependence means you are attached to the person or thing. And attachment means that when the person dies or leaves you, or when you lose or are losing the object, you will know emotional pain or discomfort.

The longer the relationship, the deeper the attachment, and the longer it takes to heal the disturbance.

There is a common exception. If you are unhappy living with a person in an intimate relationship and you leave them with a sense of relief, the other will know pain and suffer. Or the children will. Someone has to suffer where there has been attachment.

And it is most likely you will still suffer in the aftermath of such a break-up. You may have to face being without your children, or legal proceedings, or financial loss. Or a multitude of other possible causes of aggravation and frustration, or simply the harassment of your own feelings of guilt, anger, self-doubt or self-justification. Suffering somewhere or other follows attachment.

If you look at your life you will see that all this is true. You can't escape where you've been attached. Nobody escapes until things are consciously set right. It may appear that you've escaped. But the potential for pain from things left undone will remain inside you and manifest to confront and worry you in some other area of your life and relationship.

When the whole life is set right, there's no more emotional pain, no more suffering. That's the way of things in the bigger picture.

To be reading this book you have to have suffered from attachment. And from the experience of your living life you have to have distilled sufficient self-knowledge – sufficient maturity – to follow what I'm saying in your own experience.

The only maturity is self-knowledge.

This section and much of the book is a guide in how not to get attached to people, objects or situations – without avoidance. Also how to address situations where there has been attachment, and most important, to demonstrate the power of detached intelligence – real love – that you have inside you which makes detachment possible.

Parents

Honesty based on giving and free of intent to get, induces an openness and willingness to listen.

2

Love is Giving Now

With parents whom you love and who love you it is important, while they are alive, to give back something that is usually over-looked. This involves what I call having an intelligent conversation with them. An intelligent conversation is one in which you give. If you don't speak to your loving parents like I'm going to describe, when they die you'll feel you haven't really communicated the love you have for them.

Many adults tell their parents that they love them. They do things for them. They send cards or presents on birthdays or anniversaries. They pop in or phone regularly and have a chat. But none of that is as meaningful as an intelligent conversation.

Love begins with giving. Not giving things, as pleasing as that can be, but giving of yourself. In this matter of parents, I am of course talking about your peace of mind after they are dead. This may not seem so important now, but it will be. So I suggest you have an intelligent conversation with your loving parents as soon as possible.

Sit them down and tell them that you love them. Don't emo-tionalise. If you do tears will come to your eyes. Your parents will then get teary and the atmosphere will lose its crispness. Speak as straight as you can (without emotion) and keep going. Tell them you have something to say that's very important to you. Ask them to please hear you out without interrupting. This should not be difficult if they love you.

Now tell them how grateful you are for all they have done for you throughout your life.

Sincerity

You must be sincere. If you haven't a real perception of your parents' sacrifices on your behalf, I suggest you review your childhood, your teenage and early adult years. I'm asking you to be honest. You are not looking to recall your mum or dad's negative reactions in the past. You are looking only to see the good they did for you.

Negatives are inevitable in childish experience where discipline and guidance are necessary. If you reappraise in that area you'll open up a can of worms. This will lead to other negatives in your life not related to your parents. You'll have started to open up your emotional past which has no good in it whatever.

It's an uncommon wisdom that when you review the good others have done for you, and really appreciate those actions, you are not in the past. Any perception of the good not associated with excitement or winning, is simply a response of gratitude within – and that is in the present.

3
Mutual Love But...

There are many different problematical situations involving parents. Let us begin with one of the easiest, where there is mutual love between you but they try to tell you how to live your life. Or perhaps they're critical of how you are living your life.

At an appropriate time sit them down with you and say you have something important to tell them. Would they please hear you through without interrupting? It's crucial not to get into a discussion either during or after. You're the one making the statement. Any responses or discussion will break down the communication you're aiming for.

Before mentioning any problem, it's most important to acknowledge the sacrifices made by your parents in bringing you up, and the things they've done for you since. But you must mean what you say. When you're thanking someone and just use words without the genuine ethos behind them, you create similar superficial words of response in the other person. Nothing meaningful is then achieved – only an exchange of words.

Begin by telling your parents how much you appreciate all they've done for you in your life; how they looked after you as a child when you were sick; how they sat up with you at night when they themselves were tired and had to go to work next day; how they got up in the early hours and drove you down to the hospital or to the all-night pharmacy, and all the other little things they did for you which you can't even remember but have the sense of. In other words, how they cared for you, loved you and looked after you.

No Blaming

You can then mention the problem. But in doing so it's essential that you don't accuse or blame your parents. You are speaking to them for your own good, for your own peace of mind. If you accuse or blame you introduce emotion into the situation. This will create a defensive attitude and probably protests. Mum and Dad will close up and you might as well go home.

Also you are not there to teach them or change them. You must be simple, straightforward and keep to the point. You are making your statement for you, not for them. You are thanking them first because that's the honest thing to do. Such honesty based on giving and free of intent to get, induces an openness and willingness to listen in the other party.

Say to your parents that because you love them you are troubled when they persist in criticising what you are doing with your life. This makes it difficult for you to enjoy coming to see them. It is your life and you can't have anyone, even them, trying to tell you how you should live your life, or what you should or should not be doing. You welcome their advice. But it must be given without insistence or expectation.

Say that you respect them and their experience and that you know they are only trying to help you, perhaps in order to prevent you making the same mistakes as they did. But that was their life and like everyone they had to live it as they did. And so must you.

What you're speaking of is your precious life, the only one you'll ever have. No one can live it for you or try to. Neither can they try to live their life through you. Tell your parents again that you love them and thank them for hearing you through. It is best then to leave as soon as you can, saying you'll be in touch or back in a couple of days.

Getting the Idea

If when you speak with your parents again they start criticising your lifestyle, remind them of what you said. If they make excuses and try to begin a discussion you'll have to say, 'I have to leave now. You've not heard me. I'll be in touch later and try again because I love you.'

You must not try to follow verbatim what I've written. Don't memorise or conceptualise it. Get the idea. Once you've got the idea the right words come.

4

Disapproval of Your Spiritual Life

A tricky parental situation can be when you are moved to tell your parents that you're practising a spiritual teaching. Or perhaps they already know and don't approve, making their disapproval clear each time you're with them. You feel torn between love, or respect, for your parents and your knowledge of the rightness of the teaching.

Let's deal with these two situations together so that you get the general idea of how I suggest you proceed in either case. Really, where spiritual teachings and parents are concerned, there's likely to be a normal reaction of suspicion.

You'll notice that earlier I didn't say your belief in the teaching. Believing in a teaching is an open invitation to be disappointed or disillusioned. In essence a spiritual teaching has to be practical; practical means universally demonstrable in anyone's own experience. Having faith is understandable. But faith in a teaching is not going to convince your parents.

Mum and Dad probably have faith in something else anyway, even if it's only faith in their own opinions or prejudices. To counter that, you have to be able to have an intelligent conversation with them. And that means what you say has to make sense.

So let's begin.

Sit down with your parents at an appropriate time and say you want to tell them what you're doing with your life. You're moved to do this because you love them or respect them. Ask them to hear you through without interrupting, if that's possible.

Say you've realised that offspring seldom confide to their parents what they are really doing with their life. You've seen that this creates a gap – probably what's called the generation gap at all ages. You've been remiss in this way in the past. But now you want to correct that by telling them what you are doing that is pivotal to you.

Start by saying that you are endeavouring to be a better person by getting rid of the negativity in yourself. By that you mean anger, impatience, resentment and that sort of thing. Say that it's a long process and that you frequently fail. But you've got the idea now of how to practise it and you sense that in a small way you're having some success.

At this stage you may be asked a sensible question such as, 'How do you do this?' Your reply should be simple and to the point: As I've said it's a process, but the short answer is by practising getting your intelligence there before the emotional reaction. I can't explain any more just now. But I'd be pleased to give you a book or an audio recording if you're interested.'

Of course, if the parents are receptive, you may be able to explain more. But do know that the next time you see them it's possible they won't be so receptive. After hearing something important like this, parents are sure to think about it and this may create a doubt or two. This applies to most people when they're informed of something new relating to a personal interest.

No Discussion

Tell your parents that you're not trying to teach or change them. You are speaking just for yourself. And you're only working on yourself because you've seen that while these negative emotions are in you they tend to influence and control your life, making you and others around you unhappy.

It's extremely important not to get into a discussion. Not every parent is going to ask a sensible question. You're more likely to be interrupted by one or the other giving their opinion on these matters, or pooh-poohing the whole thing.

In that case it's best to remind them that you only wanted to tell them what you are doing with your life. You didn't come for their approval or disapproval; you simply came in love to inform them. Then leave amicably as soon as you can.

Another question could be, 'Where did you get these ideas?' This is indeed a contentious area. Normal parents tend to be suspicious of spiritual teachers or gurus. Such prejudice is understandable given the frightening and sometimes horrendous media reports of the activities of some so-called spiritual movements and the effects on their adherents. Even so, all prejudice is a belief based on second-hand knowledge.

Answer honestly that the idea comes from a spiritual teacher you've discovered. And if the teacher is BL, add that the teacher says that if what he says makes sense to you, the living of that is what's important, not him.

To communicate with your parents without provoking unnecessary resistance you must be able to give a down-to-earth description of the value of the teaching you're practising. It has to be a value that any normal person can accept. To say that you are endeavouring to be a better human being by ridding yourself of anger, resentment and impatience is something an ordinary sensible person would tend to appreciate or even applaud.

Whatever teaching you are following, it's probably not going to be helpful to say the teaching is about finding God, the Absolute, or becoming enlightened. These are general terms. Finding God is easily dismissed by someone who doesn't have a sense of that state.

Belief

If your parents are believers or members of an established religion they will believe that that's the only way to God. Also enlightenment means nothing to an ordinary person. It's a word coined by the unenlightened and you'll have a very rough ride trying to define it in acceptable terms outside its intellectual meaning.

The word 'belief' has to be kept out of what you say. To believe in anything means you don't really know the thing you profess to believe in. If you did, you would say I know, not I believe.

Parents are likely to believe in many things as most people do. One belief is likely to be that any spiritual teaching (other than the one they believe in) is a sham, a rip-off or a cult. And they don't want to see their offspring misled, manipulated or brain-washed by some shonky organisation or so-called guru.

All of this means that in speaking to your parents you have to avoid any mention of what you believe or believe in. In other words you have to know what you're talking about. When you speak from your own experience, namely your own knowledge without faith or belief, people tend to listen intelligently.

If you start mentioning faith or belief you'll stir up a beehive of opposition or hostility. Whatever you have faith in or believe in, someone else will have a different faith or belief. For most people the sensible fact is the acceptable fact.

5

The Deeply Emotional Parent

The deeply emotional parent doesn't want to hear anything from you that doesn't accord with their own constantly shifting emotions. This sort of parent is either bad-tempered, irritable, touchy or moody, or a combination of the four, which unfortunately is not an uncommon family phenomenon.

Let's say your mother or father can't listen without getting angry. They emotionalise or personalise whatever you say. For years you've learned to tread lightly around the parent and not to say anything that might upset them. Their emotional reflexes are just too much to deal with. You can't communicate anything that's real to you. So you've compromised, surrendered to this familial tyranny.

Perhaps you thought you surrendered out of love for the parent. Perhaps it was love at first – but now, is it love or fear? Perhaps now you don't see the situation quite as you used to and are wondering what you can do to regain a sense of rightness, or your own integrity, which seems to be missing here.

To be free of fear the cause of fear has to be faced. This requires no fear of losing. Most of humanity lives in fear and true spirituality is facing up to it and being rid of it wherever it appears in your life.

Be Direct

In facing fear you can't be fearful. You can't be emotional because emotion is fear. You have to face the parent by speaking straight which means not speaking through the medium of your emotions. Emotion is less likely to rise in you if you know what you are doing, why you are doing it and are prepared to pay the price for your freedom.

The next time your parent assails you emotionally say, 'Stop. I will not put up with this any more. Keep your emotional poison to yourself. If you ever again talk to me like this I will not come and see you and I will not even speak to you.'

The last words may evoke an emotionally defiant interruption, something like: 'I don't care. Get out, etc.'

Prepare to leave. As you are going, say to your parent: 'It's because I love you that I've told you this. I'll phone in a few days to see if you've heard me and can speak to me normally.'

If the parent attacks you when you phone again I suggest you go quiet at your end as long as it takes for the other to stop talking. Then say, 'Because I love you I'll phone again in a few days.'

You'll have to be prepared for your parent to hang up on you and not to speak to you again. That's the price you have to pay for having compromised in the past. By remaining strong and not giving in to the pressure of your sentimental attachment, one of you is going to undergo a fundamental change, probably you.

In love there's no fear or compromise with yourself. Love is straight, honest and freeing. Sentimental love is emotional, dishonest and the cause of future pain.

6

The Apoplectic Parent

Sometimes a deeply emotional parent can get so apoplectic when upset that family members are afraid he (or she) will have a heart attack. So they avoid telling him anything they know he doesn't want to hear.

This is understandable. When he later dies everybody will feel comfortable in that nothing they said could possibly have caused his death. But is such consideration right? Is it sort of playing God in reverse?

Say your deeply emotional father is a rational or scientific man, perhaps an atheist, who doesn't believe in anything spiritual. You are living a spiritual teaching and out of love would like to tell him what you're doing with your life. You know that such information will make him angry and emotional. And everyone says his emotional reactions are so violent that if you tell him you might kill him.

Suppose out of consideration for what you fear might happen, you don't tell him. Say he later dies of natural causes. How will you feel that you never told him the truth as you were moved to do?

Did your consideration do him any good? It certainly would have been good for the family members who never told him the truth as far as they were concerned and therefore never needed to feel guilty about upsetting him. But isn't that selfish – to get comfort out of withholding the truth from someone?

And what about the natural guilt that gathers in time of not having told the truth to the parent you loved so much? Will this just go away? Or will it lie somewhere inside to trouble you intermittently and disturb your peace of mind?

The beloved parent of course died with his deep emotion intact. Did he live longer because no one told him the truth? Or was a disservice done to him by denying him the chance to face his emotion and perhaps see through it with the intelligence that comes from age and being close to death?

Doctors seldom tell terminally ill patients and their family members the truth. They don't want to have to deal with the emotional reactions it invariably causes. So they treat the patient and loved ones with a mixture of their potions and hope. Then everybody is reasonably happy until it's obvious the patient is dying. Sympathy instead of hope is then handed around on the basis that everyone has done their best. But have they? Or did they all just opt out of reality by avoiding the truth?

If you haven't got the message from what I've written so far, I can't advise you on what to do. It comes down to what's important, or putting first thing first. And only you can decide what that is. All fear is based on assumptions; only in the doing do we discover the fact.

And incidentally, a man who says he's a rational man is not a logical man.

7

The Parent Who Has Died

There is no death. Whether you believe this, deny it, or hope that it's true, is irrelevant. There is no death. Certainly the body dies. But love does not die. If you really love someone who has died that love is the means of communication.

Many people love emotionally. But emotional love doesn't have the power to cross the void of death. People who have lost a loved one usually try to reach them by thinking and imagining. Mostly, such attempts fail, although there can be the psychic appearance of a dead person, or the sense of their presence without form.

Psychic events, although convincing at the time, gradually lose their immediacy. They can become just a memory or even be dismissed as imagination. Little lasting knowledge as a reality of life comes out of the experience.

Love

Love is the only real means of communication across the void. Suppose your mother or father died recently, or many years ago. And that you are troubled because you never really got your relationship right with them; or didn't get around to telling them how much you loved them.

Unlike the mental and emotional world we live in, love is not bound by time or distance. Your parent could have died fifty years ago and today you can start getting everything right with them inside yourself, provided you love them.

Here is what you do. If you truly love, that love is within your body now. As you relate to the love an image of the person may appear, but not necessarily. The love is instantaneous. It has always been there beneath all your thoughts and emotions. That's the mystery of love. It's always there now. And the amazing thing is that the deceased person's love of you will be there too, immediately.

You may reason that your mother or father didn't love you. You've had this thought because they didn't show much love for you while alive; or perhaps they abused you and yet you still love them. Or you were too young when they died. Or they walked out when you were a child and you never saw them again.

None of that is relevant in the void beyond. Love can connect with anyone that you love. It's like calling them up. But where love is involved there is no information in it, no voices, no apparitions, nothing to remember – just the immediate knowledge that communication has occurred.

To register the communication there has to be an acute sensitivity within. You have to have put aside the normal expectations of getting a response, getting something tangible, or substantive; the sort of proof the scientific mind requires. This will not happen.

You don't have to be concerned about being sensitive enough. True love is the sensitivity. And it works because your intention is not to get, but to love, to give; to love across the void to the other.

Sit quietly and alone. Be still. Connect with your love of the one who has died. Say within, 'I love you. Nothing else is important, only that I love you. I wanted you to know. I love you.'

The one that you love in the void beyond is now love. All that they were as a person was left behind. 'Their' greatest joy is for you to know that they love you and always have. This, the loving dead are constantly endeavouring to communicate. But really it can't be done from there. It requires our love here to penetrate the void and make the connection.

8

Sexual Abuse by a Family Member

Recently a woman wrote to me about sexual abuse in the family. A sensitive highly-educated professional in her mid-thirties, she longed for the fulfilment of a long-term intimate relationship. However she felt scarred and afraid. Her grandfather who'd introduced her to many good things as a child had also sexually abused her.

She'd blocked out most of the memories but was disgusted by what she did recall. Physically she had closed up and a series of health issues had led her to have a gynaecological examination, which had proved difficult. She'd tried therapy and had tried to forgive her grandfather, to little avail. She felt there was still something inside her that needed to be worked on and asked for help.

My reply: Therapists cannot help you. You have to do it yourself. First, you have to discover (as I know from your letter) that you loved your grandfather – and still do. Your love of him is buried under your very learned mind and emotions of resentment, abuse and disgust.

None of your emotions are true; nor are your thoughts. They just keep you tight and unloving. You long for love but you hold on to your ignorance of love. How could you possibly fulfil an intimate loving relationship while clinging to what is not love within you?

I suggest you be alone, quiet and still. Do you love your grandfather? The habitual mind and emotions will react and try to obscure the truth. You must practise this as long as it takes for you to see the truth and connect with the love. Your mind cannot connect; nor can your emotional self. You connect with Being, your being of love which you really are. This is in the inner stillness.

Love is Forever

Love is forever. Bodies die, are burned or buried and never seen again. And with them dies all the selfishness, ignorance and inevitable offensive events (to someone or to many) the body and its ignorance perpetrated, or was involved in. What endures and goes 'on' is the love.

The love in your grandfather is the only reality. And I can tell you that he really loved you, loves you, and that that love is in your body now. But your morally conditioned intellectual person can't see that and doesn't want to. It prefers to keep your body (which is made for love) tight and impenetrable because you permit this by holding on to the past and not letting go.

So what's your answer? Do you love him? What's the truth? And no but, but, buts... See that you love him and the job's half done. There are no buts in love. 'I just love you.'

The other half of the task is for you to know the truth of existence. But you'll only be able to follow me if you've found, without qualification, the love within you; in this case, the love of your grandfather.

The Force of Sex

Sex (the drive for power over others and not my self) impels existence. It is not personal; it's a psychic force that drives every body, particularly man, until real love is discovered and lived.

Sex without real love is ignorance. And if you look at your own life and that of everyone around you (despite appearances) you'll get the point. Everyone is sexually unhappy, frustrated or stoically (tightly) holding on and making the best of things which, until love is real-ised, is the worst of things.

Your grandfather was driven by a force greater than himself. That is not to excuse those events. It is simply to explain them in truth. Are you so pure? Have you not done to someone, or to others, what you now know you did not really want to do?

Do you persist in blaming your grandfather but not yourself for your transgressions? Are you now saying 'but, but, but...', being holier than him? Or are you glimpsing the vast truth of life behind the compulsion of existence?

Your grandfather lives, is, in the love you have inside for him. That love, that reality, is him. And it wants you to know, through me, until you realise it for yourself, that he loves you – and that's all he wants you to know: 'I love you.'

Where there is love there is no death and no need, even of forgiveness. 'I love you Grandad.' Isn't that beautiful? He is inside you now in love, your love and his.

Such love will free you, heal you or cure you.

And in all this I am not speaking of survival. I speak only of the intelligence of love which is forever.

FROM HERE TO REALITY

Children

True love is carried on true words.

9

The Newborn Child

As there is life or love beyond the death of the body, so there is life or love before the conception of the body. This 'before' and 'beyond' is a single vast state of Consciousness, an indescribably profound and unlimited intelligence.

Our physical existence of seventy or a hundred years is like a small dark tunnel within the vastness, which everything born must pass through. Sometimes in near-death experiences a brilliant light is seen or intuited to be at the end of the tunnel. This is the consciousness beyond death. That same light is at the mouth of the tunnel before conception.

The newborn child is far closer to the beginning than we are, far more recently of its radiance. And just as love is the only means of communication beyond the tunnel, so love is the key to communicating with the newborn.

The newborn can't speak any more than the loving dead can. And the ordinary feeling of love is not going to communicate to the reality of the child, any more than it can reach across the void to the beloved dead.

Immediately after being born the child is usually held in the warmth of someone's arms; ideally in the embrace of the mother and on her breast. The close-held warmth of another's physical body is extremely important. It contributes to the natural sense of wellbeing in the baby.

With regular physical contact and cuddling by both parents (if possible), and later physical games together, the child will have a sounder psychological foundation for the growing-up process and the adult life. A basic subconscious sense of love will be there. This will flower in some way in later years, given that many other influences, including the negative, will have their effect.

What is not commonly known, and therefore denied the newborn, is the next most important communication. This is to speak to the baby, telling it what has happened to it in being born.

It should not be forgotten that before leaving the womb the child was in an all-embracing, fully-supportive environment: no need to breathe, eat, drink or be concerned with heat or cold. Now, suddenly, it is plunged into a strange and relatively hostile environment.

True Love Speaks

The common stance is that the baby is not yet rationally intelligent enough (meaning experienced) to understand words. This may be true. Nonetheless, the mother invariably speaks to the baby of her love. She knows instinctually that even though the child may not understand what she's saying, something precious is being communicated. This is true because true love is carried on true words like electricity is carried on the agency of a wire.

If the parent loves the baby and has a degree of awareness beyond the commonplace, he or she will get the idea of what I'm saying and be able to communicate to the baby a very special message in their own words. Something like this:

'You have left the world where everything is one and entered a world where everything is separate. A separate physical body has been made for you so that you can exist here. It came out of (me) your mother, and in that sense you are part of me. I love you and will look after you as best I can in this strange world. Your body will grow and as it does you will grow in experience or learning of this world. Experience will help you to cope with it.

'Living here is not easy. But deep within every body here is the world of life and consciousness that you so recently left. But it soon gets covered over by experience, and forgotten. Nothing here is permanent. Your grown physical body will one day die and the love that you are will wake up again in that wondrous place of life and consciousness.'

That is only a suggestion, a start. It's important to speak to the baby regularly in words you would use in speaking to another intelligent adult. You'll find you have many things to say. Once you start speaking like this the right words and subject will come to you. But always tell the infant of your love. And as you do, hold him or her firmly to your body.

Here's another suggestion:

'There is much beauty here in this physical world. It is the beauty that appears when the incomparable beauteous oneness of where you come from is split into fragments.

'I will show you an example when we see a rainbow in the sky. The rainbow consists of several beautiful colours. Each colour forms a separate bow within the rainbow which stretches in a great arc above the ground. The bow is caused by raindrops which I will also point out to you and let you feel on your little hands and face. The light of the sun which shines here has no colour but the raindrops split the light and the beauty of the rainbow is the result.

'You are a drop of light and colour from God which is what we call the place you came from.

'All the beauty here, as I've said, is only a partial reflection of the real beauty in that place. And just as the raindrops split the light and make the beautiful rainbow, so you have been provided with a brain that splits the light of the other into all the separate objects that make up this world.'

Another suggestion:

'Your body is really a spacesuit. Your spacesuit creates the space which allows every object to be separate from you. The spacesuit body is created by the genius of almighty God which is the consciousness out of which you came.

'People here have little or no appreciation that their body is a spacesuit essential for them to exist here. The only spacesuit they know of is one they've invented to travel deeper into the space of this world. They can't exist in that space without putting on the other spacesuit.

'I will show you all this as you grow up and tell you more and more about the wonders of your God-made spacesuit. Wonder here in this world is quickly forgotten.'

10
The Two-Year-Old

At around age two the child usually is able to speak and understand words. This makes worldly communication easier. But for some time the parent will have noticed a rebellious energy starting to arise in the child. When the energy is there it stiffens the young body, makes the face go red, destroys the usual sweetness of the looks and produces defiant behaviour.

It is not commonly appreciated that the energy is psychic; that it is not natural in the child's body and is a sort of minor possession. Everybody as a child is subject to this, more or less. And it is extremely difficult at the time for the parent to know what to do to cope; and even more difficult to understand what has happened.

The possession is so common that it's accepted as being normal with the result no real attempt is made to understand it – where it comes from and why. Understanding at least brings a degree of freedom from any difficult situation.

So let us endeavour to understand what is happening here and why. We might just be able to make a difference in the child's future.

The Negative Bridge

The psychic invasion of the vulnerable child establishes a bridge for the negative energies in the psyche to cross into the brain, especially in the later years. The energies are responsible for all the negative emotional reactions that plague humanity such as anger, resentment, moodiness, jealousy, fear and self-doubt.

By speaking to the child from when it is born, a parent is using consciousness. Psychic negatives are unconscious and the presence of consciousness (real love) in the parent tends to weaken the bridge.

This doesn't mean that the child will be free of psychic reactions. But it does mean that as the child is growing up the tendency of the negatives to sometimes dominate the behaviour will be reduced. There will be more likelihood of being able to communicate and shorten the time of the temporary possession. (A parent who does not have the time to love the infant child enough will be unable to make the rare communication I've spoken of; also the parent will find communication more difficult in the later years.)

The driving force in the modern world is intellectual materialism and every child is in danger of losing touch with its body and living in a mental world. Modern technology with its computers and digital games is part of that drive. So are the scientific stories of the Big Bang and the rest of speculative cosmology which have no reference to love or truth, or how to live a more fulfilling and conscious life.

The advance of intellectual materialism as progress in our global community can't be stopped. But something can be done in, and by, the individual who is willing and able to listen consciously. Consciousness is simply having the continuous knowledge of something greater than can ever be explained or described.

The two-year-old has to be kept close to a hands-on knowledge of nature and the earth. This means taking the time to wander with the child in the garden and on walks to point out the simple wonders of nature with a little story:

'See those ants, how busy they are. Let's look closer. They're collecting food to take back to their nest. They live in the ground or a log. Just like humans they have babies in the nest, thousands of them and they all take a lot of feeding. Ants have six legs. See how fast they run. Let's see if we can find where they're heading.'

A similar routine with a little story can be followed in respect of particular flowers, trees, grass, rain, birds – any example of nature at work. And always while you look together encourage the girl or boy to voice their own discoveries and observations. You must be interested and fully engaged in these little expeditions. If you're not right there, the child won't be.

The child's attention span at this age is usually brief so don't labour the exercise. Factual stories about nature will help to hold the interest.

Wholehearted attention to this basic spiritual need of the boy or girl will help to fill what would otherwise become a kind of vacuum. That vacuum is usually filled with mental and intellectual activity in which there is little or no real love.

Love of nature and the earth, as a practical affirmation in the early years, starts to open the child subconsciously to the possibility of being able to really love and to know what is not love in adult relationships.

11

The Four-Year-Old and Onwards

The ages I'm giving are only a guide. The ideal is that the parent has been speaking intelligently to the child since it was born. Nonetheless, if what I say makes sense to the parent it's not too late to start, probably up to puberty. After that the going can be more difficult.

At age four and long before, if possible, it's a good idea to inform the child of the first 'rule' of the home. That is (provided it's the parents' conviction) that unhappiness has to be kept out of the home as much as possible.

'Unhappiness is when you are emotional, that is, when you are crying and whingeing for what you want. Or when you are moody and horrible to Mummy or Daddy. Unhappiness comes into you when you forget that you love us and forget that you love us loving you and looking after you.'

The parent has to use words from their own experience. The point is to communicate what is right and what is not right in the home, what is allowed and not allowed. This of course also puts an onus on the parents. They too have to do their best not to get emotional, not to lose their temper, argue or shout at each other; in other words not to do what the child is told not to do. That is the beginning of justice in the home.

Of course there will be failures by child and parents. But failure is not the important thing. The important thing is for all the family to get the idea that emotional people spoil the harmony in the home and that they tend to make others around them emotional. This applies to the whole life.

All the suggestions I've made so far will not just benefit the child. The one who'll benefit most is the parent. The child will be conditioned by many outside influences yet to come. But the parent has been through most of those. And the next stage for the parent, if they are willing, is to grow in consciousness; doing some or all of the suggestions will be a major contribution to that.

School

When the child starts school it will encounter more of the ignorance of the world. There will be much emotional behaviour among the other children. Bullying may have to be coped with. It is impossible to counter all the negatives the child will be exposed to. Teachers will encourage competing, as well as the celebration of birthdays and other events. The child must not be discouraged from this, which would make them seem odd to the teacher and their classmates.

Celebrations are a sort of game and entertainment that are there to be enjoyed by the young who haven't yet picked up the adult burden. Explain the reasons behind them in pleasant story form. Take Christmas and Easter which will allow you to tell wonderful factual stories without undermining later Christian associations:

'Christmas in the very ancient world of the northern hemisphere [all of which you'll later have the pleasant task of explaining more fully] was a time of the year for rejoicing with feasting and dancing that the shortest day of winter had passed. And Easter was the time in the ancient world of celebrating spring, the start of the season when the sun gets stronger and all of nature tends to produce new life. Today chocolate Easter eggs are a way of reminding us of the celebration of life; although in the old days, when chocolate hadn't been thought of, people actually gave gifts of real eggs.'

Apart from the parents dealing with particular difficulties as they see appropriate, the best protection for the young that will serve them all their lives is a solid foundation of real knowledge. Real knowledge is not learned from a whiteboard or a book. Real knowledge is of life as it is. The other is mostly information.

More suggestions for speaking to your children:

'Children and adults are often cruel to each other. They hit out and hurt, sometimes for no apparent reason, because they have a deep unhappiness in them. The less unhappiness, the less you hurt others. But few people know this. And you can't tell people.

You just have to stay away as much as possible from hurtful people.

'Mummy and Daddy have endeavoured to get you to see in yourself how hurtful emotion can be. Only by seeing things for yourself can you really know. Because other parents don't necessarily speak to their children as we do to you, it is not wise to try to tell anyone what you know. They are likely to laugh and poke fun at you. Best to just keep the knowledge within you.'

Again: 'You make friends at school. Teachers can be kind. Not all people are hurtfully unhappy. There is much good and kindness among people. It is important that you see the good when it is there.'

Again: 'When you are drawing or doing something that seems hard, don't try to do it. Just do your best. If you are running in a school race, do your best. Even if you lose and have done your best there's no failure. If you continue to keep trying to do things and fail, you'll feel you've failed. People will tell you to try. But no one can do more than their best. Trying makes the body uptight and it can't perform as well.'

Parties and Presents

'We give you a little party with your friends on your birthday and some presents at Christmas or other religious occasions. We don't want you to appear different to your friends or for you to feel that you are left out. But as we have always told you, parties and presents are not something to get excited about. You simply enjoy them. To start getting excited about anything brings up a speedy emotion. It keeps you awake at night. And the emotion usually makes you cranky and unhappy in a day or two.

'Whenever you are unhappy the thing to do is to tell Mummy or Daddy why. Tell us the reason. Then we'll do whatever we can to make it right for you again. But if you continue to whine and whinge and say you don't know why you're doing it, you are being dishonest. And we won't be able to help you. You must always be able to say why you are crying. Otherwise the crying is not real.

'The toys, parties and presents we give you are because we love you and you love us. Love means harmony and pleasure in being together. But if you start whingeing and demanding without good reason you are being emotional and unloving. You are making the home unhappy. And you know in your brighter moments, like now, that that's not right.

'If you go on being unhappy and are unable to say why, you're not being responsible. So we may not be able to give you the next toy you ask for. We're not going to give the toy to your unhappiness. It's up to you. If you can't say what's causing the unhappiness the unhappiness is not real. Not real means you can give it up, now, straightaway. That's being responsible.'

12

The Psychic World of the Child

There are occasions when parents may have to deal with psychic happenings involving their young children. The scientific and intellectual materialists of the world tend to dismiss the psychic world as imagination. Maybe it is, but maybe it's not. The doubters are those who've not had first-hand experience.

Nonetheless, innumerable ordinary people do have involuntary encounters with the psychic world. This frequently happens after the death of a loved one. But the experiences are seldom publicised and often not recounted for fear of ridicule.

Children, as I said earlier, are much closer to the womb and therefore nearer to the reality out of which we all come. Their perception of the 'other' is far more acutely natural than ours. As adults our natural perception is burdened by memory and the mind's incessant interpretation of experience. This, young children have not yet acquired.

A mother who has been with the teaching for several years wrote and mentioned that her four-year-old daughter, Ellen, started to want to call herself 'Lisa'.

'I was alarmed,' said the mother, 'something didn't seem right – though make-believe games are usually normal. I let it ride, knowing she would talk to me when she was ready.

'In the bath one night she started talking of Lisa as another person. I inquired about this and here is what she said: "Lisa is a little girl like me who comes to visit me at night when you and Daddy are asleep. Her mum and dad were shot and she was very sad and cried, but she is happy now. She has a little brother. Sometimes he pinches me and Lisa slaps him and tells him not to. But I haven't seen her for a little while. Do you know where she is, Mum?"

'I asked her if Lisa was like her and if she could be touched, like me? She said, "No, she's more like a dream. Is she a dream, Mum?"

'I told her that I didn't think she was a dream, that she is real but just comes from another place and that that place is very much like dreaming. When she asked where Lisa had gone and why she didn't visit any more, I told her Lisa had probably found her way back home.

'But I also told her that from now on I didn't want her to play games and call herself Lisa. I said it was best we didn't speak of her for a while because otherwise she may be drawn back to us and away from her home. As she didn't belong here with us that would make her unhappy.'

I was struck by the intelligence of the mother in the way she handled the situation. She didn't deny the child's experience but explained it in a realistic way and then firmly and compassionately put an end to it. Well done.

Sometimes children can seem to be speaking to nice playmates or creatures who are not visible. What then? To me, a parent should not ridicule these sorts of happenings to the child or say the child is being silly or scold the child.

A simple enquiry like, 'Who are you playing with or speaking to?' would seem best to me. That way the parent can have an opening dialogue with the child. And the child won't feel any sense of rebuff or rejection by the parent of its 'playmates' which are very real to the child.

Children do imagine playmates and usually it is quite evident that they're using their imagination. But psychic events – whether we believe in them or not – do happen to many people, as I've mentioned, and are more common than we suspect among young children.

It seems to me the wisest way to deal with the situation, after being ready to listen to the child, is to respond with sensitivity and wisdom as the mother above did. Every loving parent who is not closed off to any kind of dialogue with their child will know instinctively how to handle the situation.

13
Preparing for Puberty and After

A Sense of Order

It is difficult to find a way to handle extreme independence in an adolescent. Best, as always, is to start early in the child's life so that a sense of order and responsibility is already there when puberty arrives.

For instance, the child should be taught that it is responsible for the room in which it sleeps and plays. 'Let's tidy up together,' is a good start. The child learns more readily from cooperative efforts with parents. Once it gets the idea it will tidy up on its own, albeit with occasional grumbling protests.

The point is to communicate to the child that its room is a place in the home which is 'his' or 'hers', just as Mummy and Daddy have their room. Also that things are easier to find when they're put back in their place. So after playing, toys should be put away and not left scattered on the floor where people may step on them and break them. Then, when a particular toy is wanted for play, it can be found more easily.

It is important for the child to have an early introduction to what it means to run a home. This because the child is going to grow up and one day have a home of its own; or in the case of a teenager, a pad of its own. This should be acknowledged to the boy or girl. When the time is right, they will have a place of their own.

What does that mean? 'It means that the electricity bill has to be paid, like Mummy and Daddy pay it here. And if you leave the lights on unnecessarily it's going to cost you more. Then there's the rental of your place to be paid, like we pay it here. And the food. And many other things. We give you pocket money each week so you can start to get the hang of managing money for yourself. You have to make it last out until the next week, just like we have to. It's part of our responsibility as parents to teach you these things as best we can.'

Toys

Toys of course are not only to entertain children but to teach them in their own experience. Practical toys such as building sets, coloured pencils, crayons and painting books are the norm.

On the less positive side, toys are also for children to break as they must, instead of letting loose their awkward experimental enthusiasms on things around the house. But, 'If you deliberately break a toy you'll not get the next one you ask for. And you won't be given another one until you show that you can be responsible for your toys by looking after them.

'This doesn't mean toys don't break by accident, or through using them, or that other children may not be as caring as you and break your toys. All we want to see is that you look after your things as best you can, like Mummy and Daddy endeavour to look after the things in the house.'

A piece of garden, even a window box, is a great thing to compensate or supplement all the electronic toys and computer games. But again the parent has to 'garden' with the child. Always a parent should be alert for any sign of a particular aptitude and be prepared to acknowledge and encourage that by giving time and energy to it. In particular any artistic inclination should be encouraged as soon as it shows. Leaving instruction only to teachers, or to the boy or girl themselves, is not good enough.

The parents have to involve themselves by going to libraries with the child, buying books together, reading together, going through the dictionary or looking up things in the encyclopaedia together. This energetic and intellectual participation shows love beyond the normal in this very busy world.

Punishment

The question of punishment will arise sooner or later. It's a difficult area because opinions vary so much. Some people apparently oppose the idea of any punishment being necessary at all, but I suspect they've not been parents. Who can say what's best? I certainly can't. I can only say what I've found to work.

Discipline of the young is necessary. It implies some sort of penalty or punishment in default. I found that being just and fair with a stepson led to him eventually deciding a suitable punishment for himself.

This of course didn't happen all the time. But it was wonderful to see when it did. It was made possible by the child learning from a young age to be responsible in most of the ways I've described. In this I was joined by a very intelligent partner. Children have an innate sense of justice and fairness that can be awakened by treating them intelligently.

Penalties and punishments should be kept at a minimum. The idea is not to hurt the child, but to make the simple point that the particular behaviour or conduct is not acceptable. This assumes that the child has already been informed what is acceptable and understands why the other is not acceptable. Understanding the reason for things is the key.

Sometimes a smack is necessary. This should be around the legs. And there should be purpose in it, not blind rage or revenge. By purpose I mean that the child should know why it is being smacked. It's not being smacked only because of what it has done or not done, but to bring the intelligence back into the body.

A smack may not be suitable on many occasions. But it's inclined to work when the child is in an emotional tantrum and unable to listen. The intelligence is then out of the body and a smack is intended to bring it back where it belongs. Of course, the child should have been told long before what such a smack is for and already know from its own experience and the parents' instruction, what it means to be out of the body.

When you or your child are out of the body, either one obviously is temporarily insane; hence the old saying, 'beside himself in rage'. Sometimes parents get so exasperated by a child that there's a very thin line in the moment between rage and intelligent restraint. That's living. As long as physical violence is absent, what parent is going to throw the first stone of accusation?

Prolonged slapping around the legs at one time is not a good idea. It may make the child physically defiant and the parent determined to win the battle of wills. Best to desist and allow time for both to cool down. A later approach in love and then an explanation of what happened is likely to communicate everything both were trying to say. 'I love you', with an embrace seldom fails.

Introducing the Good

In our society what is 'good' and what is 'acceptable' are moving things depending on circumstances. In the case of the home the parents have to convey to the child what's acceptable according to the 'good rule' of keeping the home free of unhappiness. But the parents mustn't forget that because it's been agreed to be a good rule by all the family, the rule applies to them too.

There are other strategies to help to make this possible. The child from the earliest age when it can sit up and talk should be given a practical demonstration of what is good in its own experience. The good I'm speaking of – not the exciting or indulgent good – introduces the idea of God without the child having to believe in anything.

This is how: when the child is in an easy and receptive mood, say, 'We're going to play a new game together today. Sit on that low cushion on the floor and cross your legs. You love Mummy and Daddy, don't you? Now, that love is inside your tummy. It's a feeling. Feel it?'

You have to use your own words and not rush the child. Play this way for a few minutes every day if you can. And proceed from there. The child needs to learn that the good or wellbeing is always inside its body and is not dependent on getting, winning or receiving something.

This of course is the beginning of meditation. If you do not practise meditation yourself it will help you, as well as the child, to obtain a copy of my audio recording, *Start Meditating Now*.

Once the sense of an inner good is established in the early years, together with the beginning of a sense of order in the boy or girl's own experience, there is more chance of meaningful communication between the parent and the adolescent.

Puberty

At puberty the driving and maturing energy of sex starts to enter the body/mind. Its effects are usually more intense in the boy. The girl longs for romantic love and the boy wants sex.

Both are driven to experience according to the mores of their contemporaries and particularly to explore and experiment with the instinctive attraction to the opposite sex. Much of this is done in the imagination, but eventually physical experimentation is inevitable.

The sexual energy also produces a deepening independence and self-will. Advice offered against an offspring's likely disastrous action may have a delaying effect, if it's not resented or rejected outright. But finally any advice will usually be overwhelmed by the prospect of the experience.

The sex energy keeps the world moving. It drives teenagers into pitting themselves against the world so that through their mistakes they will eventually know the world and be better equipped to cope with it. The sex energy is the same energy that drove Columbus and all the early explorers on into the unknown. It drives nations to go to war. It is behind amazing feats of courage and endurance. The suppression of it causes fear. Sex is responsible for both ends of the human spectrum. There is no escaping it, one way or another.

Predispositions

Sometimes in the teenage years there is open disobedience or rebellion. There are no guarantees against this. One of the influences we can't control or predict is the predispositions the child is born with. In this regard every child is different. And in some quarters it would be referred to as karma, the repetition of the past in human affairs.

If the boy or girl has been brought up with a sense of communication with the parents, as I've endeavoured to convey, there will be more openness, more real love and more appreciation of what is good and right. Remember, love is the most profound communication.

14

First Love and the Teenage Girl

He's going to break your heart. No matter how much you love and trust him he's going to leave you – for another girl. You're going to cry and sob and wonder how this could possibly happen when everything seemed so good between you. Especially, but not necessarily, if you have been making physical love with him.

If he's just broken your heart and you're reading this because someone suggested you do, it won't help much now. The pain will be too great. But perhaps what you're reading here will be important to you when you are a mother. Perhaps you will be able to advise your daughter before the inevitable happens.

Not that it will make much difference to the way our society is. But perhaps, in time, what I'm saying of the reality behind the terrible pain of the betrayal of first love and its tenderness will pass from mother to daughter and in some future generation make a difference.

The boy is not to blame. He is just an unconscious part of a great movement of life that here in existence will destroy any union based on human love and not on the love of God, the reality or the invisible other. The human dilemma is that the force of love, the irresistible sexual attraction between the genders, occurs before there is much experience in existence of God or the other.

A teenage woman is virtually defenceless against the divine lure of sexual attraction. Certainly she can build up a mental or emotional resistance – a smart knowing – due to abuse or promiscuity. But the defence won't last. She'll still submit her body, if not her mind, to man's sexuality. It is the way of things here. It is the way man has chosen in his ignorance to make the world – based on lack of real love.

So is it God's will or man's will that your heart has been broken? It is both. Man in the beginning (and the beginning is always now) turned away from love, away from the true love of woman, and used her to satisfy his sexual nature. In doing that he set in motion the creation of a world of his own, not based on love but on sex and its drive for power over woman – and things. In other words the society we live in.

God's in Charge

But God or the divine intelligence remains in charge. As such it continuously breaks up unions not based on divine love. In that sense the break-ups are not bad at all but a divine endeavour to bring about the realisation that human love, or man's notion of love, is flawed and troublesome.

What chance has a girl got? None. Well, not much, since not every teenager suffers a broken heart; only a bent heart, a mauled heart or the puncturing of her tender romantic expectations of what love with man will be.

But it's not God's fault. When you read on you'll see that God made the earth and that man made the world; that God gave man the right of secondary creator to make a world for himself and his children as he saw fit. Man could have made a world based on love, for true love (God) is fundamental to his being. That's really why you loved the boy so much: unwittingly you saw the God in him.

He was driven by sex but you weren't. You just wanted love and naturally thought that he did too. He did, in a way. But the sexual imperative in him, in man, is too strong. And he had to go with that. Sexual love eventually satisfies itself. The man then moves on to new pastures – like all the male animals.

And that's the clue. Man's sexuality is an animal thing. It was created by God for the continuation of the human race. But now, man's inventive nature has devised so many means of contraception that propagation is less accidental and the old-fashioned restraints of fear of pregnancy no longer apply, particularly among teenagers. But still, according to God's will, the unwanted pregnancies occur, particularly among teenagers.

What hope is there then? None in man's world, for everything here dies. And there's no hope for man's love because it's part of his world. The only hope is that the individual woman, the mother, will embrace the greater love of God, the reality within, and put that before her love of man. Then the union will endure, not only in life but in death. For in God's creation there is no death of anything, only of the physical appearance.

So in true love you don't need hope.

15

First Love and the Teenage Boy

He also is disillusioned. Not necessarily by the girl, but in himself. He often feels a failure. The bravado and swaggering talk of his buddies has persuaded him that he should know 'how to do it'. But of course he doesn't. And in his innocence when the opportunity comes, he knows he doesn't.

Instead of just letting his body do it, which is natural, he adopts the concepts he's garnered from others, including the examples of actors in sex scenes in the movies. Accordingly he behaves tough, 'cool', dismissive or sexually demanding. But behind the facade he's awkward, nervous and uncertain. All he really wants to do is make love with her. But no one has told him how, why and what it means.

His greatest fear is that he's going to ejaculate early. And in most cases he does, sometimes as he's about to penetrate her, or sometimes immediately after. Mostly his immediate passion dissolves with it. He feels perhaps not so much a failure, as a suppressed sense of guilt at leaving the girl in some kind of heightened expectation, which he can't fulfil. He talks and acts his way through it, probably makes a series of excuses, or perhaps, depending on his sensitivity, apologises.

The girl, if it's her first time, is not likely to react to his premature ejaculation. She is more passive than he is and deeply absorbing of what is happening. He's more inclined to be carried away by the action. She may feel disappointment but if she loves the boy she can quickly rise above it. If she's made love before with other boys and doesn't love this boy she may be critical and complain. Any complaint will go deeply into him and make him hesitant or fearful when he comes to make love again.

Gradually he will get used to his premature ejaculation and perhaps delay it to some extent by masturbation. Young girls of course have to get used to it. As they sometimes have to get used to his abrupt withdrawal at the moment before ejaculation.

The teenage boy as much as possible has to give up thinking about the female private parts. His continual sexual imagining stimulates his male sexual drive. This not only increases the likelihood of premature ejaculation but fires the need to masturbate. There is nothing wrong in itself with masturbation. It just perpetuates the need to masturbate.

Woman doesn't have the same natural pressure for sex as man. Her pressure arises first, from man putting sex without love into her, and second, from her thinking that she's missing out on sex. The combination often leads to masturbation. 'Missing out' arises from woman's continual comparison of herself with other women, particularly the completely false images in the glossy magazines and with the just-as-false sexual and romantic antics of actresses in the movies.

At every age woman who has not become bitter about man is a giver. Her greatest delight is to give to man in love – and to be taken in love.

A Fortunate Liaison

A fortunate sexual education for the teenage boy is if he attracts an older experienced woman. As a rule she will encourage him in a right way so that he is not so excited before coitus. He can become a good lover under her repeated tuition if she is giving enough.

For an older woman experienced in man's sexual using of her without much love, to intimately embrace the fresh and relatively innocent body of a teenage lad, or a younger man, can be a great delight.

But she must know that the youth is going to grow in sexual experience, confidence and perhaps guile. Although she must love, it is not wise to fall in love as eventually he probably will want to make love with other women and leave her. The same applies to the youth – as she may leave him first.

Falling in love is a form of trance which usually results in a traumatic awakening.

The two should know that something precious is being done and avoid as much as possible becoming attached. Togetherness in this situation is something to make the most of while it lasts as it is fraught with potential uncertainty. Of course the same unpredictability is implicit in every partnership. But some contain more risk than others – yet again with no certainty of misfortune.

FROM HERE TO REALITY

Work

The idea of working is to have a job you enjoy.

16
Workmates

When you're living the idea of the spiritual life as BL teaches it, the emotionality of workmates can be difficult. Most people don't realise that their emotions make them and those around them unhappy. And when you're endeavouring not to be emotional the presence of emotional people can be quite confrontational and testing, especially if they're the boss.

Let's deal with workmates first, the boss later. What's the best course? As always the best course is honesty. As soon as possible tell the people you're working with that you're endeavouring to live a more spiritual life. Say in your own words at an appropriate time:

'If I don't join in any arguments or discussions about the past please don't think I'm being stand-offish or aloof. It's only that I've realised that arguments achieve little and that talking about the past tends to perpetuate worrying about the past. I'm trying to live that.

'I frequently fail. But the important thing I've found is to do my best and not to be concerned too much about failure. I'm not trying to be perfect. I just want to change my self and the way I've been living most of my life in allowing my emotions to dictate most of my actions.

'I'm not implying in any way that I'm better than you or ever will be. I'm not out to try to teach you anything. What I'm doing is for me alone. I've no desire to put my belief onto you or to try to persuade you from your belief.'

People may rubbish you. Some may joke and call you different high-sounding names like guru or reverend. But the essential thing is for them to know from the start what you're doing and why you're doing it. Most people can accept this as long as there's no sugges-tion that you're better than they are, or that their beliefs are not true.

There may be the bad-tempered, aggressive or even vicious workmate who'll have a go at you at any time. Coping and responding to that is part of the spiritual exercise. If you do respond, do so as much as possible without emotion or fear. Don't react. Keep to facts. 'What have I done to you?'

'You're a so and so, so and so.'

'That may be true. What have I done to you?' Avoid discussions with an emotional person.

Rehearsals Seldom Work

It's all very well to rehearse responses but seldom do they fit the actual situation. Even so, the point is to remain as unemotional as possible and to keep to facts. If the other person can't hear and doesn't want to, you'll just have to keep away from them as much as possible.

The spiritual life with all its challenges is not something you are living independently as it so often seems. Inside you is the intelligence, the spirit of life itself. It can change things and people amazingly – mostly when we've learned the lesson it was all about.

The finest course is to surrender your discomfort to God, the inner reality – and to stick to facts.

17
The Boss

Your boss more than likely will be emotional. To be unable to see or communicate straight, to dither, to confuse issues and to rely on the authority of a position rather than the facts, are sure-fire indicators of emotionality.

An emotional person has an unresolved problem within. The more emotional the deeper the problem, and the more aggressive and unreasonable the person is likely to be. The best way again is to speak only in facts and not to get emotional or to exchange accusations. What's the fact? Keep to that if you can.

A boss has the advantage. And an emotional boss will inevitably let you know it by glossing over facts, misquoting and generally confusing issues, especially when they're having a bad day. A bad day for anyone means the normal frustrations of being normal, and not natural, have got the better of them.

We don't really know what's troubling the person – domestic problems, their love-life, career worries or just general discontent.

It's important to have a job description and to know what's in it. It helps you to keep to facts if the boss is confusing an issue. In the face of unreasonable demands or attacks you keep to that – what you are being paid to do. That's not to say you shouldn't give more to the job than you were hired for.

Finally, in an extreme case of working for an emotionally unreasonable employer you may have to be prepared to lose your job (be fired or quit), rather than go on compromising.

Enjoy What You Do

The idea of working is to have a job you enjoy. In our goal-driven modern society this is not always easy or possible. There are many busy people who appear to enjoy their work but who really enjoy the stress and strife involved and not the job. A job can be demanding at times but not all the time.

A person who enjoys conflict and struggle in a job has unresolved conflict inside. They may moan and complain to others about the work but if they lost or quit the job they'd be lost inside for a time. Such people are then likely to enter into a conflictual partnership by creating one.

The best guide is to do what you have a talent or aptitude for. That you will enjoy. Often the put-off is that there's no money in it. But you can practise your craft or skill while you take a job that pays enough to live on.

When you don't have the means or the luck to begin with, it can pay off to improve a long-held interest or natural gift into a commercial possibility. It's amazing what can be done with sufficient application. It just takes time – which is really the test of any earnest endeavour.

Sometimes the individual can't see what sort of work they would really enjoy. If they enjoy something this week they're likely to be tired of it next week. Then there's the self-indulgent desire to be paid and do as little as possible; or to collect the dole and do nothing.

It takes all kinds to make a world.

But what people seldom realise is that the world we live in as it affects us is a mirror of what we are within.

FROM HERE TO REALITY

Going Deeper

FROM HERE TO REALITY

The Torment and the Good

I didn't say it was easy; I said it was simple.

18
Your self

The biggest problem in everybody's life is their self. Your self is what does what you don't really want to do, and doesn't do what you really want. You can see from that sentence that there are two very different impulses working in you. The question is, which one is real?

The answer is in finding the one that's not real. When you've found what's not real, what remains is real. It's as simple as that.

To start, all you've got to do is to honestly, which means consciously, admit to what disturbs you. I'll start the ball rolling and you see if what I'm saying is true.

You're disturbed when you are frustrated, confused, resentful, moody, angry, jealous, miserable, depressed, discontented, restless, grieving – in other words, when you are unhappy. These are all negative emotions and forceful expressions of unhappiness, even though some are retained inwardly. They disturb your natural enjoyment of life and also affect the people around you.

Those emotions, and the many others I haven't mentioned, are your self. Your self is one complete bundle of unhappiness. It consists of all the emotional ups (passing excitement) and downs (disappointments) you've had since you were born. All have coalesced, fused, into the single discordant entity that shares your body and your life with the reality you are.

Your emotional self is cunning and clever. It has a convincing kind of intelligence. That's because while it was forming in infancy and childhood there was a real intelligence there – your fine natural intelligence. But the force of the coarser emotion hijacked the subtle intelligence.

Not all of it, of course. But enough to fool you into repeating experiences that cause you conflict and confusion. Your own intelligence so often tells you not to go along with your emotional choices; but in difficult situations the pressure and demand of the self is often overwhelming.

The Poseur

Throughout your life your emotional self has been posing as you and making most of the decisions based on personal feelings. All such feelings are emotional. Your pure intelligence is far more intelligent. Given freedom from the burden of your self it would make decisions based on a clear analysis of the facts.

That's precisely what happens when you begin to claim back the intelligence usurped by the emotional self. But the full power of your intelligence can only be gained by denying the emotional self its control. You do that by looking intelligently at what, for instance, makes you angry.

You have to see that you are angry because you can't get your own way or because you want the impossible. If you can't get your own way and can't see a way around the situation, give up. Stop trying. See what practical action you can take. If you can't see any, look again next day and the next. Life is always moving on. But most important is to discover there is no validity and certainly no value in being angry – except self-satisfaction.

The same applies to all negative emotions. They are based on assumptions, presumptions, misunderstandings and emotional attachments to events and people.

People have told me that some good has come out of their person being angry. That may be so in some cases. Yet the same can be said of nations which, after long provocation, go to war. If you're on the winning side, that's good. But is it good if you're on the losing side?

Usually, people feel better after an outburst of anger. That's because of the build-up over time of negative emotions in the self. Finally the emotional tension reaches breaking point and violent words or actions follow. The person feels better. But they often leave the people around them disturbed. They have vented their anger, and someone who they probably say they love is left with the aftermath. Anyway, the relief is usually only temporary before the tension starts building up again. The cycle then repeats itself.

Anger, like all negative emotions, is a psychic possession. Each time a person gets angry a psychic bridge starts to be established to this very troublesome and unreliable part of the psyche. In the case of an habitually angry person the bridge becomes so solid that anger is a distinct part of the personality. The person genuinely can't help getting angry.

Understanding Anger

It is better for everyone to understand anger as soon as possible. First, that it's a possession. Second, that it cannot be justified or excused. Anger, to begin with, is due to identification with a particular situation. Certainly, situations arise where action has to be taken against people or events. But whether it's legal action or any other practical action, there is no need to be angry. Is there? An angry person can't extricate themselves from anger while they justify their anger.

The bridge over which anger crosses into the brain has to be dissolved continuously. This is because existence itself is a potentially anger-stoking situation and, indeed, a tension-making one. To start with, we are all in separate bodies trying to relate to other separate bodies and things. As weird as it may sound, that is unnatural.

When we are attracted to someone we may not have the looks or body that appeals to them, and none of us is without the need of the good fruits of attraction. Then there's the prospect of other persons, other bodies, being successful materially when we who have tried so hard are still denied even modest wealth.

In every such case there's a stirring of emotion, a feeling of failure, or not being good enough, of disappointment or inadequacy and self-doubt – in other words inner conflict.

And if the search for material success or someone to love and be loved by continues to be unsuccessful, a build-up of tension occurs subconsciously. The result is discontent, jealousy, resentment, or the urge to hit out, hit back or the sexual feeling of missing out – each one an element in the building of the bridge of anger.

To put a stop to the inevitable mounting tension that plagues everybody in existence, it is necessary to consciously examine every single negative emotion as it arises; to identify the circumstance causing it and to realise that each disturbing feeling is a reaction of your unhappy self. That is self-knowledge.

How does your self manage so convincingly to make everything seem so personal? By you continuously interpreting events from a personal point of view; by reacting to what pleases or displeases you, instead of simply seeing events as they are without identifying with them. Until we master our self, we are slaves to our self-ishness.

19

Pure Intelligence

The purpose of living with all its ups and downs is for you to discover the pure intelligence you are.

The process is long and often difficult with many misleading twists, turns and false assumptions. And there's no guarantee of ultimate success. But the more you are conscious in your living life and relationships, conscious of what inevitably spoils them, sours them or deadens the initial vibrant interaction, the more intelligent you become. You are then reclaiming some of the intelligence and vitality that your emotional self steals from you to sustain itself.

Frequently during the process you'll feel you are dying. But it is not you or your body dying. It is your bothersome self. Since everybody clings habitually to being their self, they mistakenly presume their self is what they are. The dissolution of the self is then taken personally. And what's left of your self suffers.

The symptoms of such suffering are desolation (being forsaken), wretchedness (a sense of unworthiness), deep loneliness (in the midst of people and loved ones), sadness, hopelessness and aching despair.

Nonetheless, behind it all and directing everything for eventual good, is the pure intelligence you are.

But I repeat: it is not what you are that is suffering. It is not you who is being demolished. But it certainly feels like it.

Pure intelligence is the natural intelligence of the body. It is the intelligence behind the eyes looking at these words. Sight feels nothing. Sight just sees. Hearing doesn't feel. Hearing just hears. And so it is with all the body's senses. No one can say what this intelligence is. It's simply there. And it never moves.

'My self' calls itself 'I' all day long. It says, 'I love you', when it doesn't; 'I am happy', when it's unhappy, and 'I am honest', or 'I am sincere', when it is not. And yet there are other times when you say, 'I love you' etc. and really mean it. Which I are we talking about?

Then there is I who love my father but when he is cruel to my mother I still love him but I don't like him. Which I is real? Then there's I who love my children and I who put my own interests before them; I who like many things but I who dislike many other things. How many 'I's are there in the body? And which is real?

None of those is real. Every one is simply an aspect of your self. Each I rises and declares itself according to the dominant emotion or vested interest at the time; or the words are uttered habitually or robotically like a machine: 'How are you today?'

Is there any real I in the body?

Yes, several, in descending order. But they are not accessible to the mind which is an instrument of self. Each 'real' I is at a different level of the pure psyche. Each is a finer rendition of the one before until finally all vanish into the one-and-only Supreme.

Confusion from the East

Some confusion regarding your self is also likely if you've been exposed to Eastern teachings. Eastern teachings refer to a higher Self with a capital 'S', and sometimes to a lower self with a small 's' which can only be communicated in the written word.

More recent versions of Eastern-based teachings also refer to the self as ego. This is another red herring introduced by the self so that people won't take immediate responsibility for their troublesome self. There's no more up-front and meaningful word in your experience than 'my self' – once you admit to the menace it is.

As for your higher Self, no one can describe that or tell you about it, other than to say that once your troublesome self finally surrenders, I, the consciousness of God, am there immediately and unmistakably.

Then I disappear…

20
'I'

'I' enable you to know. I am the knower of everything in your memory and experience. Without my reflection you can't know anything. When you're asked a question I reflect instantaneously on the particular object or subject and come up with an answer. The reflection is so quick and natural that no one notices the split second it takes, except where I need to ponder and ask for time to think about it.

Although I'm the only knower, I'm not the intelligence I seem to have. My intelligence is only a reflection of the pure intelligence in my body. And a reflection – like your reflection in the bathroom mirror – is not the real thing. As I am the closest thing in existence to intelligence in the body, everyone calls themselves I.

There are two things I reflect on in every body – first, what the senses are reporting and second, my self, which is the sum total of my feelings, accumulated and preserved since the body was born.

Everybody's knowing life begins with their feelings and that's where I-the-knower begin. As my feelings become stronger and my experience of the senses widens, I reflect on both as myself. Since I am the means of all knowing, I then assume that my self and my memorable experiences are real. But they are not real. *I am the most real thing in existence – as long as I am free of all identification.*

I am the thinker, the reasoner, the rationaliser and the interpreter of events. If I were not, nothing in particular would make sense. The whole of human existence depends on I.

The spiritual life begins when I start to realise that my emotional feelings and opinions are no longer as meaningful as they used to be. As they are reduced I sink deeper within and become more intelligent. At the same time I sense there's something more real within that I can't name.

The Camera Effect

The process is something like a camera. The senses are the lens, the receptors of the environment. The intelligence behind the lens (and the camera) is unmoving. And nothing happens unless there's film in the camera.

My self is supposed to be the film. Like a good film it's supposed to record only the images that come through the lens. It's not supposed to distort the images with its own conclusions. That would be a very unreliable film. You'd never get the picture you focused on; you'd seldom see things as they are.

That's just what's happened. I as my self started interpreting the pictures, giving them a self-ish bias. This is equivalent to the ludicrous situation of the film taking over the camera and cutting out the intelligence behind the camera! Result: confused and sometimes chaotic images.

My original and legitimate job is to watch through the lens of the senses for any happening or situation that might endanger the survival or wellbeing of the physical body. *I judge events against previous experience with what I call my mind.* If the result is all-clear I relax the body after having got it tensed ready for action. If the result is threatening, I initiate immediate evasive action by the body.

That would be all very well if I remained the reflection of the body's pure intelligence. But I've identified myself with my feelings. My feelings are personal and permeate my memory, putting a personal slant on what would otherwise be a simple act of perception of facts.

Even so, the body's pure intelligence is completely beyond my comprehension; but not beyond my power of observation. Its speed is amazing. By comparison my mind is laboriously slow. My body touches a hot stove or a piece of dry ice and the hand is withdrawn immediately – while my mind is still trying to work out whether the object was freezing or hot.

Pure intelligence is instinctual, that incredible immediate response which protects and guides all living creatures and organic life. It is divine, cosmic.

21

Power of the Good

How do I as an adult continue to be so attached to my trouble-some self?

By considering my self – by thinking about the emotions or feelings I've identified with. The enlightening alternative is to reflect on the good in my life which, if I look intelligently, far outweighs the not-so-good. But the magnetic habit of self is so strong it usually overwhelms the innate intelligence I am.

By omission I've allowed this irresponsible emotional self to build up inside the physical body. It copies and uses my reflected intelligence. But being a reflection of my reflection, it's only mentally clever and not intelligent as I am.

Self is devious, cunning and self-serving. And while it is in control I cannot be the intelligence I am.

Your self has no life of its own. To survive it has to suck at the natural life and vitality of the body, quite often destroying the sense of wellbeing. The result is that you and practically everyone on earth can't for long enjoy the simple wonders of life presented by the senses. Your self turns life into the stress and strain of living – until its spurious authority is dissolved.

Nonetheless, life is always within. And life – which is of divine intelligence – frequently interrupts the confusion and emotional tyranny of the ruling self. Life makes it possible for everyone to go on – and of course to enjoy their life. Except in those cir-cumstances where the hopeless feelings of self throttle the rising fountain of life and sometimes even force the body to murder itself.

22

God and self

As everything comes from the Source, what is the divine purpose of self?

Paradoxically, self is essential for the realisation of God.

The deepest realisation of God occurs when I as my self completely disown my self. This is only possible when I become sufficiently intelligent to see the suffering caused by my self's ignorance.

Self is psychic and not subject to physical limitations. On the surface where we live with it, self is all the stubborn negativity I've described. But in its deepest depths self is responsive to the light of intelligence from within and can be transformed.

When I as self finally disown my own superficial ignorance I do so as a total conviction. Simultaneously I 'perceives' and surrenders to 'That' within which I know to be the one and only good. Then I realises that That is the ever-present supreme consciousness of God, the Source. I am no longer self. In other words, God has realised God in existence.

Here's another way of explaining it.

Every single thing is determined by God's Will. Therefore selfish ignorance and suffering are created by God. But by consciously seeing enough of the suffering caused by my self in my living life, I, the reflective intelligence in the body, finally separate from my self. Then God is realised, or the consciousness (as the intelligence has then become) realises God.

In other words the whole seemingly dark story of personal existence, emotional pain and emotional suffering is simply so that God in the midst of ignorance may realise God.

23
The Psyche

Our physical life is not as complete and self-contained as we imagine. For the most part we are psychic creatures. This means we are basically ruled by influences beyond our immediate control – psychic influences.

These in the first instance are registered as feelings.

The psychic realm is immediately inside or behind our physical bodies. It comprises all the emotional feelings that men and women have ever had in the past. That's a great bulk and variety of emotions and a great deal of past. But all are recorded in the ethereal medium of the psyche, along with the thoughts that accompany them.

This is not so amazing when you consider the quantity of data a modern computer can hold on a tiny physical chip or two. The psychic realm is not restricted by physical limitations; it is abstract, without form, and infinitely impressionable and sensitive to feelings in the physical. It is an immortal record of the trials and tribulations of life on earth. And it is because of the psychic realm that these trials and tribulations keep repeating themselves.

The psychic realm is only the first of three states comprising our inner reality. These are the psychic, pure psyche and spirit.

Sweetness and Joy

Like all the inner states accessible to us, the psychic, the first realm, becomes finer and more reflective of ultimate good the deeper the individual's intelligence penetrates it.

The coarsest level of the psychic is next to the physical, as described. But deeper in are the sweetness, joy, giving, and truly loving aspirations of humanity. In between the coarse and the fine, and merging somewhat into either, are the true and not-so-true offerings and beliefs of the followers of the established religions. All feelings are in the psychic.

The psychic finishes by blending into the next realm which is the pure psyche. The pure psyche is infinitely deep in extent compared with the psychic.

The pure psyche is all good, a very fine reflection of the good of God, the supreme consciousness. At its deepest it contains no images, no words and of course, no feelings. The communication is simply that of immediate goodness and rightness and of the sweetness and perfection of the reality behind the projection of the physical earth. The pure psyche gets finer the deeper it is accessed and finally disappears into the realm of spirit.

Nothing meaningful in human terms can be said about the spirit. Sufficient to say that it is the spirit of God, the supreme consciousness. When the spirit is accessed, any residue remaining of the pure psyche and psychic is immediately dissolved in that moment. Hence that moment's pure vision. The human mind, its aspirations and supposed reasons for existing are completely obliterated in an inflow of inexpressible knowledge or gnosis.

The uninterrupted realisation of the spirit is what would be regarded as enlightenment. But enlightenment is an unenlightened word of the mind and so has no real meaning in the uninterrupted state of this realisation. The best that can be said from the spirit about enlightenment is that enlightenment is being now and being now is being innocent of all wanting. Being now, not just living now, is a great rarity on this earth.

The most important point about this model of your inner reality is that the three realms – psychic, psyche and spirit – are present or active within you now and every moment of your life.

There are no divisions really. The only delineation is how deeply the individual can access their own reality. Does he or she remain mostly reacting and focusing on feelings while loving and giving as best they can? That's the psychic. Is there acknowledgement of the sweetness and goodness of life and nature? That's the pure psyche. Is there in the midst of the living life a continuous underpinning love and expressed gratitude to God? That's the spirit.

Bridges

The psychic is the dominant influence in human affairs. All wars, cruelty and violence are due to its effects.

At the lowest or coarsest level the psychic contains all the emotional expressions of anger, resentment, jealousy, impatience, hatred, sexual excitement and deviant pleasures, greed, envy and dishonesty – in other words all the negativity that living on earth has engendered in us and our forebears. This collective mass represents a great negative force pressing down on us.

Anger and other negative emotions that we harbour provide a bridge for the same negativity to cross into us. This reinforces our emotions and helps to perpetuate them.

Thus, in living the spiritual life, it is essential to begin eliminating our negative emotions. We can do this – if we can see the truth of it – because the power of the pure psyche and the spirit is always present and with us. Once done – and it can be done – the psychic cannot invade our consciousness. And we realise a great freedom.

Our personal emotions arise from the fact that we are sensory creatures divided from each other by physical bodies. This persuades us that we are separate persons. The ignorance – lack of consciousness or presence – inherent in that misconception allows the psychic to impose its disturbing emotions on us.

We are indeed separate bodies. But the gradual journeying of intelligence within reveals a consciousness behind the physical in which the essence of every thing and every body is an undivided whole.

The inherent nature of the psychic and psyche is to reflect back what man and woman put into them. This means that if you live an emotional life it repeats itself by attracting situations and circumstances that keep making you emotional. Or, if you are a complaining person who can't help judging others, you'll bring more of both to you. The more you judge others the more you judge yourself which makes you unhappy.

Similarly, if you are predominantly giving and loving you will receive these blessings back into your life. The difficulty for many people is that they fail to see and acknowledge the good that keeps emerging in their life because of a focus on problems. Problems arise mostly from thinking about difficulties instead of taking action.

The validating power behind the unstinting generosity of the inner realm is God, the uncreated creative intelligence. It is God's pleasure to give back to man and woman what they love or concentrate on most. This should be a divine gift. But, because of human unhappiness, God's giving back has become a great burden on humanity.

This is no reflection on God. It's a reflection on countless generations of men and women losing sight of the good and identifying with their own personal and selfish aspirations. It is not God's fault that it's all gone wrong and that everyone must receive back their own negativity and ignorance.

Originally there was no troublesome psychic world. The whole psyche reflected God's benevolence, beauty and wonder. Early on when the population was much fewer and man and woman were intimate with nature and the earth – God's gift – there was far less negativity and far more knowledge of God and the natural good. But psychic pressure was developing amidst the good and thus arose man's self-made afflictions. Even so it was known that God was merciful, compassionate and magnanimous to God's creatures. And that finally God's greatest gift for all living things is the compassionate fact of death.

24

Pure Love

In physical existence the reflection of pure intelligence is love. Not emotional love which characterises most human love, but pure love. Pure love is free of attachment to the feelings and therefore is not a relationship, not a dependence.

In pure love I simply love. Understandably the question arises, 'How can I love without feelings?' But that's the point. When you truly love you don't need feelings. Love is sufficient.

Such love of course is rare between man and woman. The only way they can really love each other in a vital trouble-free partnership is to love God or the unknowable first. Then no attachment to the other is necessary and what were once feelings become simply the knowledge of love of the other. Love is not a feeling. It is a sensation – not of the outer senses but of the inner senses, which I call the nucleate senses.

This whole book is an attempt to guide you, first, into the realisation of this love, and then into the living of it. Because the truth of it is that your essence, the undivided mystical reality of the inner nucleate senses, is pure love.

We are prevented from realising this and living a life of love because we establish a relationship with the man or woman we love. As soon as relationship creeps in, our love-life together comes under strain. The strain manifests as possessiveness, jealousy, misunderstandings and arguments: in other words, emotions.

In spite of the exchange of negativity in arguments with a loved one, all we are really trying to do is to tell the other, 'I love you.' This would be construed by most people as a weird way of communicating love. It is weird because we are trying to communicate through negativity instead of love. Still, everyone who loves somebody is guilty of it at sometime, as everyone who loves somebody enjoys the mystical sensation of pure love – even if it is only in the beginning or for a brief period.

As human beings we don't really know what love is. We don't really know what we are. We live a life of relationship with every thing, every object outside us, including the body of the one we love.

But love is not outside us. Love is what we are inside. We focus that love outside and conclude that the love is out there too.

Relationship

The delusion is universal and begins with our own body. Our first love is the body.

As a baby we instinctively responded to the body's needs of food and comfort. As children and adults we served the body more and more. So much so that inevitably, with such concentrated and continuous loving care of the body, we became attached to it. And now everyone is attached to their body, which means in relationship with the body.

Do we love the body?

No. It would seem we do due to the attachment. But there's no love in attachment – only difficulties. For example, the main difficulty for everyone in relation to the body is the fear of death. Not now when everything is okay and the healthy ones can boast, 'I'm not afraid to die'. But when the life-threatening illness or situation arrives, then comes the fear and dread of death.

And yet in the moments of really dying most people are unafraid. In fact, frequently an amazing stillness and sweetness comes into them which the one who loves them can't help but empathise with and recognise as love. Amazingly, fear and grief are no longer present.

What is happening in these moments? What has happened to the one who's dying and to the one witnessing the wonder of love unfolding in this normally tragic human situation?

Both are in love without relationship. Love is communicating. Words are not only unnecessary but useless.

Both have given up their relationship to the body. And love, which both now are, is present and communicating.

The one dying has given up hope which is the last relationship to the body. He or she knows that the body is finished, that even if it were possible to get up and walk, the body's many parts have broken down beyond repair. Who but a fool would want to go on living in such a dilapidated and malfunctioning vehicle? Only someone still in relationship. Only someone not yet really dying or ready to die.

Similarly, any bedside watchers attached to the dying body would want it to go on living – seemingly at all costs. They grieve and mourn in attachment. They can't let go, can't let what is completely natural happen. Their main concern is their own selfish loss. They fail to grasp the broader picture – that living in a worn-out body is pointless without the natural quality of life. Yet such compassionate understanding they often extend to other direly injured creatures.

Those who really love the one dying in front of them know that the body is finished. No more relationship is possible there. And the one really dying, having given up all hope, all desire for recovery, bathes in the glory of love free of relationship.

Man and Woman

Both man and woman are divine principles, each an aspect of God or reality.

25

Two Different Species

Man and woman are two different species, not unlike dog and cat. Two arms, two legs and a head – the similarity ends there.

Man is structured, dogged. Woman is fluid, feline. Dogs chase cats; cats don't chase dogs – unless cornered or enraged. Dogs are constantly on the move, appearing to know where they're going but running aimlessly in the direction of the nose, stopping here and there for a smell or a pee and awkwardly lifting a leg with little control over what gets wet. Cats squat ladylike, preferring privacy. Dogs pee anywhere, not caring who's looking.

Cats don't move without good purpose. When they do they slink along; no dogged jogging for them.

Cats enjoy comfort, warmth, being gently stroked, lying in the sun, or curling up on beds or sofas. Dogs jump on beds, get restless, start prancing around and doing rude things. Cats sleep most of the day and come alive at night. Dogs nap some of the day (when they're not jogging and sniffing around) and sleep and bark at night or howl disconsolately when the owner is absent.

Cats dig a hole and daintily bury their poo after a sniff to ensure it's theirs. Dogs crap hastily, eager to be on the move again and give a few desultory and completely ineffective back-kicks. Dogs enjoy smelling the crap of other dogs and shoving their nose in naughty smelly places.

Dogs love rolling in rotting flesh and have to be washed regularly. Cats preen their own body.

Cats have sharp claws and needle teeth which they use on dogs that corner them or get too familiar. Dogs have wide and blunted claws that are useful for burying bones but mostly for digging useless holes.

Dogs charge after sticks and balls and sometimes cleverly try to bite moving car tyres. Cats prefer to play a cat and mouse game.

Dogs wag their tail when they're pleased. Cats wag their tail when they're angry.

Is it any wonder they don't really understand each other?

Only love, real love, can dissolve their differences.

26
Man's Love of Woman

Man is in relationship with woman until he loves woman in the way she is created for.

He is attracted to her initially as a means of sexual satisfaction. And sexual satisfaction keeps him with her. But when the sexual attraction is satisfied he tends to lose interest, become familiar, take her for granted and settle for companionship or compatibility (if it's there). Or he will leave her, often assuring her that he still loves her.

A paradox.

But a paradox is a seeming contradiction. A seeming contradiction is a partly observed fact. And a partly observed fact is the result of not seeing the whole.

In man's love for woman there are really only two facts to see. The first is that the love of woman is his principal concern. The second is his irresistible sexual drive. We need to go a little deeper into this. And then perhaps we'll be able to see how the two facts are connected and appreciate how a man can leave a woman while telling her he still loves her – without any seeming contradiction.

Until man finds a woman he can really love, or until he learns to really love, he is in relationship with his sexual drive or need. The sexual relationship, a natural imperative in the male, tyrannises him all his days. And he unconsciously (and often consciously) projects onto woman the conflict and confusion it causes in him.

Man can't help this. While the sexual drive dominates he is in servitude. He cannot really be responsible for his life. He is fundamentally in the power of something beyond his control. This is self-evident in every man's love-life.

All men are sexually driven and therefore are in relationship with sex. The fact that some men don't display much interest in sex makes no difference. They are mentally and psychologically (feelingly) enslaved by it.

Such men are able to suppress the outward display of this basic drive. But their thoughts and emotions are constantly focused on the idea of woman or the vague imagining of her private parts. And so masturbation, promiscuity and sexual deviation rule – all in the hope of finding satisfaction. But satisfaction, like excitement, is a passing thing and needs to be repeated continually.

Many men conceal their sexual drive in ambitious projects, in worldly distractions that are applauded and envied by other less public men who are nonetheless busy in the world in their own way. It's all the energy of sexual frustration which has driven man since time began to secure power over other men and women instead of over his self.

Ambitious and successful men in a love-partnership with woman are champions at illicit sex. Foreign trips and distant business conferences provide ample opportunities for deceit. Prostitutes are in business not just for the rich and famous but also for the man next door. Where sex without love is involved, dishonesty reigns.

It is man's world. He made it as it is down through the ages with his sexual drive. He used woman as a personal beast of burden, to produce children as familial slaves to help plough his fields, care for his animals and if necessary go to war to protect his property. He dismissed his daughters as chattels and expected woman to give him a male heir to perpetuate his selfish and loveless way of life.

Today his cruel and violent history of war, abuse, deceit and mayhem continues under the westernised cloak of comfort, convenience, lies, compromise and sophistication.

Honesty

Only love can transform the sexual tyrant in man. That love begins with honesty. Man has to admit and face up to the first fact within himself – that the love of woman is his principal concern.

Here I'm not speaking of the love of a particular woman. I'm speaking of man's love of Woman – a completely different reality.

Both woman and man are divine principles, each an aspect of God or reality.

Thus in the six billion mass of people on earth there is only one real principle behind each of the two genders. This singularity amid such diversity creates enormous confusion in man's love of woman. With his dominant drive for sexual satisfaction he mistakes woman's individual body for the divine Woman he truly loves.

Thus, in leaving a woman he will declare quite honestly (but meaninglessly as far as she is concerned) that he still loves her. He's not really torn or he wouldn't go. But he has seen something of the divine in the woman which the man who just abruptly leaves has not seen.

Man's inability to realise the divine principle in woman is due to his sexual drive. This, through no fault of his to begin with, is superimposed on his natural ability to love. The drive is far coarser than the love. It excites his sensuous nature which continuously submerges his love – even though the love keeps subtly tugging at his finer being.

Return to Love

Two other facts contribute to the difficulty that man and woman have in coming together in an enduring, vital and conscious union.

The first is the assumption by both that they are the same when they are in fact completely different. The result is man despairs of understanding woman and woman despairs because he doesn't understand her. Where there is attraction compromise follows.

The other fact is that man and woman are part animal – animal bodies plus pure reflective intelligence which animals don't have or need.

Man's sexual drive is fundamentally animalistic. Instinctively the drive is for the propagation of the human species. But his normal reflective faculty – the ability to think about sex – destroys the natural animalistic innocence. The return to love is the return to innocence while still in an animal body.

27

Woman's Love of Man

Woman was created for man to love. Every woman knows this in her deepest place. She yearns to unite with him in love. But so often, due to experience, she despairs and gives up, turns her back on man, or compromises with his sexual nature for the sake of peace or comfort and convenience.

Woman is not as obsessed with sex as man is. He wants sex, she wants love. But women in our westernised civilisation have become increasingly sexual at the expense of love. Man has made her this way by his sexual use of her: by his sexual excitation of her and by putting his male sexuality into her in lovemaking without sufficient real love. And this with her connivance, cooperation, compromise or consent. He has made her something like himself; in some cases even psychically possessed by the male sexual drive. Woman today is between five and sixty per cent male.

The transformation has been very gradual, handed on psychically in woman from generation to generation. Our psychic nature means we are basically controlled by emotional feelings – not unavoidable physical feelings such as pain, hunger and sensations.

The idea of love between woman and man is to eliminate emotional feelings from love and therefore from life. This is the next stage of the evolution of intelligence on earth.

The current evolution marked by man's scientific ingenuity in tinkering with the species – from plants, to animals to humans – is a subtext. The subtext refers to external progress. But the elimination of feelings is an inner evolution that for humanity will take many centuries and innumerable generations.

Woman's True Nature

Nonetheless, a start has already been made by many individuals, especially the men and women who really practise the whole of my teaching. The majority of the casual people who come to me out of interest concentrate on my teachings on love-making, as described in my book and audio recording entitled, *Making Love*. But the making of real love, that is, love that alters consciousness, cannot be practised without years of self-denial, self-surrender and an increasing love or gratitude to God, the unknown behind all good.

At this early stage of the evolution, woman is the key. This is because woman's true nature is a hundred per cent love. She has to be true to that and give up being true to her feelings. Man's true nature is ninety per cent love and ten per cent something to do.

With his ten per cent, man is supposed to have built a world based on love. But the reality is that he used it to build a world based on his sexual power drive which is responsible for all the conflict and unhappiness on earth. Some obvious side effects are the increasing addiction to drugs and alcohol, sex shops, pornography, and sexual misuse of children – all in the forlorn hope of finding enduring excitation, fulfilment, love or something to love.

Woman has been used abominably by man to serve his appetite for sexual gratification. Is it any wonder that subconsciously she tries to get even and so often actually makes his life a misery? But despite man's misuse of her, woman has been a willing accomplice and cannot be excused. Finding little love in man's sexuality she still gave him what he wanted and in the process became more or less possessed like him.

What else could she do? The male-dominated religions, cultures and society offered no alternative. The true love of man that she naturally craved didn't seem to be here, except perhaps on her side. She felt she must be mistaken. Love was not what life was about. The failure must be her fault.

So she settled for the passing feelings of sexual stimulation and excitement – receiving at the same time a faint echo from within of her pure God-made nature which is to please man and give him pleasure. Woman loves giving man pleasure and pleasing him – in love. Just as he in his innermost nature loves to love her, care for her, delight her and protect her in this very hostile and difficult world for love and woman.

But woman's surrender to sex without love has made her deeply emotional and therefore largely unlovable to man. She simply cannot understand what has happened to love, which to her is God. Instead of being true to her knowledge of love she is true to her feelings which lead her into more emotional situations and discontent.

Woman's Responsibility

Man cannot really love woman until woman takes responsibility for her true nature. He is too steeped in sex and not helped at all by the readiness of deluded women to give him what he wants instead of what she knows in her deepest place is right.

Today the passage of time has entrenched the feeling of the sexual imperative in the majority of women. The sexual imperative basically is the compulsion to procreate. And procreation, due again to man's tinkering with natural processes, has been subverted to satisfy sexual urges.

Sexual desires are natural. But they degenerate into random sexual urges when real love is absent. Woman often resorts to procreation in the vain hope that the love of her offspring will compensate for the lack of love or even bring her and her partner together in love.

Many women have revolted and turned away in disgust from man. But that only perpetuates feelings – feelings of distrust, discontent, intermittent rage and self-doubt. These are all the aftermath of man's lack of love and her mistaken acceptance that she cannot do anything about it.

28
Man and Woman in Partnership

The intelligent question for both is, why are you together? And the intelligent answer is, to enjoy being together.

What happened? In most cases when you first came together there was joy and delight. Soon after, you probably made beautiful love. Why did those golden moments fade? How could they fade when the splendour was so vital, immediate, real?

That's the question you have to ask yourself in every partnership. You have to discover what the spoiler is.

Not that the let-down in a partnership is always sudden. It can be very gradual. Instead of making love once or twice a day you make love once a week. One of you may get immersed in an interesting hobby at the expense of being together. Maybe one or the other will be staying back at work because 'it's necessary' when it wasn't necessary before.

A climate of familiarity, casualness and compromise begins to set in. One, or both, starts taking the other for granted. You don't kiss as often, as lovingly, or as meaningfully as you used to. And if you or the other questions what is happening to your love the excuse of a billion former lovers may be heard: 'The honeymoon doesn't last forever, you know'.

Why doesn't it?

Where I come from the honeymoon does last. It goes on indefinitely. But it can't last while the lovers allow themselves to be controlled by the spoiler – their emotional unhappy self.

Know Your self

'Know yourself', proclaimed the ancient sage. But he didn't say how, and he didn't say what your self is. So it's become a comfortable intellectual saying that gets quoted by people who don't know their self.

There's no better way to get to know your trouble-making self than in partnership. It's your self that makes you repeat the same sad routine as lovers have been doing for countless generations. It is a pity when we've made such progress in everything else that's less important.

In any good and fulfilling situation your self sooner or later will take the shine off it or ruin it. That applies also to the self of the partner. But your first concern has to be your own self – and why it so often gets away with its dirty work.

Your self is your emotions and feelings. Your emotions and feelings seduce you in two ways. First, as moods. Moods slide in like a thief in the night and you're suddenly thinking about being uncertain, doubtful or afraid of making a mistake. You then have second thoughts about your lover or the situation and perhaps start being cool or distant to him or her when there's no real reason.

Your feelings of doubt and fear tell you that something's wrong. It's not the situation that's necessarily wrong; it's your doubts and fears that are wrong. And if the partnership does go wrong you'll think you should have been true to your feelings earlier.

But that's your self thinking. It was your self that spoiled the partnership anyway; or that clouded your natural intelligence by lulling you into a sense of security which is false in any situation. Nothing is secure, and there are always signs before something goes wrong.

The other way your emotions and feelings are able to seduce you is because of their swiftness. They are so quick that they take over and you find yourself saying harsh things or a nasty word that you know will provoke an argument. And should the argument keep developing you may suddenly hear your self exclaim, 'I'm leaving' or 'I'm through' while you walk out the door wondering, 'Is this really happening?'

It's happening all right. And you are going to have to handle the consequences because the culprit, your self, will have ducked for cover; actually disappeared. But being psychic it just changes form.

In its new guise your self makes you feel wretched, lonely, and if you're a woman, guilty. Your self enjoys going over the events in your mind, rearranging the confrontational dialogue and trying to find some sort of justification for the disaster it has caused. Madness! Yes, the self is mad. And it has made a mad world.

Natural Intelligence

What can you do to outwit and outpace your self?

It's a matter of you being your natural intelligence. Your self is not naturally intelligent. It is clever, scheming, cunning, persuasive, deceitful and reactive. It does not see life as it is because it abides in the dark of ignorance inside your body.

Your self's impressions of the external world are second-hand. Your intelligence registers the world direct through your senses. Your self has no senses. It relies on interpretations of what you are seeing based on emotions of the past. Your self can never see existence as it is now. But you can.

What you have to do is start to distance your natural intelligence from your emotions and feelings. This is not difficult. Throughout your life you will have already seen or glimpsed the damaging or ruinous nature of your self. And by reading this book you will have got the idea more and begun to separate somewhat from your self – thus becoming more naturally intelligent by knowing your self.

Your natural intelligence is immediate. I'll show you. Look at any object now. As long as you are just seeing the object you are there immediately. But you mustn't interpret what you are seeing. It's not necessary anyway. If you are seeing a chair, do you say, 'That's a chair'? Of course not. The cognition and recognition is immediate.

But if you infer something about the chair such as that it's the one your mother gave you, you are interpreting. Your intelligence is not immediate any more. You've gone into the past. That's where your self lives. And before you know it you will have thoughts or emotions about your mother or something else associated with the chair. Knock on the door of your self and you get an almost instantaneous problematical answer.

While you remain in your senses and practise not interpreting situations unnecessarily, your self with all its speed and cleverness can't get in. There is nothing swifter than the intelligence of immediacy.

29

The Broken Heart

Most people at some time have their heart broken and experience the accompanying intense pain, anguish and futility of carrying on. The cause may be a failed love affair or the death of a loved one. The cause doesn't really matter. What matters is that the heart, the central place of love and life in the human body, is felt to have been broken.

What is the value of such suffering? Since it happens to so many people it must be necessary in the way of things. How? Why?

The human heart is actually a necessary psychic blockage in the free flow of pure psyche through the system. However, in the mirror world of limited human intelligence, the heart is understandably described as a kind of pump that keeps the blood circulating – a reverse concept to what I've just said.

The pump concept is true in our mirror world of substance and matter. But it's not the truth because every image in a mirror is reversed. Moreover every mirror-body vanishes, dies – when in truth nothing dies.

The physical body is enabled to continue and function internally as a living organism by the constant immortal inspiration of life (inspiration from the Latin 'to breathe' or 'to infuse as life'). Unchecked, the flow of pure life would destroy the human organism. But the divine instinctual intelligence within every animal mirror-body creates a physical heart to partly block the flow of vital life. The substance of vital life in our mirror world is blood.

Since the physical human heart is in truth a blockage, it's also a blockage in the psychological system. The psycho-logical system is what allows man and woman to realise God or truth. Its mirror image is the mind and emotions which cannot realise God or truth.

Due to the human mind the heart is saturated with emotions. It is the emotional centre of the body. The deepest emotions are instantly felt there. The heart is a living reservoir of attachment. Attachment arises from ignorance of love.

A real broken heart is supposed to release all the emotions that have accumulated there since birth.

But how many broken hearts are real? And how do you tell?

Once the heart is purified it's no longer a blockage. An extraordinary psychological change follows. The pure psyche flows unimpeded through the system and all attachment to the world and the body vanishes. The body is then known to be necessary for existence but not vital for life. In other words any fear of death of the body is completely erased.

The Weeping Heart

When a lover leaves you, or a loved one dies, your heart is endeavouring to free itself of attachment to that person. It's not you that weeps in the first place. It's your heart secreting (from the Latin, 'to separate and give off', extending to excreta and the excretion of waste matter).

But because of the ignorance of society and its teachers, nobody realises this. So people repeatedly get attached to those they love. This doesn't mean the love is deficient. It means that by continuing to keep attaching themselves to the objects of their love they ensure another potentially meaningless heartbreak.

Some people, of course, through repeated disappointments and heartbreaks resist the urge to love the opposite gender out of a sense of self-protection. This in one way is unfortunate. They protect themselves from assumed future suffering but deny themselves the opportunity to purify the heart.

Catch 22 here is that if they fall in love they'll attach themselves and suffer again anyway. The solution of course is to not fall in love but simply to love without attachment.

Few people escape the death of someone they love. This is heartbreak of a different kind. The cause then is the subconscious human conviction that death of the body is the end of the love.

The heart again weeps but never is the heartbreak sufficient to purify the heart totally. The only heartbreak to do that is the sense of separation from the love of God which is so intense that complete self-dissolution occurs.

Sometimes the sheer frustration of not being able to love or find love, despite a consuming inner urge, leads to suicide. Intense attachment to drugs or alcohol and the failure of these to give enduring fulfilment can also lead to suicide.

No case of suicide can ever be really explained. Death in any form is determined by the divine intelligence to which human reasons are completely irrelevant.

FROM HERE TO REALITY

Ego

Instinct and ego are I-dentical – the pure intelligence in every living thing.

30

The Popular Misconception

Ask most people what ego means and they'll probably say the word is used to describe a selfish, self-centred, arrogant person. Thus, egotist, egomania and the well-worn ego trip.

But that's not the ego at all. That's the troublesome self. The ego is the most impersonal, unconscious and essential function in the human body. Through ignorance the self has succeeded once more in deflecting attention from itself – this time on a popular world-wide basis.

There is no 'I' in the selfless ego. The ego is the body's pure intelligence. And as such it has another name recognisable as being selfless in everybody's own experience. The name is instinct.

Instinct and ego are I-dentical – the pure intelligence in every living thing.

The function of instinct is to protect the body from injury and to ensure its survival as much as that is possible. It does this in every animal, plant, insect and bacteria without distinction or consideration. Ego rules in all for good. Thank God.

The Many Faces of 'self'

*The deepest realisation of God occurs when I as my self
completely disown my self.*

31

The Historical self

How, in the first place, in our modern psychology-based society, did the personal self get mixed up with the divine impersonal instinct? Because the uninterrupted realisation of God or Supreme Being was absent in the founder of psychoanalytic theory, Sigmund Freud, and those who came after him.

With God-realisation the whole human perspective changes. It gives a clear inner instinctual knowledge of the origins of humanity and its evolved psychological structure, as well as a clear outer view of the facticity of life through the senses. Inner and outer come together with clarity – which means with no speculative or theorising self in between.

I know little about Freud apart from a bit of history I've read. He was certainly gifted and there's not a great deal in psychology that doesn't go back to his formative insights. He seems to have been the first to have coined the word 'ego' as a division of the psyche.

Freud saw pretty clearly into the influence of the psychic on human behaviour and proposed sexuality as a basis for it. His whole method, however, was historical – studying the past in people and himself to arrive at present behaviour.

Self-analysis

Freud, from what I've read, also attempted to know himself through self-analysis. Self-analysis is partial. It depends on self revealing itself. And self is no fool when it comes to self-disso-lution. Being cunningly resourceful it reveals relatively harmless historical fragments as well as shamelessly invented fragments – while all the time adding to itself through the living life.

To even partially penetrate self, a sincere and serious state of consciousness is necessary. This Freud demonstrated through his lifelong dedication to the investigation of the psyche.

Even so it takes more than analysis to really know your self.

It takes an intense and continuous love of God to finally break through. This is not to imply that Freud did not love the unknowable God; nor Einstein, and all the other great, dedicated contributors to human knowledge. But the critical test is the living life of relationships – to external objects and people, to your body and to your self. There must be harmony, peace and fulfilment in relation to all. Only the deeply God-realised enjoy this state of grace.

Hypnosis

Freud, in confronting his self, is said to have been thrown into turmoil, as he apparently expected. He is said to have suffered from 'a powerful psychoneurosis' which sounds like an academic way of describing the agony one must go through to realise self and be free of it as a problem. Apart from physical pain, the only agony is the dying of self.

Freud was reportedly tickled pink when his first psychoanalytic efforts, assisted by hypnosis, seemed to prove successful in the treatment of a girl exhibiting severe symptoms of hysteria after her father died. The 'talking cure', as the patient named Freud's method, worked. But then another doctor demonstrated that he could use hypnosis to induce all kinds of conditions of spontaneous hysteria. Freud carried on and re-jigged his theory of the origins of hysteria.

To me, everyone suffering from emotional problems is a victim of hypnosis – the hypnotic suggestions of an ignorant world and society. The power behind this hypnotic effect is the global fear of death as an end. Remove the ignorance and the condition vanishes. But what a task, when most of humanity is more or less hysterical about death.

The Id

Freud intuited and, as far as I know, named the id. Id means 'it' in Latin and to me it (id) is the foundation of the entire human existential system. It is the sum total of all the *animalistic forces and instinctive impulses* in the body. At its instinctual level it is God beneath existence.

An ongoing close study of your self will reveal the power and effect of 'it' in your living life. It is like a volcano. It simmers away in every body causing actions beyond volition and understanding and from time to time erupts unpredictably and often violently, defying reason and restraint.

Freud regarded the id as the reservoir of blind instinctive impulses endeavouring to work their way into existence through what he called the ego. Fair enough. The id, however, is only apprehended as being blind by our rationalising self-consciousness. It is utterly conscious in its own right. Freud certainly glimpsed this. He also conceived the id as containing the hereditary influences, and apparently connected it with the primitive past of humanity. This is so. The id is the undifferentiated summation of the historical self extending back to the beginning of time. The past then determines the future which is the present.

The primitive in the id is the more pure 'animalistic' beginning of humanity when there was very little emotion or past in the body. 'Animalistic' can conjure up thoughts of brute or beast. But that's a far later definition made by the self-conscious self to separate man from the animal which he substantially is.

The word 'animal' derives originally from the Sanskrit, the most ancient of languages, and means breath, life or soul – quite different to brute and beast. But self, being devoid of self-knowledge, doesn't know this. You only have to look at an animal to perceive its innocent beauty, the presence of instinctual intelligence unburdened by self. (Man and woman sometimes reflect this sublime beauty – when they are truly surrendered to love or when self is truly absent.) Animals of course are always being what they are; human beings seldom are.

Karma

The primitive past of humanity is within each individual physical body because our physical bodies are products of the past.

Fundamentally the id is behind all our drives – self-conscious and unconscious. And it is not just the primitive past. It is the potency of all past. Its Sanskrit name is karma. Karma is the power that repeats the past in different forms and conditions in order that the past may at last be consciously faced and neutralised to become the present.

Contrary to most theories our bodies have not evolved. The human body began (begins) as a pure idea in God's intellect in the deepest part of the psyche. From there the body has simply come further into manifestation, into physical appearance. The effect is not unlike seeing a vague dot in the distant sky coming towards you, at a closer point recognising the shape as an aircraft and finally the full close-up view.

What may be mistaken for the body's evolution is the effect of the vast train of karma on every body ever born since time or past began. Every body in a particular genetic lineage exhibits at birth one or some of the karmic effects appearing in or on some of the earlier bodies. There is a compounding, yet gradually diminishing, effect as some of the past during the life of the body is converted by increasing consciousness into the present.

In this you will see the origin of hereditary influences and properties associated with DNA by modern biological science.

You will now also be able to appreciate why the human body remains forever a radiant purity in the divine intellect – behind all the karmic effects and properties influencing the endless procession of countless bodies into existence. And the amazing thing is that the consciousness of this purity beyond all time and past can be realised here in the present.

32

The Evolving self

All that has evolved in the whole of immemorial time is the emotional self and its agency, the human mind.

Together, with the saving grace of divine intelligence, they are responsible for progress. Thus progress consists not only of a mad rat-race in pursuit of selfish interests but also of inventions, discoveries and medical procedures that help to heal and reduce pain in the physical body. These practical altruistic inspirations are from the sixth dimension – and are a gift from God, the pure psyche.

Our physical universe is defined as being four-dimensional – capable of being measured in length, breadth, depth and time. The fifth dimension is the psyche behind the universe. And the sixth dimension is the divine world of pure idea, the origin of which is explained later.

Emotions are the source of hardness and force – the projection of ignorance into existence. So under the influence and pressure of the evolving self the human body has become more substantive (psychic) and substantial (material). This means that with the passage of time physicality has become more and more solid – and the world more and more hard.

The Instinctual I

Most people, including Freud, refer to humans as being conscious. This again is the self putting a gloss on the fact. Humanity is self-conscious, not conscious. Consciousness is a profound inner state in which very little remains of reflective self as ignorance of life and God.

To sum up at this point: the divine instinctual intelligence, termed the unconscious, is really the conscious state behind the evolving historical self. Evolution of the self continues as it always has, but the unconscious in every body remains precisely as it is and where it is – outside time and yet ever-present.

The Genius

Fortunately, all that is not important. What's important is that your body dies and the self-conscious burden – everything you think you are, apart from true love, which can't be thought about anyway – dies with the body. The fact remains that you are love and you are truth to a far more profound degree than you can know or think about.

Your essential being is the unconscious, the inner instinctual presence which contains every level of the pure psyche. This, from behind every historical influence, constantly directs your living life towards a greater reality.

The greatest reality is death. So either through physical death, or being freed while alive from attachment to the physical body or the world, I enter the pure psyche according to my state of consciousness – my self-knowledge.

The genius behind it all is the instinctual unconscious.

Human history as evolution can be known theoretically and speculatively through the study of myths, anthropology and fossilised discoveries. But the unconscious as instinct cannot be known. It can only be approached by love and appreciation of its ever-present but unfathomable mystery.

33
The Pirate self

When uninterrupted God-realisation is absent, the evolved human self pirates the divine intelligence of instinct. It does this by thinking and rationalisation, which are other words for reasoning.

Then the self thinks, 'I am this intelligence' – just as you can imagine, 'I'm in the supermarket', when you're not; or you can reason that two-times-two equals four when you have no apples or counters in front of you.

Only when the sense mechanism is free of thought, interpretation or rationalisation can the facticity of existence be seen. Otherwise the reasoning faculty causes complications, conflict, comparison and discontent.

Second Thing First

Reasoning is legitimate. But it must begin with first thing first and continue by sticking to facts without consideration of feelings. Scientists have supposedly got rid of feelings but have fooled everyone with their theories by not putting first thing first. First thing first is self-knowledge.

Most of humanity (like scientists) put second thing first and confuse issues even further by trying to reason emotionally with feelings. The result is confusion and chaos in human relationships, communication and dealings.

As you have seen, first thing first in a love relationship is to enjoy being together – all the time. The only thing that spoils that are the feelings of the emotional or pirate self

A prime example of the pirate self at work is when the theoretical physicist deduces, from what has been previously reasoned, the distance of a star from the earth.

The physicist then says, 'I've proven my deduction by actual phenomenal observations and measurements.' But what his I hasn't realised is that anything deduced with conviction in the mind then appears to be affirmed in the phenomenal world. Science already knows that the consciousness of the observer (the scientist) has an essential effect on experimental results but amazingly ignores this out of self-consideration.

Not just the scientists, but people from all walks of life project their convictions onto others, as well as onto events, and see things totally differently from less identified observers. This happens particularly where strong emotions are involved such as love, hate and sexual excitement.

Fervent national or group emotions over an event often leave outsiders cold and wondering what is happening. Two examples in modern times of mass emotional projection verging on hysteria were the amazing effects nationally, and seemingly globally, of the assassination of President Kennedy in the 1960s and the accidental death in the 1990s of Diana, Princess of Wales.

The value of present scientific inquiry, of course, is a deep-rooted group conviction, particularly among scientists. They keep following a broadly selected route. There are other routes needing enlightened inquiry, such as love, truth, inner peace, frustration, discontent and a heap of other causes of physically damaging unhappiness in people.

These are dismissed as the domain of philosophy and religion. Science prefers to stick to theorising and inventing its own problematical reality through ignoring the pointers to what's actually real. Love and truth are well and truly off the scientific menu – except when the scientist arrives home.

What if every scientist had to put their self through the terrible rigours and discipline of self-knowledge? The self, comfortably ensconced in scientific avoidance, ensures that that doesn't happen. And so, blithely and blindly, ignorance as materialism leads the way.

The Value of Science

Science is only of value where a study is made of a particular object or organism for the purpose of reducing physical pain.

Once the inquiry focuses on extending the life of an organism, particularly a human being, self-ishness or corruption of motive creeps in.

Science should exist for the good of humanity, not for the good of science. But medical science – because it is not self-knowledge based – has developed mostly as a process of experimentation: everyone treated (with the best of intentions) is a guinea-pig hopefully adding to the bottomless chest of medical knowledge and experience.

This applies particularly to radiotherapy and chemotherapy, the darlings of those doctors who don't have cancer yet. (Not to mention radical surgery, an option often recommended – by surgeons – followed by a course of one or both of the above.) Undoubtedly some people have survived for many years after having radiation and chemo. But would they have survived anyway? An undoctored register of how many cancer sufferers survive and how many die after having the treatments is not available. Even doctors are amazed at times by remissions they can't explain.

Radiotherapy can indeed temporarily reduce localised pain in the spine from cancer – provided the operatives administering it don't make a mistake. It can also create fierce pain in unrelated tissue.

The fact remains that radiotherapy and chemotherapy are purely experimental and therefore haphazard, despite all the expert opinions to the contrary. You may survive them and you may not. But the cover-up is that if you die, it's the cancer that killed you.

It may be true that few people die directly from radiotherapy or chemotherapy but no one really knows. The effect on the human system, particularly of chemotherapy, is so debilitating that the natural immunity is pretty well shot.

Chemo certainly destroys the quality of life and the carrot for putting up with it is – perhaps – a few more years of living. When the patients mostly die – after going through terrible deprivation of the quality of life, added to the insidious effect of the cancer – there is much shaking of heads and well-meaning sympathy from the doctors. And tears all round among the closest survivors. But no one's responsible. Everyone has done their best.

Have they?

No, they haven't. But they can't help it – because no one is responsible for their self. When you're not responsible for your self you can't be responsible for what you do. And as the mass of humanity is not responsible, no one's responsible and so everyone soldiers on as best they can – mostly hoping for a miracle or a lottery win.

.

34

The Suffering self

Fear is the generic name of self. We fear tomorrow; we fear we will die; we fear our loved one doesn't love us; we fear what people will say or think; we fear failure. It is all the activity of self which loves to suffer, even though you think you don't. But if you think about your personal life you inevitably project emotionally into the future or into the past. And you suffer.

Self being psychic also enjoys the opposite to suffering – excitement or emotional highs. But self-knowledge teaches us that such highs invariably lead to sadness or discontent – even if only because they end and then you can't help *thinking* about how good things were.

Physical Pain

There is no suffering in physical pain.

This might seem an outrageous statement. But please test it in your own experience next time you have physical pain. Meanwhile I'll explain.

Physical pain is unavoidable in these vulnerable human bodies. You kick your toe, gash your arm, have a medical injection or operation, break a leg, wake up with a migraine, fall over – and all the other unfortunate happenings that can afflict the body.

But only self suffers – because only self thinks. Without thought you don't suffer. There is only the physical pain. Thinking makes physical pain worse: an emotional element is added to the pain. As you stop thinking about the pain you reduce it by anything from twenty to sixty per cent. This of course doesn't stop the pain, but it removes the element of fear which can be considerable.

Physical pain is true feeling. Thinking about the consequences of physical pain, about future effects on you or others, arouses feelings, emotional feelings, which are not true; as well as worry, which is even less true.

But most people fail to make the distinction between physical pain and emotional pain. Emotional pain is certainly feeling. But it is not true feeling. Emotional pain is self-made and avoidable. Physical pain is natural and therefore unavoidable. Physical pain may be reduced with modern medical substances and in extreme cases controlled and made tolerable with narcotics. But such pain is pain. There's no virtue in it as far as we can see – except in the bearing of it.

From this has arisen the perceived virtue of stoic forbearance.

Imagined Suffering

It is popular and fashionable to think that starving third world people are suffering. This is not necessarily so. It is possible to starve to death as it is possible to fast to death without suffering. But there must be no thought about food or the absence of it, no imagining. In such cases there is simply the physical pain that accompanies contraction in the organism.

Starving to death is tolerable, as people in the West with 'everything to live for' have demonstrated in their misplaced pursuit of physical beauty. But in the famine-stricken third world to starve or not to starve is not an option, not a decision. Compared to us these people live with a minimum of hope and expectation. Theirs is a simple waiting on the facticity of life which we in the West with all our choices and options can't even imagine. Compared to our world and most of us, these people are truly innocent, not unlike the beautiful instinctual animals that bear pain without thought.

No Decisions

Emotional pain is the most common pain on earth.

Emotional pain comes from previous choices and decisions. Choices and decisions – the accepted way of life in our modern civilisation – are the product of ignorance which is simply lack of self-knowledge. We can't help descending into ignorance after we're born. The question is how long we stay there before realising – through self-knowledge – that nothing is what it seems, particularly the antics and feelings of our self.

Instead of making choices, why not do what you prefer? All animals eat what they prefer and bypass what they don't prefer while conditions offer their preferences. Should their preferences not be available animals will eat a lower grade of preferences. In either case they won't make a choice. They do what comes naturally – and that's what they prefer.

Choices come from likes and dislikes. We develop likes and dislikes from childhood. Parents, relatives and society encourage us to like and dislike things. We get into the habit of saying what we like and dislike. This creates a disjointed and self-projecting way of looking at things and judging them. The self feeds off these polarised reactions. Best not to say what you like or don't like. 'No thank you,' or 'not just now' is a better way; or a simple 'thank you.' Be guided by preference. As you give up likes and dislikes you'll get the idea.

The spiritual master, the Blessed John, who in London in 1968 had a great transforming influence on my life, used to say: 'Don't make decisions. Go for the biggest yes.'

Just as the unhappy self lives off choices and likes and dislikes, so for its own good it forces us into the habit of making decisions. Most 'decisions' are not necessary. You only think they are. Best, as the Blessed John advised, to go for the biggest yes. There's nothing sharp or staccato in that. There's a nice pause while you sum up the facts – not influenced by your feelings. That's the intelligent way.

Stop saying, 'I decided'. You'll be amazed at how unnecessary the word is in your life. You'll also be amazed at how often events work out and make decisions irrelevant. You may be in for a bit of nail-biting for a while as you wait without making a decision until what may seem the last moment. But if you're true, life will be true too and surprise you. Only the valiant get the prize.

35

The Child and self

You are born with innate instinctual intelligence. This is focused on the inner senses, the nuclear senses within, a psycho-spiritual complex. This is behind the physical senses. Although the physical senses are activated, the body at this stage has not manifested in the baby's experience. The baby for the most part is responsive to the needs of the senses within, as it was in the womb.

The nuclear senses are instinctive and present before the body. And the innate instinctual intelligence behind them is none other than God, the indescribable power and presence behind everything.

To describe God's presence in practical existential terms, God is instinct. You don't need a university degree to know instinct in your own body, or to observe this amazing intelligence acting immediately and without interruption inside every human body and every living thing.

The Inner Sun

God, the inner Source of instinctual intelligence, is the incredible original mighty sun within, the Source of the perceived brilliance and power of all the galaxies and lights in the starry sky and the lights below.

The unbearable glory and genius of the Source is made bearable, understandable and recognisable by way of several divinely designed incremental densities – the levels of the psyche. The densest density is the physical body. Such density allows the apparently distant fiery firmament to be seen, appreciated and perhaps recognised as infinite beauty.

But the point is that the external universe is merely a sensory reflection – an outer projection through the brain of the nuclear reality within. By nuclear I mean the minute divinely radiant centre of all things.

The Source of I

In the new-born baby's experience the physical body has not yet manifested. Experience and time are the source of self. As experience and time (ageing) increase so does the presence of the body and so does the self, as I. The baby, now a child, confidently begins calling its self I.

From the unknowable unconscious depths within, God the Source of light or intelligence, lights up the entire human subconscious where the notion of self resides. As self is only a figment born of transient experience and time, the divine light passes unobstructed through the self into the physical senses.

This provides sufficient intelligence for the physical world to be perceived as it is and as it is created every moment by the Source.

The self, however, having no inner knowledge, no inner light of intelligence, assumes that the divine light shining continuously through it into the physical world is its own illumination! The self sees itself as the source of all and concludes that I am in control – the original disastrous case of mistaken identity!

The Shadow

Being composed only of thought and impressions, the self casts an illusory thoughtful shadow onto existence. As the shadow has no reality, this happens only in the thoughtful personal subconscious where the self abides.

Although the self has no effect on the actual facticity of existence, it has an almost overwhelming effect in the subconscious of the individual. There it creates intermittent and sometimes intense personal stress, anxiety and depression. This happens because the self as the person *interprets* the world from a *self-conscious* point of view. Self-conscious means seeing things through your feelings and emotions – seeing through the distortion of self.

The result is completely personal.

We don't just see objects. We interpret them according to our emotional identification with them. If a number of people are looking at a building and have no emotional association with it, they all see the same thing. But if one of them owns and treasures the building and it's being sold, that person will interpret the scene personally and not see the building simply as it is.

As all persons are personal and perceiving self-consciously most of the time, they share the same emotions stored inside. This enables other persons to usually understand or sympathise with what another person is going through. What makes human beings human is that they reflect off their emotions instead of simply being.

36
The Reflective self

Awareness is the intelligent means by which the physical world is seen through the physical senses. Without awareness there is no physical world and no you or me. But as we saw in the previous essay, awareness in most people is corrupted and distorted by self thinking or reflecting on its feelings.

Feelings form an emotional memory in the self from psychic impressions of past hurts and excitement. When self reflects on this memory it stirs up feelings of the past which are then projected onto current events or persons.

The self's other memory is the mental or intellectual memory. This is the storehouse in the subconscious of past mental impressions of events and conditions not overtly associated with emotions.

Emotional events stir mental reflection – worry, fear and confusion. Mental reflection stirs the emotions – excitement and various levels of depression. Together the emotional and mental memories make up our whole psychological self, the human psychonomy.

Living is made tedious, emotionally exciting and mentally worrying by self-reflection. Each time you think, you reinforce your self which makes you have to think again. Each time you are emotional, you again reinforce your self which makes you have to be emotional again. This to-ing and fro-ing is how self stays lodged in the human subconscious.

Self is never present in the moment. When self is absent in the moment you are aware and present. You are not self-conscious then. You are more conscious. But because you will think and be emotional again you're unable to remain conscious for long. The pressure of your self to exist through using your innate intelligence is too great.

Nevertheless living is a process of discovering that I no longer want to be controlled by my self. Self is so firmly entrenched in the human subconscious that it can take consciousness many recurrences for this to happen. But once you get the idea and start to practise refraining from aimless thought, and not thinking about your feelings, the separation is already under way.

But it can't be done by an intellectual or emotional decision. Action based on such decisions soon wilts. Practice endures once you've lived long enough to start waking up to your self.

Self-interest

Lodged in the dark of the subconscious and never seeing the world as it is, self forms impressions of what the awareness is perceiving. It interprets everything through the bias of self-interest. This becomes our emotional involvement with the world, in other words, our feelings. In direct awareness there is no interpretation, no feelings. Events and things are seen precisely as they are.

Due to self, nearly every body in existence is constantly reflecting – thinking, speculating, imagining, wondering, fanta-sising, theorising and so forth. And what is self reflecting on? The past, because that's all self knows. Its interpretations are the past. Self also constantly thinks about the future, not realising that there's no future to reflect on, except what the mind and emotions project as expectations from the past.

Prediction

There is a future in anyone's living life that can be glimpsed in the present. Clairvoyants sometimes demonstrate this. But it's not advisable to act on such predictions. The danger is too great of self influencing and distorting the prediction. All predictions are still in the tricky psychic realm where self rules as the human subconscious.

However, not all the psychic realm is misleading. Like all levels of the psyche, the deeper region of the psychic, where it adjoins the pure psyche, is considerably free of self.

Into this region at death everyone must go – and stay or pass through according to their lights. Predictions or communications from the deeper level are mostly reliable. But due to the lower psychic trickster, it is best to be cautious and to simply wait and see whether predictions or communications come to pass.

Self and Experience

Self, like the body, does not exist without experience. This means self is dependent for existence on experience and the appearance of the body. As experience literally formulates the body – makes the inner senses manifest outwardly as form – so self is inextricably identified with the body. That identification results in emotional attachment to the body and this creates the fear of death. The attachment has to be consciously dissolved. There's only one way that can be done and that's through the experience of living.

As we have seen in this and previous essays, it was the gradual appearance of the baby body through increasing experience that brought self into being. Finally self has to go out in reverse to how it came in – by intelligence dissolving self's attachment to experience.

Poor self. Its first name is fear and its last name is attachment. There's no way out for it except by dying – not by your body dying but by your self dying willingly and consciously to its own ignorance.

37

The Subconscious and self

The human subconscious really should not be there inside you. The space it occupies was originally pure psyche, the untroubled unconscious. But the space has been taken over by self. And as I've described, this began at the beginning of time marking the manifestation of the body.

The purpose behind the living of a real spiritual life is to empty the subconscious of self and return it to its pristine state.

At birth a baby is the instinctual intelligence of the unconscious. For a few early years it is between the unconscious and subconscious. Due to the influence of the unconscious, a child may exhibit exceptional and inexplicable abilities along certain lines, or make extraordinarily perceptive observations. There are children who show spontaneous early signs of genius such as Mozart, Schubert and Mendelssohn, all of whom began to compose before the age of twelve, and numerous other children outside the field of music. But in many cases the subconscious fog of self gradually impairs or frustrates the genius and the adult fails to meet early expectations.

The physical body is actual. The self is imaginary. It is extremely difficult not to confuse one with the other.

Your self is how you feel about people, conditions and events. Such feelings are the painful love of a person, the love of an object, fear, self-doubt, frustration, jealousy, hate and every other negative emotion. None of these feelings are of your body. They are all due to assumptions, presumptions, interpretations and judgements by your self.

The body's 'feelings' on the other hand are confined to direct physical stimulus such as a blow, an injury, a sudden pain, an ache, heat or cold, fatigue after physical effort, hunger, thirst, excitation of the sexual parts, natural excretory calls: those sorts of actual feelings, as well as the relief of them.

Joy, Love and Knowledge

There are other intimations from within that are not of self or the body and therefore are not feelings. These are spontaneous joy and love without an object.

Spontaneous joy is associated with the knowledge of wellbeing, of all being well. And love without an object is the love of God, the unknowable Source within. It is possible to love somebody without doubt and pain to the degree that God is loved – by putting love of God before love of the other. Utter love of God enables utter love of woman or man without problems.

Spontaneous love and joy emerge from the instinctual intelligence of the unconscious, via the inner nucleate senses behind the physical senses.

The inner senses are completely abstract, an aspect of pure psyche. They are pure, undifferentiated, radiant energy resonating at a frequency far beyond the register of the mind or emotions. Our physical senses are an externalised and separative projection of them. The inner senses are divine.

Love and joy rising out of the unconscious resonate to the radiant frequency of the inner senses. Thus love and joy are sensed to be divine.

Resonance means to intensify and enrich as a resounding quality – just as a finely made violin or guitar depends on a shaped resonance chamber to produce a pleasing mellow variety of tone. Without attention to resonance there is the raw sound of twanging and striking – something like the rawness of feeling that derives from resonating to the troublesome vibrations of your self.

The key to getting the idea behind this is in the word 'knowledge'. Knowledge is what the ancients called gnosis. Gnosis is pure knowledge, meaning knowledge that rises spontaneously from within without any reflection by the mind. What the world calls knowledge is not knowledge. Worldly knowledge is simply the result of the mind synthesising, or combining, past information and experience. Pure knowledge – self-knowledge

– contains none of those elements. It ascends from the depths of the unconscious and as such is divine.

The body and especially the self are too coarse to register pure knowledge or the divine intimations of joy and love. Joy and love arise in everyone – because no one is special – but until the sub-conscious is cleared, they have to pass through the shadow of self. This automatically distorts and converts the knowledge into emotional feelings. The extraordinary divine purity is then smothered by feelings. The emotionalised feelings are indeed recognised as joy or love. But they lack the original power to fulfil and so tend to add to the person's involuntary discontent.

To the degree that the subconscious self has been dissolved and transformed, some kind of exceptional knowledge or power of spiritual perception is evident in the individual. Spiritual masters have this power – but again only to the extent that self is absent. And only God knows that.

With the power or inner light of intelligence the externalised physical master penetrates the self of the student or devotee from without while simultaneously the light of divine intelligence inside the individual works on his or her self from within. Both are the same selfless consciousness doing the same job.

This intelligence is in everybody at this moment. But the constant focus on the feelings of self degrade the intelligence into the cleverness of mind. The effect then is like trying to pick up a pin with woollen gloves.

38
The Nature of self

There is nature. And there is human nature. Human nature is the nature of self. It is human nature to worry, to mourn the dead and fear death, to be spiteful, moody, envious, self-doubtful and to have all the rest of the unhappy negative emotions that spoil life on earth.

Everyone to begin with has to take on the persona of human nature which means being loaded with a share of human negativity. Because of this everyone tends to forgive, understand or sympathise with others who are having a bout of suffering from the persona's negativity.

The subconscious or involuntary rationale for this is that if I accept your bouts of suffering you'll accept mine when I have them. In other words, by excusing another's negativity I excuse my self. Even worse is if I react emotionally to another's negativity. Our two personas then get locked in a gladiatorial fight in which even the winner doesn't win.

And so the great merry-go-round of unhappiness in human affairs continues unchecked because nobody is really taking responsibility for human nature.

The Mask

The words 'persona' and 'person' derive from the Latin meaning 'mask', especially a mask worn by an actor. As an extension, actor became person and then the analytic psychologist C. J. Jung (a breakaway student of Freud) defined the persona as 'the social front or facade an individual assumes to depict to the world the role in life that he (or she) is playing'.

That's true. We're all involved in a role simply to exist. So everybody has to have a persona. But does the persona have to be the hideous mask you see over your face in the mirror when you're deeply emotional and crying from the intense feeling of that pain? Or does it have to be the mask that appears on another's face, including the child you love, when unresolved human nature has possessed the individual?

The child can't help it. But you can. You must discover what's behind the pain behind the mask. The role you are playing by simply living your life is okay. It may change. But whatever role you're playing for the time being you don't have to be unhappy.

The beggar sleeping on the streets and eating from garbage bins is not naturally unhappy. Only if the human nature starts to possess him and he begins comparing his lot, his role, with another's, will he be unhappy. The beggar is not prevented from ceasing to beg and living a new role. But he can't try to change his situation by a decision. Decisions are made by unhappy people. And the beggar completely in his role is not unhappy. He enjoys his life, his role, as it is for now.

Are you enjoying the character in your role? The character is okay as long as he or she doesn't start trying to act out another role which means putting an artificial character, another mask, over the original character. Disaster is the result. But we've all got so used to the disaster that it's no longer seen as a disaster. It's just accepted as the usual fluctuating conflict of human nature.

Behind the Pain

What is it behind the pain behind the mask?

Jung calls it the anima. Anima is from the Latin meaning 'wind, air, breath, life, soul, spirit, essence'. Jung concurs, describing it as an individual's 'true inner self'.

So far so good.

Anima is the root of animate which means 'to enliven, endow with breath or soul'. Both anima and animate extend in meaning to animal. And lo and behold, out of all the definitions comes, 'the passive or animal soul' and the quality of 'animal instinct' – none other than the pure instinctual intelligence that is essential within every body, a quality not associated with human nature or the human self.

Then there's animus meaning 'consciousness, courage, heart, will (Will?) and purpose'. And finally there is the affectionate animula: 'little soul'. And animulus: 'darling'! Have you ever seen an animal in its natural state that wasn't darling? Have you ever seen a true loved one in her or his natural state, that wasn't darling? If not, you'd better look again. For darling, the essence of consciousness and courage, is what you are.

39

The Sexual self

Self is sex. That's not to say that sex is bad. Sex is essential for the propagation of all the species. And sex between man and woman can be and should be enjoyable – a peak of physical expression of love for the other. But self has pirated sex as its primary vehicle and made a problem of it where none really is.

Sex breeds problems only when self is involved. Sex then becomes an unconscious *drive* – a search for self-satisfaction. But self can't be satisfied for long before discontent sets in. Self then compounds the self-seeking element in sex by using it to try to fill the unfillable emptiness of discontent.

Sexual discontent, being a self-ish emotion, is then unwittingly projected onto other events and persons – as anger, moods, emotional demands, unpleasantness, unreasonableness and other forms of unhappiness. *All unhappiness can be traced back to lack of love – and particularly sex without love.*

Only by loving and being loved can selfishness be removed from sex. This is a tall order in our sex-driven society. Two questions need to be asked. First, do the two partners know what real love is? The answer probably is no. Second, but even more important is, do you know?

Let's go into this together.

Normal love is based on sexual attraction. There's nothing wrong with that. Problems arise only when we endeavour to possess the other; when we badger them with emotional demands; when we settle for satisfying sex and at other times display little enjoyment in being together; when we put personal and unnecessary things before the partnership; when we fail to realise that two physical bodies can never be one; when we compromise with a partner for the sake of comfort and convenience; when, while living together, we've grown apart into casualness, familiarity and habitual acceptance of each other; when we put the children before our mutual love of each other.

Remaining Alert

True love arises out of being more conscious. More conscious means being able to see more clearly the fact behind the appearance of things. As far as a partnership is concerned it means not sitting back and assuming that everything's all right.

This doesn't mean that you should doubt the other or be suspicious. But it does mean you should remain alert for any sign that love in the partnership is being taken for granted. And the first place to look is in yourself and your own behaviour.

Are you 'too tired' when you come home from work to embrace and sit down with the other and tell them that you love them? And how much you enjoy living with them? And coming home to them? All this before unloading on the other about your busy day? Perhaps you can't be bothered? Perhaps you make reasonable excuses for your lack of love? These are all signs that you are at fault, deficient, in the relationship. You are not loving, not giving, and not conscious.

The Parasite

Self, as described earlier, begins to enter us soon after we're born. Self is a parasite made of elapsed time or past. It lives off the immediacy of the body's instinctual intelligence and covers that over with a mounting thickness of ignorant past. Self then assumes that it is the intelligence and therefore is in control.

In its ignorance self doesn't realise that the intelligence it has assumed is a cloudy and sluggish flutter of intelligence that manages to shine through the self, not unlike how an intense light may appear as a dull glimmer through a very thick layer of opaque material.

With its very limited intelligence, and being down in the dark inside every human body, self has nothing to reflect on but itself – a vault of confused and vague memories, impressions, emotional hurts and excitements of the past. The result in most people is almost ceaseless thinking about the past. Most of the thinking is aimless and much of it negative and destructive in that it stirs up past emotional depressions and emotional highs which distort the facticity of life.

The parasitic self lives off the natural vitality of the human body in the same way as all parasites live off the host organism. In humans, the parasite self reduces the body's wellbeing and effectiveness (except in short determined bursts) and causes unstoppable worry and indefinable physical fatigue.

The most powerful instinct in the body after survival is the drive to mate with the opposite gender. We make love with our physical bodies. If the bodies were all that made love, there'd be no problem. Bodies essentially are animalistic, instinctually intelligent. So all the natural animals mate without problems. Bodies instinctually know how to mate, and in our case, how to make love. So making love is not problematical in its instinctual purity. But the parasite-self absorbs some of this vital power and uses it to *reflect* on itself – specifically on its memory of past sexual excitement. This produces in every body sexual selfishness, sexual wanting, sexual manipulation, sexual dissatisfaction, sexual frustration, sexual discontent and sexual dishonesty – *more* or *less*.

It is unavoidable until sex is transformed into real love.

Real Love

Real love begins with the *living* of the knowledge that something greater than yourself is within, and that that something is directing your life, despite all the external difficulties and unresolved emotional pain. Real love also depends on you surrendering to that power in times of stress and anguish and giving up your will and expectations of what is best and what should be.

At the same time it is imperative to offer silent or verbal gratitude for what you have. You are offering this to the unknowable power within for that is where all good in your life comes from. There must be a sincere discernment and appreciation of what you have.

People generally overlook the blessings that they can walk, see, enjoy nature and have the pleasure and presence of the people they love around them. If you are going to learn to truly love, you can't afford to take these things for granted. You must express your thanks more and more often, pausing frequently in your busy day to do so.

People will say they do this already. Fair enough. But I'm speaking to you. 'Already' means that already you haven't got the idea. You express gratitude to the inner reality *now!* Past performance is irrelevant.

At some time you'll be amorously in love with someone. Inasmuch as you've given *conscious* thanks to the unknown for your life you will avoid suffering. People generally only know the emotional pain of suffering but don't understand its subtlety. By this I mean living with a partner you think you love who takes you for granted or abuses you. Or you compromise with the absence of loving attention because you're compatible and live like friends.

Love of God

Love is vibrant but you are the one who has to be vibrant without putting that expectation on another. You can only be vibrant within in your love of the invisible reality. Such love can transform another who loves you in time. You have to stay with the inner love – for that is God.

For a partnership to endure God must be loved before the partner. Most people love the partner first and so partnership in time becomes an inevitable compromise, burden or pain.

The gratitude I've advised is the initial way to start realising love or God.

If you pray, use it to offer thanks for what you have. Endeavour if you can, not to ask for anything. But in times of deep loss and distress it is not out of the order of things to ask God for help.

Eventually you will be continuously thanking God – from a conscious unconscious state within – for the love you have of

God. Without exception all true love is God's love – not ours. When you are dead you are completely immersed in that love, though again you may not know it.

40
The Transformation of self

Self is the only thing in human existence apart from the body. I am self, you are self; everybody is self. Self starts out as being the one-and-only in everyone's experience. Due to its conflicting desires and discontent, self often tires of itself without realising that itself is the cause.

Living is an almost constant conflict for the self: sometimes winning, which is good, and then trying to hold on to what is good, or to improve what is good; always confronted with some sort of challenge to win or succeed again; never satisfied or content for long. Strangely – and perhaps wickedly – all these feelings, good and bad, that keep the individual in an almost constant condition of stress, are nourishment for the self and keep it alive.

As living is devised by God, the paradox has divine purpose. The purpose is for the intransigent and unyieldingly ignorant self to realise God: a prodigious, massive undertaking.

Living is a process of disappointments. Whatever is accomplished or gained loses its initial glow; ageing of the body is relentless and often through accidents and persistent or terminal illness, the hopes, wishes and expectations are dashed. The self, being psychic, recovers quickly and builds up new interests and distractions to keep at bay the truth that living is transient and every body must die in the end.

But because God the Source is behind everything there is the constant, extremely subtle unconscious pull back towards the Source from which all things emerge. Thus do all things deteriorate and eventually pass away, and even the rocks of the earth erode.

But within every body a light of greater intelligence shines, despite the materialistic and self-serving focus of the self on the external world. And when self through its own greed and blindness plunges into depression, there's a chance in the temporary cessation of the outward drive for I, the intelligence of the individual, to ask, 'What's it all about?' That question is prompted by a sliver of light getting through.

The outwardly driving self has no knowledge of this. Because self is not only psychic but fills the entire human subconscious, the surface self is like the tip of the iceberg with seven-eighths of it down below. The whole of self is so vast that it's responsible for all the ignorance in the human race; for all the violence, wars, abuse, arguments, deprivations and suffering. It is an amazing and astonishing psychic force, a cloud that seeps through and contaminates all of human existence.

The Light Divine

But despite the immensity of self as the accumulation of all human unhappiness since time began, it is vulnerable in its deepest regions. For down there in the depths, buried under immemorial time and adjoining the self, is the original pure psyche – the unconscious.

The divine light or intelligence of Source is continuously working in this region where the unconscious actually adjoins the beginning of self. Here, self is not all ignorant darkness; it is dim but there is light in it. Here, a process of attrition goes on as a slow infiltration of Source converts ignorance back to the light of the usurped pure psyche.

Self here has some power of inner self-reflection, incipient self-knowledge. Here I question the validity of my self and begin an awakening, depending on the strength of the incoming dawning of pure intelligence.

The psychic weirdness of self allows it to be two things at once. This is in most people's experience of their self. At its superficial levels it is ignorance; at its deepest it 'knows' the truth.

Am I speaking of humanity or am I speaking of your self?

There is only your self. Humanity is a concept of self to divert attention from the one integrity – your realisation of the pure consciousness of God within. Even so, the concept of humanity and its massive subconscious as I've described it, is true for all who

129

believe there is such a thing as humanity. But it's not true. Only individual consciousness is true.

As individual consciousness you don't have that great density of self I've been speaking of. If you did you wouldn't be reading this work.

Every time you sincerely appeal to God to help you in desperate or tragic situations, a sliver of light from that great sun enters your subconscious. When you consistently acknowledge the good, which is God, in your daily life and give thanks, you are again transforming your self. Your self is becoming more intelligent, more I.

So your self started out as I, the one-and-only arrogant and self-assured controller of your life. Now, your intelligence perceives two aspects of your self. There is a knowledge of God and at the same time the presence of your self. The two frequently seem to clash. Sometimes your self takes over; sometimes you just have a knowledge of your devotion to God the unknown.

Opportunities

Living as devised by God provides numerous opportunities to increase your pure awareness. A kindly action at the expense of self; giving time to help someone by taking the time from your own interests; desisting from blaming and accusing others – are a few examples of how you serve the good and become more intelligent.

There is no guarantee of how long it takes to fully and uninterruptedly realise the consciousness of God – if ever in this one projected life. If you do, however, it will be in your transformed self that the realisation occurs. For there is only self in this projected existence.

The task, as I've mentioned before, is for the self to become so tired of itself at its deepest level that it realises itself to be the cause of all suffering and disowns itself. By that time of course your self has a great awareness and focus on the power of God within, and has become really intelligent. Accompanying this lightened state is likely to be a distaste or even disgust for the self-made world of ignorance.

With God-realisation I am now one again. But I'm completely different to the one I started out as. In truth I cannot now be described or named. Nor can I name what I am because now I am not even I.

I myself have disappeared through love into that which I loved.

FROM HERE TO REALITY

The Source of Life on Earth

The single divine principle of Man/Woman may be said to be the immediate constant impulse behind life on earth.

41
The Divinity of Man and Woman

In the deepest region of the psyche, Man and Woman merge into one divine principle or idea, and as such are indistinguishable from spirit, Source. Being divine, they are united in the ethereality behind existence as a single dazzling spiritual light.

This exquisitely powerful and creative light, radiating down through the levels of the psyche, is the enduring impulse behind life on earth and all that that involves.

The ultimate potential of each individual man and woman is to be this immaculately profound light of intelligence. Although this may only happen in death after sufficient self-knowledge has accrued, there are many exalted degrees of the light that can be realised while we are alive. The following sections explain why this is not only possible but inevitable in time.

The Spiritual Hierarchy

Every thing and condition in existence has to take a subordinate place to the level above, in line with the descending order of 'authority' in the spiritual hierarchy. This is repeated in human affairs at every level of governance, from presidents and prime ministers down through echelons of officials to voters/supporters; in corporative business from chairpersons and directors down through executive officers to shareholders; and even in the 'pecking order' of the natural species.

A further effect in the sensory physical world at the bottom of the hierarchic spiral is that, in every subordinate level of human organisation, the numbers of people or machines involved increase along with more complication, confusion and misunderstandings.

The spiritual hierarchy begins with the indescribable spirit or Source as the 'highest authority' and extends down through successive subordinate levels of the psyche to the physical.

Just below spirit is the deepest level of the psyche and this is apprehensible as the ethereality. Ethereal, the dictionary says, 'relates to regions beyond the earth, lacks material substance and is marked by unusual delicacy and refinement'. The ethereality is the abstract reality of life as it appears on earth, whereas spirit is the source, not only of the ethereality, but of whatever else might be outside of life on earth.

For us the ethereality is the accessible reality – accessible because it repeats itself in different forms down through every level of the psyche. And to our evolving consciousness, the many levels of the psyche represent a giant abstract staircase which we are all subconsciously ascending with the power of self-knowledge – bearing in mind that self-knowledge is beyond the reach of our self-conscious surface minds. However, to be able to read and enjoy this book over time is a clear indication of self-knowledge at work, especially when it comes to relating to descriptions of the ethereality and the spiritual hierarchy.

The Seven Heavens

In spirit everything is one, silent and unmoving. This may be called the *seventh heaven*. Although not acting, the sheer presence of spirit stimulates the entire psyche.

The ethereality, the deepest level of the psyche next to spirit, is the *sixth heaven* and it introduces the first sign of movement and differentiation. The differentiation – the beginning of difference or separation – is so hazy as to be amorphous and the movement so swift that the ether oscillates constantly and instantly between unity and incipient differentiation. The whole impression is of shimmering ethereal light.

The next deepest level of the psyche, the *fifth heaven*, repeats the constancy of spirit and the ethereality and introduces pure creative power. This can only be described as the divine spirit of MAN, as God or Self. MAN as God or Self has no gender.

The next subordinate level of the psyche, the *fourth heaven*, is created by the superior spirit of MAN translating itself into the single divine principle of Man/Woman. Man/Woman may be said to be the immediate constant impulse behind life on earth.

These highest four heavens are so abstract that they can be likened to spirit. From here on, the psyche is less abstract and the effect of the spirit more substantive – although, as yet, far from substantial.

As the *third heaven*, the influence of spirit creates the original brain (or psychic brain as I call it in *The Origins of Man and the Universe*). The original brain, having the immediacy and profound intelligence of the abstract psyche, controls and executes simultaneously every aspect of life on earth on behalf of the Man/Woman principle – and represents the endless presence and marvellous complexity of the one life. The brain does all this as an idea, vaguely similar to how we develop an idea mentally into a plan of action. But in the enormously swift time of the original brain there is no delay between idea and action. The original brain carries out so many functions instantly and simultaneously that our brain pales into insignificance by comparison.

For example, the original brain translates the divine Man/Woman principle and its constancy into the untiring inspiration of life or love; then into the intangible idea of the earth along with the immutable laws of nature.

The realisation of the presence of the original brain is synonymous with the enduring realisation of immortality and divine love. To us, of course, the original brain is realised as a distinct aspect of God or Self.

The original brain produces the *second heaven* in the level below. It does this by converting the Man/Woman principle into two abstract ideas: the inferior imperatives of male and female. The enforced separation of one into two creates a potential of stress. This results in the irresistible dynamic of attraction between male and female in all the species (including humans) as each, much further down in the physical, strives to repeat the union of the greater reality behind.

As far as we are concerned all the heavens are abstract and potential, but may be realised, that is, made real in our consciousness *in the moment*. For instance, the realisation of the second heaven – a brief sense of divine union – occurs in orgasm which is virtually momentary. (Prolonged sexual stimulation can also convey a sense of 'heaven' but the longer a pleasurable sensation is sustained in polarised existence, the greater the risk of attracting the opposite of depression or discontent.)

The *first heaven* is the level of the psyche closest to the physical and this is the inner space where we think, imagine and dream. Once, this was pure psyche, a true heaven that, being the mirror of the divine intellect, reflected back to man and woman their love of goodness, rightness, truth and God. But as man and woman began focusing more on problems than the good, the psyche absorbed the negative emotions and thoughts and, as a perfect response, reflected them back on demand. So problems brought more problems and worry. This made man and woman increasingly unhappy, and permanently contaminated the closest part of the psyche.

Eventually the original brain graciously divided the first heaven into what men and women seemed to want – a hell, as well as a heaven. From then on the first degree of the first level of the psyche became hell, or the place where men and women while alive suffered from their own negativity.

The heavenly part of the level, being divine, is far vaster and deeper than the human-made hell. And with very few exceptions the individual consciousness of all men and women initially gravitates to this heaven at the death of the physical body.

Next, the original brain, impelled by the divine light shining through the entire psyche, produces the physical world. It does this by reproducing a replica of itself in sense. This is the flesh-and-blood human brain.

Despite the enormous limitation of being a physical structure, as well as being the last step down in the psyche, the human brain retains something of the creativity of the spirit. Being forced by necessity to repeat the pattern of the original brain above, the physical brain sets about reproducing itself and at the same time dividing what was two, the abstract elements of male and female, into many.

It does this by creating billions of replica flesh-and-blood brains in the reproductive male and female bodies of billions of men and women. And it continues the ceaseless flow of human brains by attempting to merge the two flesh-and-blood genders through physical intercourse – a futile endeavour however, since union is only possible in the abstraction of consciousness. The result in the physical is the stress, frustration, misunderstandings and sometimes bitterness that accompanies relationships between men and women.

The Reproductive Mortal Bodies

The reproductive bodies of men and women, and all the species, are mortal, and must die. But the principle behind each man or woman's reproductive body is not only beyond death, but extends back through every level of the psyche to divine spirit. That is our journey and potential in consciousness and self-knowledge.

No Genders Beyond Existence

Male and female occur only in existence. There are no genders, no sexes, beyond the physical – because there are no bodies with sexual organs (or intestinal tracts for that matter). However, a psychic apparition of a dead person may be recognised by someone alive as the male or female they knew in the past. The flesh-and-blood brain, being itself a reproduction – a product of the past – converts the invisible abstract psychic energy into a past sensory form it can recognise.

This applies to every object and condition in our sensory existence. *Every thing and every one is a psychic emanation vibrating at a particular abstract frequency.* At the human level, however, the brain doesn't have the refinement to present or register the wide-ranging differences in self-knowledge or reality in people. So everybody appears pretty much the same except for the brain's emphasis on appearances which, like the brain, are superficial and mostly misleading.

In times of severe illness, pain or a major spiritual crisis, a higher level of the psyche may reveal itself to the brain as the visionary presence of a helpful and supportive being(s). The being will be distinctly seen to have no gender. This is the angelic realm. Angels, being well beyond the physical but always present in consciousness as an aspect of the eternal good, have no gender.

Heaven

We use the word 'heaven' or 'heavenly' in our day-to-day language to describe a situation or happening that provides an inner sense, albeit temporary, of completion or fulfilment. This means we already have an idea from previous recurrences of what heaven really is.

At the death of the physical body the consciousness of everybody passes into the first heaven and the immediacy of pure knowledge. The immediacy wipes out all previous sensory awareness of separation from the environment. In the first heaven the consciousness is one with all that previously was separate from the physical awareness. This however is not realised since all memory has been erased. What is realised is the simplicity of being united with the source of all.

Of course this is only the first heaven. But heaven is heaven, as fulfilment is fulfilment for different people. And there is a great range of difference for different levels of consciousness in the first heaven. The determining element is self-knowledge which determines where the consciousness gravitates to.

For instance, there is a form of dreaming in the first heaven – far more real than most of our dreaming – but still a dream. In this 'relatively real' dream it is possible to meet parents and other loved ones known on earth; it is also possible to communicate in different ways with people on earth. This is not memory as we know it but the relative reality behind memory: more real, but not real.

The first impression of the first heaven is often of the presence of pure love. Love is realised to be all. And love *is* all here, because the ambience of the first heaven – the pervading and uniting atmosphere – is love or God. In our sensory experience, the equivalent pervading and uniting atmosphere is space.

The consciousness of deeper self-knowledge doesn't linger in the first heaven but proceeds to other levels of resonance similar to its own. Heaven is always heaven because fulfilment is fulfilment at every level, although the consciousness or self-knowledge varies enormously. In the deepest or higher heavens fulfilment is only greater oneness with God.

42

Peace on Earth

All women are indeed endeavouring to realise, and then to be, the consciousness of the divine principle of Woman. The same applies to all men and the principle of Man.

Woman, however, cannot realise the female principle as a completion in existence until she is purely loved by man for that which she is. For this she must rise above her emotionality and human expectations of love – an extremely daunting task the way society is. But by loving God, the other, and putting that before her love or longing for man, her emotionality steadily dwindles.

It is true that woman does not need man for her to realise the pure love of God. But such a realisation is due to an inner state of self-knowledge outside physical existence. In that sense it does not contribute to the divine purpose in existence of man and woman's irresistible attraction for each other. The purpose is to bring about peace on earth – the end of all war and violence. For all war and violence is due to the fundamental division between the genders, and the frustration, discontent and dishonesty that this causes in both.

Two physical bodies, no matter how close, can never merge. The merging into a state of union has to happen in the consciousness within the bodies. In this sense, although the bodies are two, the consciousness realised is one.

Peace on earth for everybody is an impossible altruistic hope. One of the many reasons is because it concerns the desires of other men and women, many of whom don't know what peace is or don't want it. But for the individual man and woman in loving partnership such conscious union is possible. Then, where they are, there is peace on earth. And just as astonishing: in such uninterrupted divine love between man and woman the actual circumstances surrounding them serve their union. In other words, they live in some sort of external paradise – for them, but not necessarily in the view of others.

Isaiah, the great Hebrew prophet of around 700BC, makes an oblique reference to this extraordinary state of consciousness. He speaks of a time when 'the wolf shall lie down with the lamb'. Perhaps today it can be said that 'the dog shall lie down with the cat'.

Death

You are the consciousness of deep dreamless sleep or death in the profundity behind your brain and self.

43

Everybody's Regular Experience

To our consciousness, physical death represents nothing and that's why we fear it. Death means the end of our objective awareness or self-consciousness – no more thought, memories, sensations or emotional feelings.

Yet everyone alive experiences the state of death without realising it – and without any sign of distress. Just the opposite. We relish it.

Our living experience of death happens in deep dreamless sleep when our entire psychological self and its sensory existence sinks into apparent oblivion and disappears. We look forward to sleep and the disappearance of our self every day. We're not afraid of it. In fact, we can only bear sixteen to eighteen hours of sensory existence before 'dying' to go to sleep.

Since dreamless sleep is 'nothing' that we can remember, we can't know how often we slip into it from our more superficial dreaming. But dreamless sleep is the reason we wake up in the morning bodily refreshed, vitally nourished and ready for another busy day of effortful existence; until exhaustion – the depletion of our sustainable energies – again drives us back into the inner mystery of death that we love so much.

Deep dreamless sleep is the same state of consciousness that persists after physical death when no perceptible existence is possible.

As we wake up each day here in bodily existence without any seeming interruption to our continuity, so in death we wake up in a completely different consciousness.

Can this non-existence consciousness be defined in our living experience?

It can somewhat. The consciousness of both deep dreamless sleep and death is pure knowledge, knowledge in which there is no memory or past. It is self-knowledge, pure knowledge, uncontaminated by thought. And it can only be appreciated where there is sufficient self-knowledge. For example, have you ever woken in the morning in the familiarity of your bedroom, yet, for a brief moment, without knowing where you are? This is the intermediate state of consciousness between living and death, and living and deep dreamless sleep. You are in existence as your senses but you don't know where you are. You're not really here yet because you haven't gone into your memory and thought where you are. Immediately you think by recalling, you leave the intermediate state of pure knowledge, and enter the world of knowing.

Dreams

There are three modes in the human condition: awake, dreaming and deep dreamless sleep. Let us look at dreaming.

Dreaming occurs in several deepening layers of self or memory before the descent into dreamless sleep. Surface dreams are like the ticking-over of a computer before you start using it. The dreams are random and inconsequential ramblings and babblings of self in the memory (just like aimless thought in the waking mode).

A deeper layer is where the dreams have some significance in possibly revealing areas of the living life where there is emotional disturbance not yet faced and perhaps indicating a course of action to neutralise the problem. This is where therapists like Jungians work in dream analysis. Or past stressful situations, long forgotten, rise and re-enact themselves and so disturb the sleep.

A deeper layer still is where dreams are clearly predictive or prophetic and are usually recalled when the dreamer wakes up. This layer, being deeper and closer to the inner light, has a greater *possibility* of some reality. There's a sense while still asleep that the dream is 'real', a lucidity. And usually because of this the waker clearly recalls the dream and intuits what needs to be done in the living life. ('Real' here does not mean the common experience of believing, while dreaming, that 'this is too real to be a dream' only to wake up and find it was a dream after all.

Perhaps such a dream does have significance but I'm speaking generally here in order to convey the idea.)

Nightmares occur at a range of depths in the subconscious self. At one level it's possible to really scare yourself! Some horrible memory from your life may arise, a phobic fear, or what you've read or heard – and you're so relieved when you wake up and find it was only a dream. Again I'm not implying that such dreams are without significance. But our limited power of introspection makes conclusions dubious.

The difference between nightmares and other dreams is that the disturbing energy of the nightmare persists on waking. You only have to think of it for the uncomfortable feeling to be there.

The deepest level of terrifying nightmare is when the energy of the Band of Death rises out of the pure unconscious through the subconscious to the level of the sleeping dreamer. These nightmares range from impossible tasks to the sheer terror of impending extinction. Extinction is correctly apprehended by the self because, along with all its beliefs, opinions, theories and fears, it dies with the physical body.

The fact remains, however, that there is no death. The presence and consciousness of deep dreamless sleep shows the futility of any attempt to understand death through reasoning or rational thought. The Band of Death is a static area in the psyche of *no experience*. To even get near it scares the wits out of self.

Physical death is the natural process of the intelligence passing through the Band of Death, the purification of the individual subconscious and the birth of a new consciousness.

44

Help From the 'Other'

The 'other' is a very chancy area. But it has to be mentioned because I know that 'people' who have died have communicated with the living.

I'm not speaking of seances or the attempt from here to make contact with the dead. I'm referring to spontaneous phenomena where there is no deliberate intention. Spontaneous events are more acceptable to me. There is less risk of imagination and wishful thinking creating a psychic illusion. This whole area is mostly in the psychic realm of the subconscious. Although the psychic is purer towards its deeper levels, it *is* the area of much delusion and mischief as I've explained.

Because the mass information media is steeped in cynical materialistic ignorance we seldom hear of the many 'inexplicable' experiences that living people have after the death of loved ones. Occasionally when news is short the tabloid press and especially the jostling magazines ask their readership for such accounts. (The 'serious' broadsheets of course eschew such nonsense.) The result is usually more responses than can be printed in one issue. Publication is for titillation with no intention of taking respondents seriously before getting on with the next bit of exciting scandal, sexual beat-ups, glamour and celebrity deaths.

The numerous psychic happenings in my own experience are beyond doubt as far as I'm concerned. You can read about them in my autobiography, *My Life of Love and Truth*. And in my many years as an international teacher I've received first-hand a lot of extraordinary accounts. I've made no attempt to remember them, probably because I know they are true.

One I do remember concerns a man at one of my meetings. He said that a close male friend who'd died sometime before had advised him to give up his current occupation and work in another field. He said he did what his friend had said and it resulted in success and inner fulfilment. I was dubious and questioned him for the reasons stated above. But I listened and from his seriousness, sincerity and simplicity in asking me about the event, I knew he was telling the truth. I'm afraid he wasn't too impressed by my caution.

As a rule the identifiable presence of a dead person will gradually fade as their consciousness moves on. In earthly time, the presence may be 'around' for (say) *up to* three months. But, as in everything, there will be exceptions.

The most common phenomena after a loved one dies is the unquestionable impression of their 'presence' in the room, without any appearance or voice. This may happen at the time of death or days after. The important thing for the person still alive is that they know without doubt it's their loved one.

The Divine Fingerprint

Each of us possesses what may be called a divine fingerprint at our fundamental level of being. This identifies what we are through every level of the psyche. It's psychic, but is more than psychic, the deeper our consciousness or self-knowledge. The fact that no two physical fingerprints are the same arises from the divine fingerprint principle, which of course is infinitely applicable by comparison.

Thus every body alive has a distinct psychic presence. Each lives their living life mostly as this presence inside the physical body. Our preoccupation with the physical body and those of others has caused the presence to be referred to as a psychic body. Hence apparitions appear to have physical forms. But the forms are not strictly true. The human flesh-and-blood brain when faced with a psychic presence will endeavour from memory to give it a familiar form and appearance. But really, without the presence of a human brain, the energy behind the appearance has no form.

The Psychic

Despite sensory appearances we are mostly psychic creatures. It's not difficult to see that the intelligence we are now is far more potent and capable once disembodied.

Yet nothing is clear-cut or necessarily as it seems where the psychic is concerned. Sometimes an entity itself will assume a pain from a physical injury or illness while they were alive in order to be recognised. The pain, being a psychic transference, is actually felt briefly by the living person.

Telemetry is an extraordinary psychic gift that some people have. In physical science telemetry is the transmission of data via an electrical apparatus. But the psychic gift is much more simple and demonstrates how widespread these impersonal psychic impressions are which science refuses to acknowledge.

A psychic with a genuine telemetric capability can inform you of much to do with your living life from holding in their hand an object worn constantly near your body. Picking up a tool like a hammer, the psychic may hear swear words.

Then there are entities in the psyche who were angry or discontented for much of their lives. These entities inhabit the coarsest level adjoining the physical. Like parasites, they live off the living who unconsciously cooperate through their habitual attachment to anger and discontent. Here also are the forces of sexual obsession.

However, the living are protected from the negative psychic by the divine order of things. Without the willing cooperation of the individual, the psychic is powerless. Dabbling in the 'other' for 'fun and games' or out of curiosity is not advisable.

Nonetheless, there is much that is good and harmless in the upper psychic. This is demonstrated in the experiences of many people who have been helped from this area or found comfort in knowing that the one they loved is not dead. Yet I have to say it still remains an area that is seldom as it seems.

Love

The key to reality is love. The more real the love the less the negative psychic can interfere.

Thus the return of the presence of anyone who has died depends on love – either the love of the one who died or the love of the living person for him or her. Often the dead love far beyond the knowledge of the living. Their self has gone and they are now a totally different intelligence to how the living person remembers them. Through the miracle of love they are constantly attempting to communicate the love they now are through the heavy judgemental past of the living. This often happens (as explained earlier) in cases where the one who's died was responsible for sexual abuse of a child or teenager in the family whom they actually really loved.

Intelligence

The intelligence at every level of the psyche has the power to temporarily return to the level or levels it has already passed through in existence. Thus the psychic realm is able to continuously enter and influence the physical. But it can't go deeper. This is the origin of the occult term 'the ring pass not'. No intelligence can pass to a deeper heaven than that which it is now in – until its light is made more brilliant by recurrence on earth. (Recurrence and 'lights' are explained in a later essay).

In other words, going deeper into the pure psyche is determined by the speed of the intelligence or consciousness. The speed is determined by the power or brightness of the lights – which in turn depends completely on living in existence. Intelligence can't go deeper until it has truly experienced, faced and risen above the play of circumstances in the physical.

The idea is expressed in my epic poem, *Man the Thinking Piece of Sand* (published in the book, *Where the Spirit Speaks to its Own* and the audio recording, *Barry Long's Epic Spiritual Poems*):

How to understand death without dying?
How to understand failure without failing?
Today's accuser is tomorrow's accused
The slaughterer, the slaughtered
The fiend, the friend
The coward, the martyr
The brute, the God
Thus does My Highest Man look back on all with infinite
    understanding and compassion
And therein lies the hope of bewildered beast
And shuffling, suffering man.

Ghosts

What about ghosts?

I have a ghost story which may give you some idea of why such apparitions appear. On this occasion the ghost was indicating something that even the person to whom it appeared didn't realise.

It was during a seventeen-day seminar (Master Session) I gave annually at Cabarita, New South Wales. A woman attending on her own died of natural causes in the same hotel where the man was staying. She died on a Sunday and the body wasn't found till Tuesday. I was informed immediately but we didn't announce the death as that would have served no purpose.

On the Wednesday afternoon I was speaking privately to the man. Among other things he happened to mention casually that he had seen an apparition of his dead father standing in the door of his room.

I pressed the man for details. He said his father didn't say anything and that anyway the figure seemed to be lifeless so he just dismissed it as one of those things.

I asked him what surroundings the figure appeared in.

He said it was standing with the closed door passing through it.

What was behind the figure?

He paused for a few seconds and said, 'There were a couple of men wearing stove-pipe hats sitting on a carriage. I think it was a hearse.'

I then told him of the woman's body lying undiscovered in her bedroom at the time of his vision.

Another case of a ghostly appearance with significance was popular when I was a teenager and is still quoted sometimes. It concerns 'Fisher's Ghost' as the media called it.

Fisher disappeared from his home west of Sydney amid fears that he had been murdered, but neither he nor his body had been found.

Someone who knew him reported seeing a ghostly apparition of a man sitting on a local bridge and pointing to a spot on the creek bank. Others also saw it and it became a big story in the newspapers because when police dug at the spot, Fisher's body was found. He had been murdered.

Ghostly happenings like these are far more common than we realise. People fear ridicule and keep quiet. But in most cases apparitions are indicating something meaningful – if only to the observer.

45

Death, Masters and Limbo

Love of a deceased spiritual master is different to the love of another individual. While alive a true spiritual master has realised God at the deepest level. At physical death his consciousness passes into the first degree of the psyche – the Band of Death – and then into the divine 'heaven' he has realised.

Individuals who really loved the Master by living the truth of what he said may briefly experience his presence.

However, where communities have gathered around the master a psychic field exists. This is generated by the inevitable emotional and intellectual attachment to the master while he is alive. After his death people in the community may 'sense' his presence or have other psychic experiences relating to him. This may also happen to newcomers to the community.

But these happenings are purely of the master's psychic 'presence' – and are not real. Barry Long will never return. Nor will Krishnamurti. They're the only two I can speak for. And I trust no one gets involved with my psychic presence and that it is allowed to disintegrate – like the dream it is.

Limbo

However, there is a deeper region of the psyche called limbo. Here are lodged a collection of psycho-spiritual entities. They are frustrated pseudo spiritual masters and teachers who, while on earth, never realised the master consciousness of God but were more or less closely associated with a living master.

These entities don't have the knowledge or nous to 'go on'. They focus on the earth and take possession of suitable willing bodies to channel their considerable knowledge through. What they couldn't do through their own physical body when they had one they now do through someone else's body.

Being spiritual they have a good deal of self-knowledge. And being psychic they have great powers of seduction through having access to both future and past and by giving out high-sounding homilies. But they are not responsible. The virtue of responsibility is gained only while in the physical body – yours not another's.

A true spiritual master goes on, never to be seen or heard from again.

The entities in limbo go on interminably confined by their own inflated ignorance of God. There's no escape from limbo, the half-in-half-out region of the psyche, except to hear the truth of limbo from a living master. Chances of this are not good when the entity can only hear what he or she already knows.

It's interesting to glance at the Roman Catholic idea of limbo and to see how it is half true and half terribly misleadingly and threateningly wrong. Catholic theology describes limbo as an abode of souls barred from heaven because of not having received Christian baptism. In the above context the first part about 'being barred from heaven' is partly acceptable except that being in limbo is due to volitional ignorance, not punishment. The baptism bit, which excludes most of the world's population from God, is of course absurd.

Psychic Presence

Everyone in existence has a psychic presence. To the degree that the consciousness of God the Source is realised, the psychic presence is cast off like dead tissue. The psychic presence of a dead master would simply disintegrate but for the emotional and conceptual attachments of his followers. These keep the otherwise dead image 'alive' and the followers devoted to it. The master consciousness meanwhile has returned and vanished into whence it came.

It is one thing to simply love the master. There is no holding in real love. But every form of human love contains a selfish element of emotion and this, especially where groups are concerned, can have an effect in the finer levels of the psychic.

The effect is a sort of 'reaching out for' which creates ripples of need.

In the after-death process of a spiritual being whose consciousness is destined by his or her lights to descend to a profound heaven, the being must initially pass through the whole first level of the psyche in order to be purified of any skerrick of existence.

I recall the death at forty of my second wife, Julie, who was a deeply spiritual woman. In the interval of several days between her death and cremation, 'she' appeared at night in a recognisable nightdress to her former closest friend. Her friend intuited that Julie was being held back by the devotion of the meditation group that met regularly at our home. The friend phoned and asked me to tell them to let her go. This I did next night. And at the crematorium on the brick wall over the flowers was a brass plate no one noticed until later, inscribed, 'I am free!' Such is the wonder and power of the psyche.

It's not difficult to link such a happening to the evening after Jesus' death when he appeared to Mary Magdalene saying, 'Don't touch me. I've not yet ascended to the Father.'

Julie's wish throughout her life was simply to be with God.

Science

The speed of light is a dreary shadow compared to the 'speed' of uninterrupted God-consciousness.

46

The Past and Present

The past is usually dismissed as something 'natural' that's just there. It doesn't seem to ever have been intelligently examined or investigated, probably because all human endeavour – personal, commercial, scientific, religious, political and social – is concerned with the past.

Our whole civilisation is based on past. From the past is derived the idea of the future. That's because the future is merely the inevitable unfolding of the consequences of yesterday, the past.

The present is *now*. Now is not only what you're perceiving with the senses now. That may be regarded as now, but is not really-now because it's subject to the delay of time or past as an image travels from the object to the eye. Really-now is a state within, free of past, a continuous uninterruptible focus on the inner reality behind the senses. (The state is available to anyone in time, a natural outcome of ongoing surrender of personal attachment.)

Really-now is *direct*. Awareness through the senses is indirect. Indirect means seeing a version of what is, through the past. Direct means seeing the facticity of what is, free of past.

You can confirm now in your own experience how sensory awareness takes place in the past. It takes time for the image of an object to reach the retina of the eye. Then it takes time for the image to reach the brain through the optic nerve. Although it all seems simultaneous the fact is that time has elapsed. Elapsed time is past time, or simply past. Everything we register through the senses is already in the past.

Another example is when we hear sounds. Sound is much slower than light which transports images to the eye. (No light, no image, no see.) Sound travels around 600 feet a second. When you see a jet aircraft flying over, the sound arrives several seconds later. Count the seconds, multiply by 600, and you can estimate how far away the aircraft was. The aircraft is a long way past where the sound tells you it is.

Similarly with a lightning flash. The thunder you hear is in the past. And the lightning has vanished long before the thunder is heard.

In our usual everyday interactions the elapsed time in seeing and hearing is so tiny that we don't notice it. But as the distance (past) increases, the delay is more evident, particularly with sound.

Even with sight there's an indication that we're seeing through the past. You might have perfect vision but as you look into the furthest distance there's the blur of the impenetrable past. Use binoculars which optically seem to reduce the distance and again at the extremity of the image there's the blur of the past.

Even the world's most powerful telescopes, including radio telescopes, will be unable to penetrate the past indicated by the extremity of their range. The explanation is that the entire material universe consists of past. Like the illusive horizon, the past keeps shifting back, always just out of range and impenetrable by any device dependent on the speed of light.

Why is there no blur to start with? There is a blur. But we accept this obvious distortion as normal – because we live in the past, and because the organ of the physical brain and the instruments we use to see and measure objects are all products of the past.

With the human eye, as the distance or elapsed time increases, every object appears smaller, even in everyday life. When looking at cosmic objects the effect is the same though more pronounced. A planet like Saturn is an indistinguishable dot in the night sky. Use a telescope and the object again appears relatively larger but still nothing compared to the 'actual' size. It's all an illusion because the past is completely illusionary – being a result of the lumbering speed of light.

The Slowness of Light

Science in its own measured experience tells us that the speed of light is a fundamental constant, a sort of absolute, in that nothing can exceed that speed. A few intuitive scientists today are questioning that dogma of the past. (By the time I finish this section I trust I'll have shown you that the speed of light is a dreary shadow compared to the 'speed' of uninterrupted God-consciousness – a fact I've endeavoured to pass on to scientists for two decades.)

Light itself contradicts the concepts of fundamental and absolute. Fundamental means supporting or determining every-thing. Absolute means immediacy – no distance, no time, no accumulated past. But light from the sun takes eight minutes to arrive here. In that time a great deal has happened which the light cannot tell us. For instance, the sun could have exploded and dis-appeared and we wouldn't know about it for eight minutes. During that time we'd still be seeing and feeling the old familiar light of the sun!

The past is fundamental and absolute in existence. But then intelligence capable of achieving the immediacy of conscious-ness is also in existence – in the form of some profound people. This consciousness sees through the impenetrable past of the human mind and its concepts and clearly can be realised, in time. In fact, here in existence is the only place consciousness is realised.

The relative slowness of light in cosmic terms – scientifically measured in incomprehensible light years of past! – symbolises the slowness of the rational mind. And by describing light from any source as a constant or absolute, science demonstrates its own materialistic limitations; also that all its theories and calcu-lations are unreal products of the past.

47

What Science Has Yet To Realise

Light is material. Science of course has discovered this – more or less. It also knows that light uses and is transported through the medium of space. But what science doesn't know is that *space is also material* – finer, but still material.

An inkling of this appears in scientific theorising. But adherence to pursuing the coarse materiality of existence, and being restricted by the mental limitation of the speed of light, seems to have obscured the next critical stage of scientific discovery.

Perhaps that's because some scientists have been unable to believe, or should I say, *prove by measurement* their own intuitions, let alone realise them. I suspect that's the case.

An example of scientific ambivalence regarding light and space is that light is said to have two modes – one that it's a minute particle, and the other that it's simply wave-motion, an immaterial wave. Light seems to vary between both modes. Once the truth *of the matter* is realised the explanation is clear.

In itself, light is a minute particle called a photon or a 'quantum of radiant energy'. Quantum is a fancy word for a measurable quantity. Anything measurable is material. So the particle theory is correct.

Then there's the wave-motion mode. You've seen a moving boat throwing out waves in the medium of the sea? The boat is made of far denser material than the water. So what the scientists are 'seeing' is the quantum particle of light travelling in substantive space and making a bow wave in space's purely material but very fine medium. Hence the wave theory.

But what accounts for light's scientifically observed fluctuations between sometimes wave, sometimes particle? The fluctuating mindset of the scientist observing the experiment. Science knows from its quantum theory that the observing consciousness influences the result. But so far it has chosen to ignore this because it would mean each scientist focusing first on self-knowledge.

The extreme fluctuation between wave and particle reflects the duality in scientific consciousness. Perhaps this book will help to unify what is at present split.

Space to our senses appears as nothing. Yet it's one of the last material mediums capable of being perceived, registered or realised by the human mind; or let us say, realised by the scientific mind – since space is material. No one spiritually motivated would want to pursue this area, spiritual motivation being focused on the immaterial behind the material, the substantive behind the substantial.

Gravitation

The other all-embracing and all-present medium not yet realised by science as being material, is gravitation. Gravitation is of finer stuff than space. But again scientists are split, some theorising that gravitational waves are responsible and others that particles called gravitons are involved.

Both theories are incorrect because they imply movement or time. The gravitation that science is concerned with is an effect and all effects involve delay. The gravitation I'm speaking of is immediate throughout the entire sensory universe, and in immediacy there is no movement, delay or time.

Space and gravitation as perceived by science exist only in the past of the material universe – in sensory '*reception*'. But they may be said to be the last agencies in existence before the crossover of consciousness into intelligences. The realisation of both will mark the beginning of the New Science that is still many generations away.

The spiritual word 'realisation' when applied to material science means the capability to *consciously* use the mediums of space and gravitation. The *unconscious* use of a medium is the earlier example of a boat and crew supported by the medium of water. Conscious use turns the medium into an agency – a means by which – as in the case of water being converted into steam to generate electricity. The two mediums – space and gravitation – when used consciously will become the *agencies* for the practical application of the New Science, including – many, many generations from now – the material reality of space travel in excess of the speed of light.

Present science uses the localised gravitation of planets (and possibly to some small degree the gravitation of the sun) to give space probe machines an extra 'flick' as they pass by, thus boosting speed while saving rocket fuel. But this tactic is not the means of going beyond the speed of light that I'm referring to.

The materiality of space varies according to gravitational influence. Science has seen this in the discovery that space bends or folds in the gravitational drag of massive cosmic bodies. But the *realisation* or utilisation of the distortion of space, and of the immediacy of gravitation, will mark the entry into another time beyond imagining.

I must point out that spiritual realisation – for instance, the realisation of Supreme Being within – is completely different to realisations by the scientific or rational mind.

The rational mind is material, the source of all materiality. Its aspirations are materialistic right up to the end – which is physical death. But while one or more brainy minds are alive, the evolution of existence as progress continues. Spiritual realisation on the other hand simply reveals the immaterial truth behind existence and eliminates the need to find out more.

48

Space Travel

The space journey that science has only relatively recently begun is a journey into the past. To the brain and its executive, the mind, space travel appears to involve the future. But that is part of the illusion of the past.

As you journey 'forward' in outer space you're actually going back – not back in time but back to where you began. This doesn't make any appreciable difference while spaceships and their crews travel at a fraction of the speed of light.

But once lightspeed is exceeded the whole psychological mindset of the 'travellers' or those back on earth monitoring the situation, changes. They are then briefly conscious in the present. Consciousness of the present destroys the past. If there were human crews on board they and their bodies would be destroyed too. For human bodies and their aspiring brains are products of the past.

For this reason, the New Science will use the equivalents of robots. These will have no resemblance to human form and will be the product of a scientific consciousness on earth beyond anything we can imagine.

When lightspeed is exceeded by using gravitation, gravitation becomes a power and is no longer a force as science regards it today. Force varies. The comparative, localised present science view is that the gravitation of the Earth is weaker than the gravitation of the Sun. But the power of gravitation is its universal immediacy. And beyond the speed of light any associated mentality is advanced to a higher degree of consciousness. In other words the bending and empowering of a robotic mind in the spaceship due to the influence of space and gravitation will have an extraordinary knock-on effect in the observing brains on earth.

There will be 'reports' of contact or visions of intelligences and worlds far exceeding even this advanced New Science earth technology. Accompanying this will be the amazing realisation that what is being observed is earth science in another time.

Unlike today's plodding information technology, the communications will be immediate gravitational communications independent of light or past. And it won't be a case of receiving answers to questions before the questions are asked, as has been popularly speculated. With immediacy of knowledge there are no longer any questions. That's how it is with pure consciousness. But science can never realise pure consciousness; it must always be stuck in some form or other. So space aspirations will not cease.

Eventually, the non-existent future spaceship travelling in the immediacy of gravitation will encounter the perimeter of impenetrable space – and will end up back where it started. This will be similar to the experience of the early sailing ship navigators who set off not knowing whether the world ended at the horizon. Never reaching the horizon, some pressed on resolutely only to discover themselves back where they started.

Could such a spaceship even be said to have left? Of course not. It can't happen – even though it's true. But what is true is only true for now. It's not the truth.

Is there any chance of a total transmutation of human nature?

No. The masses can't change. They simply progress from one form of experience to another. But the psychological mindset of the individual man or woman can be converted into pure consciousness. That doesn't happen in the future. It only happens now.

Spiritual Consciousness

Deep spiritual consciousness is far swifter than any peak of human intelligence usually associated with scientists such as Einstein, and in our time, Stephen Hawking. The flaw in such intelligence is its concentration on materiality.

To attain the speed of unwavering divine consciousness a scientist would have to abandon his or her absorbing interest in 'unlocking' the mysteries of matter, and put self-knowledge first.

This in time perhaps would lead to higher consciousness and a knowledge of the inner radiant cosmos behind the sensory universe.

The scientist with all his or her brilliant insights into materiality has no advantage over any man or woman devoted to knowing their self.

Matter

Regarding matter or materiality: both words derive from the Latin mater, meaning mother. Earth is usually referred to as mother earth. The implication is that matter originates on earth. This actually is true. Even though the physical universe seems to consist largely of matter, the eyes that see, and the brain/mind that interprets what is seen, are material products of mother earth.

This implies that the whole universe of matter and substantive space are projections of our mother-made senses.

Further, that there's no life in the universe other than the sensory life of matter created by the mater, mother earth.

And even that can't be real because it all vanishes with the death of the material brain.

What's left?

Nothing.

Nothing to speak of, that is.

God

God is beyond words, beyond concepts, beyond the human mind and emotions, but not beyond simply being.

49

The Will and Free Will

Have you ever wondered how everything hangs together? How everything works – in spite of the silliness of us all, including me? That's the Will.

Then, how everyone makes mistakes: the professionals, the banks, the workers, bosses, the army, the generals, the politicians, the people who should know but don't know? How there's seldom anybody responsible any more to speak to at the other end of the phone? That's due to man's free will.

Free will keeps the mad scientists insanely busy trying to improve everything that's natural and thereby reducing the quality of life for us all. Thus tomatoes have lost their taste and it's hard to buy a rose that still smells like a rose.

Because of free will you've got a fifty-fifty chance of survival in medical and surgical matters at the doubtful price of a few more years of living and trying to find something worthwhile to live for. But because of Will and the profundity behind it, physical death is only the death of conflictual living and the return to the vastness of life.

If man and his free will had had their way the world would have been destroyed long ago: atom bombs, hydrogen bombs, neutron bombs, poison gas, world wars, cold wars, religious wars, arsenals of deadly germs – all ready for use or to break out. Just a matter of when. All the result of free will.

Yet, whatever man does to the earth and himself, no matter how much carnage and devastation he inflicts on both with his diabolical self-consciousness and free will, he is not permitted to completely destroy either.

Permitted? By God?

No. By Will. Will is the executive power of the unknowable God. God is beyond all action, all power. God is simply above all in a profound sense, and yet immediately present.

Will finally holds everything together – by the order of things that is God. In the same way Will eventually destroys or dissolves everything sooner or later. Order is in every aspect of existence – including man's life, despite his chaotic comings and goings. Even the moment of his physical death is determined by the inscrutable law of Will.

Man's Dominion

In the order of things man is sovereign over nature. With such superior authority he has the free will to do what he wishes with the earth and all that's on it. This is obvious.

You have only to look at man's history to see he's been true to his free will. He has destroyed billions of his own kind even in the name of God and religion; polluted the seas, the rivers and the atmosphere; levelled the jungles and forests; decimated the wildlife; and sent man to the planets where, in being true to his free will, he will destroy or enslave any form of life or goodness that he may find there – all in the name of progress. Progress is the progressive result of man's free will.

But what he doesn't realise is that his free will is simply the option to choose. And he has only two choices. He can choose to go man's way, the free will way. Or he can choose the other way.

Most men (and women) as you can see from the confusion, conflict and unhappiness around you, have chosen man's way. The big problem with that way is that everything achieved vanishes at death. And before death, achievement creates the fear of death, the fear of losing what has been gained.

The other way, the way of surrendering man's bothersome free will to Will, is not an achievement but the blessing of uninterrupted freedom.

Justice

Where there is law and order there is also justice. Not man's law and justice. They are badly flawed, although still an attempt to follow the order of things as laid down by Will.

Will and the order of things are cosmic. Cosmic means beyond the affairs of man. Cosmic order is maintained by cosmic law. Cosmic law is just and infallible. Behind it is Will in which there is no choice, therefore no mistakes, no chaos, no confusion – and no death.

50

God and Love

You cannot be in relationship with God. You can only love God.

When God is truly loved, God is distinguished by every word that denotes the good – words such as love, sweet, kind, right, noble, honest and so on. And finally such love – with gratitude for your life now and what you've been given – brings an amazing absence of problems – peace. On the other hand, every word and feeling that denotes what's not good is a result of man long ago having left the good to go his own wilful independent way.

Every real good is attributable to God. But man has his own personal measure of what is good, and what is not good. He interprets events against the fulfilment or otherwise of his aspirations and expectations. As a result, man's good varies whereas God's good does not.

Death is an example of what man regards as not good. But death is release from all pain and suffering. Death is really life. Man doesn't realise this. He dreads the death of himself and his loved ones and so suffers from the thought of death – and from the actuality when the inevitable looms.

Nor does he realise that death of his troublesome self while he is alive can free him of conflict and suffering. The mystics have told him this and demonstrated it through the ages. But to little avail. Death-while-living begins by detaching from personal notions of good and bad because a greater good within has been discovered. The only greater good is God.

God in truth is everything – and nothing. Everyone is an aspect of God. But the God or the good in us is hidden under multiple layers of emotional feelings and opinions imposed by our various man-made cultures. We all know this through the conflict of wanting to do good or the right thing and being persuaded by our feelings to do otherwise.

Even though we may not know it, God is always at the perimeter of our lives, always surrounding or embracing our lives. In times of severe anguish and despair, God quite often is present and is known to be indescribably good and true, removing the anxiety and darkness.

No one dies without real-ising God. For in truth death is merely the inexpressible freedom of *being* in the ambience of God.

'Forever'

Sometimes in moments of extreme beauty or love, God is realised to be an indescribable 'That', with an accompanying conviction of 'forever and ever.'

Then there is the realisation of God as happens in the mystical life. God is realised as both love and truth, or the supreme good, or Supreme Being beyond all description – depending on the depth of God realised. For God is not only unfathomable but depthless within each of us.

Nothing can adequately describe God because God to our comprehension is nothing. Nothing to speak of is God. Our psychological make-up is to objectify everything, to make an object of it that can be described or put in relationship to something else. God is beyond words, beyond concepts, beyond the human mind and emotions, but not beyond simply being.

God can only be loved here in existence. That extraordinary love can part the curtains of time and ignorance. Then is revealed the wonder of wonders – the wonder of God being God within.

51

Perfection

Only God is perfect. Even so there is a relative perfection in existence which is in the realised reflection of the consciousness of God. But the one who realises is not the one who's perfect. The perfection is the indescribable state reflected. The danger, where traces of self-consciousness remain, is the assumption that 'I am' what is being realised or has been realised.

The intermittent realisation of God happens randomly in the individual consciousness of many people behind their active mind and emotions – happenings we seldom hear about. These moments are wonderful but usually don't endure; they get obscured by coping with the ups and downs of daily living.

The rarest inner realisation of the perfection of God is an uninterrupted ever-present state of consciousness or knowledge. A high degree of this usually distinguishes a world teacher.

Nobody Perfect

Sometimes due to realisation teachers imply that they are God, or call themselves God. That to me is an error. 'I am (this)' is certainly the truth of the realisation. At every level of realisation there is the knowledge 'I am this', before I disappear.

To me God cannot be retained as an idea. When retained it degenerates into a concept. God or Self has to be realised continuously moment to moment and in that there's no permanence, continuity, or structure. To realise God is to know nothing apart from what is communicated in the moment. Otherwise I am nothing and know nothing.

52

God Being God

Everyone and everything is God being God. Our bodies are God. The food we eat is God. The table we eat from is God. Our lovers are God. The people around us are God.

So why are there problems? Why is there ignorance?

Problems exist because of ignorance. And ignorance exists because God in everything doesn't realise it is God.

Have you realised you are God?

I don't mean having a brief insight of being God, which of course is an astonishing and beautiful moment. I mean having such an uninterrupted knowledge of being God that the knowledge disappears and you are just what you are – without any more problems in your life and without any questions about God or the amazing truth that such a realisation reveals.

That realisation of God is extremely rare. But the fact that it is possible means it's possible for you, in time. Everyone who has realised God has realised God in time.

But only God knows the time it takes.

Paradoxically no one who has realised God is God. The realisation of God is only the reflection of the Consciousness and Will of God. The reality of God is still far beyond God's Consciousness and Will.

Now back to everything being God steeped in ignorance.

The unnameable purity of God is the Source of everything. It is deep within each one of us, even beyond eternity. To our mind or psychology the Source is so subtle that it is equivalent to nothing. This means it would be inaccessible to us – except for the divine way of things.

The structure of the psyche within us is the divine way of things. It is the scheme of everything that has been, is, or ever can be. It even includes ignorance, the speculations and presumptions of science, and the confused and confusing precepts of traditional and organised religions.

In the psyche's deepest depths is the region of the Source.

From there – in diminishing degrees of purity – the psyche ascends up towards our self-conscious physical existence. Each degree or level represents what would be called a 'heaven' to the level above. For us perceiving and descending inwardly, the first heaven is the realisation of immortality. This, as I've mentioned, is the realisation of being one with all life. Even so, it is far more than that.

After Death

After death the intelligence we are behind our mind and emotions passes into the first heaven. We then are immortality and not just the realisation of it. Immortal means being freed of the physical body and the fear of death. It is a wondrous state, justifiably named a heaven. And yet it is only the first heaven.

The first heaven is the nearest relatively-real heaven to our human condition here in physical existence. Physical existence is the outer extremity of the psyche. There's nowhere else to go from here but inward. The popular culture of scientific materialism is taking the human mind deeper into ignorance, which is deeper into the distraction of outer space. Inner space is the only way out.

As intelligence descends deeper inwardly there are fewer 'recognisable' forms or conditions. In other words, there is less relativity, less complication – less and less of anything. In the increasing absence of 'anything' there is a greater all-embracing knowledge and being of the reality – the Source or God.

There are said to be seven heavens. I don't know the number. All I know is the wonder of being there.

53

The Divine Circus

How the Ringmaster Does It

The Hindus refer to existence as the divine lila (leela) – the dance, play or game of God. Many others have seen existence as a prime example of crackpot stupidity. Few of them would disagree with Shakespeare's description: 'a tale told by an idiot, full of sound and fury, signifying nothing'.

You don't have to be a genius to see the fatuity of existence. We grow up in ignorance, uncertainty and fear. We live most of our lives in the past. We suffer emotional pain through attachment and physical pain is unavoidable. We start out bravely enthusiastic and eager to make our mark, only to eventually discover that no matter what we've accomplished and to what great heights we may have risen it all adds up to zero. (Only the onlookers of the fame and success of others think differently.) Gradually we are overtaken by the burden of self and ageing with all its bodily problems.

Everyone born suffers, everyone does their best to survive, cope and somehow make a life of it only to be thwarted by death. What an amazing divine circus it is. Or perhaps the odd individual would call it a form of hell.

Why would any power called God be responsible for such an incredible bit of tomfoolery?

Why are we fooled by it for so long?

And finally, how's it done?

The answer to the first question I've already mentioned but will say it again: so that God which is unconscious in every thing (including you and me to begin with), can emerge in time from the ignorance of matter, and realise God as God always is and always was – untouched, unconcerned, uninvolved and unlimited by time and existence – and bring that God-consciousness into existence. That's the purpose of the whole charade.

Why are we fooled for so long? Because the realisation of God is a universal process that's been going on since time began when man as God began to slip deeper and deeper into ignorance in the form of past and progress. It takes infinite recurrences for God to realise God and that's a long, long time. Still, God-realisation does happen, and it always happens *now*.

How is the charade of existence done? No one seems to have ever described it meaningfully. But I'll give it a shot. And I can tell you now, that as every showman and magician knows, it's all done by mirrors!

The one mirror behind existence is the mirror of inner space – the intellect. This is within every body and every living thing and makes every level of life on earth possible, and in human terms, knowable.

However, the intellect becomes finer and more powerful as it descends away from the physical towards eternity, which is the extremity of human consciousness. In so doing, the one intellect becomes three – three reflective climacterics – critical stages or turning points in human consciousness. These are the universal intellect, the human intellect, and the pure intellect. Each remains potential – that is, unrealised – until the consciousness attempting access is resonating at a commensurate speed.

The Universal Intellect

This is the source of instinct which resonates in all forms of life. It is common to all living things, including humans at physical conception. The reflective power of the universal intellect enables all the 'unself-conscious' animals to register pain and the discomfort of hunger, along with the contentment of wellbeing or 'no intrusive feelings'. Insects and bacteria are controlled instinctually by the universal intellect.

As human beings 'occupy' animal bodies that basically are unself-conscious and instinctual, we are controlled to a great extent by the universal intellect.

The Human Intellect

This is only accessible by animals which have reached a certain degree of self-consciousness, in other words, by the human animal. Self-consciousness is the ability to reflect mentally on a personal memory and emotional feelings such as guilt, fear of the future and events of the past. Traces of this faculty are seen in domesticated animals used to being in the company of us self-conscious humans. In consciousness, physical proximity has a rub-off effect.

The universal intellect, being basic to all life, continues to function within and outside the range of the human intellect.

The human intellect itself forms a circular band of concepts around the mind. Its more common name is the memory. The mind's rationalising and reasoning lacks sufficient speed of intelligence to penetrate through to the divine intellect behind. Instead, the thoughts bounce back with both old and newly synthesised concepts. These may add to the momentum of progress but seldom solve any real problem for the individual.

The exception is when the divine intelligence behind the human intellect imparts a new idea. This invariably revolutionises contemporary concepts and initiates a new direction in personal or human affairs.

Our self-conscious mechanism prevents us from admitting to, or accepting uninterruptedly, that a power greater than our personal and individual capacity is controlling the events of our lives and our responses.

The Pure Intellect

This is the divine intellect created by God for man and woman so that they may realise the truth while still alive and escape the limitations of a physical, mental and personalised self-conscious existence.

The pure intellect encompasses both the universal and human intellects. It is at the 'bottom' and 'top' of 'everything'. In reality,

178

it is all there is, an inscrutable power with nothing in it, and nothing before it or after it – God or Source.

The pure intellect reveals itself in man or woman when the consciousness becomes aware of a power and intelligence beyond the understanding of the human intellect. It follows a growing detachment from the belief that the human mind by itself can solve any fundamentally important problem. This reduces the activity of the mind and allows the pure intellect's far swifter intelligent reflection to inform the consciousness.

God or Self-realisation at each level is an inrush of this intelligence. But it must be kept in mind that God or Self-realisation is merely a mirror reflection of God or Self and not the reality itself. No body could stand the searing purity of God or Self direct without disintegrating. So by divine grace the pure intellect is provided to break down by mirror reflection the immediate uninterrupted knowledge of the indescribable omniscience of God.

Projection

Everything in existence is a degraded copy of a deeper reality within the psyche, and a projection from there. The key word is 'projection'.

Let me remind you of how projection works here in the actuality.

To shine a recognisable image on a cinema screen (or any reflective surface) the slide or movie film has to be placed upside down in the projector – and elements in the projector turn the image right side up. The screen acts like a mirror. It captures the image and bounces it back to the viewer on the reflected waves of the incoming light – just as the bathroom mirror does. But due to the behaviour of light in relation to the eye, the image arrives at the retina upside down. The extraordinary thing is that the human brain is naturally programmed to automatically reverse the inverted image so that we see it right way up! (This doesn't mean that what we normally see with our eyes is upside down. But it does mean that we don't see things as they really are. We see reflected light images of objects, not the objects themselves.)

179

Furthermore, when the inverted slide is inserted into the projector, not only does the upside down slide get projected the right way up, but also left is right and right is left; so the image that is projected through a lens appears on the screen the right way round. And the same goes for the reflection in the bathroom mirror: what you see is not quite how things are in front of the mirror, despite the brain's basic correction. There's a subtle *wrong-way-round* appearance to the reflection.

In order for us to perceive existence as an uninterrupted continuity, the human brain has to project and replace each image at a frequency of more than 60 frames a second. The ordinary household electric light bulb goes on and off unnoticed at about this rate. The mind retains a residue of the last image and we see an apparently continuous light. At a frequency lower than forty frames a second our impression of existence would be like a flickering old movie.

54

God-Realisation

Before this I was Dead

It's incredible, unbelievable, a miracle. No, not a miracle. Miracles are particular. This is everything. I am everything. No, not just everything, I am that which is behind and in everything – I am It, God, Self, Source.

But this is not anything I've previously conceived of God or imagined as this realisation. Words are absolutely inadequate.

And yet there's no sense of attainment, achievement or aggrandisement. That would be laughable. Yet I can't help laughing and smiling hugely. Because I'm absolutely free!

Incredibly, I am absolutely responsible for all that is happening in existence – wars, earthquakes, peace, the lot. And it is all perfect!

I've done nothing to deserve this astonishing state of consciousness. It's not a prize or a reward. It just is, now. I'm humbled, incredibly humbled. I'm nothing. Before this I was dead. I'm not even sure I existed. The past has vanished.

What I am now is what I have always been and always was. This must be heaven. But it can't be heaven because it's not something that I'm in. I am completely it.

My cup runs over with joy and gratitude.

The above is an attempt to present the wonderment, amazement and glory of God-realisation at a few of the levels. I'm sure to have omitted some particulars. But particulars are nothing compared to the wonderment, amazement and glory. It's the idea in regard to God I trust I'm communicating – and affirming.

Nothing is more intimately individual than 'I' in everyone's experience. So naturally the essential point at every level of God-realisation is 'I'.

It is always I who realises – I that you call yourself all day and not some imagined 'higher I'. The difference is that your intelligence has speeded up since you called yourself I yesterday, or years ago. Your intelligent way of looking at things has changed but not I. It's the same incredible I at every level of existence whether I feel happy, unhappy or am just doing and being what I am. I is the eyepiece of intelligence.

Thus God at every level is realised as *individual* consciousness – I am That which is being realised. There's no greater delight, joy and astonishment than that *I* (who am otherwise so insignificant) can be this consciousness. And yet...

55

The Ever-Reappearing I

I, the knower of it all, am the intelligence of the human mind. I come out of existence in the same way as I who am reading this arise out of the existence of that physical body; and in the same way as I who realised Supreme Being came out of the body of Barry Long. Nonetheless, I am a phantom. I, and nothing that I reflect on, has any reality. This is made clear in God or Self-realisation: in that moment I disappear, only to quickly reappear (usually unnoticed) as the know-all of daily living.

Whichever way you look at it, while the physical body lives I am the reflection and reflector on the body and existence. I am that which makes it all knowable and reasonable. But never have I been able to work it out or really make sense of it.

Indeed, I must be intelligent to know I'm intelligent; that's what I think, anyway – not realising that if 'I am' because I think I am, I'm simply a product of thought which has no reality because I am the thinker. I am notional, theoretical, and ephemeral whereas existence is demonstrably here now, substantive, tangible, specific and continuously immediate – completely beyond the understanding of I. I am not continuously immediate. I'm a 'maybe' – an everyday unreliable, unpinnable pest.

In my ignorance I have created other imagined and assumed 'realities'. I have done this in a so-called attempt to find reality. But the truth is I have assiduously gone away from reality – religiously, spiritually and especially scientifically. I am the author and ignorance behind evolution, progress, God-realisation and every other substitute for the reality of existence now.

I am the creator of the troublesome world. God is the creator of the actuality – 'what is', before I start interpreting or naming. In other words, the world is a personal imposition on the objectivity of existence, the moment-to-moment actuality which I have no hope of explaining.

The world consists of every circumstance and situation that I find myself in now, or ever have found myself in. The world is the burden I have ignorantly striven endlessly to cast off or escape from – when I myself am the world. There is *nothing* here to know but what I have created by thought and reflection. Otherwise it's simply the unknowable 'what is'.

So existence – the speck in the eye – is not the problem at all in the realisation of Supreme Being. I am the problem, I who remember and am separate from the immediacy of existence; I who strive ceaselessly to realise finer unreal abstractions such as heaven, nirvana, the absolute, nothing, the void, freedom. I am the hindrance, the problem. I who claim to have realised anything am an illusion. In following some tradition-based real- isations I even refer to existence as an illusion, not comprehending that if all is illusion then so am I who proclaim it. The only illusion is I who think I realise or know anything.

There's nothing in truth to realise or be realised. And there never was!

56
Inner Space

All intelligent activity including God-realisation occurs in inner space within the physical body.

Inner space is where I think, plan, imagine, feel, worry, daydream – and have insights and realisations of truth. But inner space is not another world or place separate from concrete existence. Inner space is simply an *abstract* extension of concrete existence.

Every profound insight and realisation of God or reality gives the false impression that it's happening in a place far beyond the body and physical existence. The impression is understandable, but not when the significance of inner space is appreciated.

Inner space, like outer space, has an extremity beyond which nothing can proceed. That is eternity where time no longer exists. Anything reaching the extremity, either as consciousness or 'thing', will be imperceptibly deflected and eventually arrive back at its starting point. This is because existence is a complete energetic sphere containing inner and outer space. And it is impenetrable, outwardly or inwardly, from our human flesh-and-blood position.

Humanity lives within the energetic sphere and there is no way out either by inner realisation or outer space travel. All must return to the solid body of existence. We don't know this yet about faster-than-light space travel. But we do know it from the masters and mystics of all ages who have realised God, and who without exception have returned to the solidity of their bodies and physical existence. *No one can demonstrate realisation without a body.*

Inner and outer exist only while I the knower am in a living physical body. When the body dies, what I call I and the whole of inner and outer vanish. Perhaps at physical death there is a universal state of intelligence beyond our individual perceptions and deepest realisations. But nobody knows – because everybody, even in their highest moments, is still in the fact of bodily existence.

The Mirror

As mentioned earlier, inner space, from the most aimless thought to the most profound realisation, is actually a mirror; the mirror is the intellect. The intellect is the God-given inner mirror that allows us to register external existence. We perceive a tree and the image reflects off the intellect onto the mind of experience (the memory) which then recognises a tree.

That's universal, meaning common to everybody.

But the inner realisation of God or truth is clearly not universal. In most people the pure intellect is blocked out for much of the time by mental reference to clutter in the memory and the clamour of emotions. Where there is attachment and any sense of identification with an object, the mind is unable to resist the personal pull and keeps circling the emotion as thought. The mind is then disturbed, can't see straight, imagines things to be as they are not, fantasises and thinks in circles – worry.

The human mind as we think we know it doesn't really exist. The mind only comes into play when it reflects on the memory or existence and thinks about the reflection. Otherwise there is only the pure innate intelligence which goes direct to the intellect and keeps the intellect relatively clear of mind. Of course, even the truly enlightened masters have to use the factual memory of the mind. But to be en-lightened means that emotional attachment has been pretty well dissolved. The master thinks straight and uses the memory for practical purposes.

The memory is the inevitable result of having been born into physical existence. It builds up throughout the life from experience and emotional involvements, screening and obscuring the pure intellect. The memory consists of layers of personal considerations, misleading concepts of life and living, and emotional feelings; in short, mental clutter and emotional clamour.

At birth the intellect is relatively clear. But from then on the gaining of experience and memory starts clouding the perception with innumerable notions, fears, unexpressed desires and personal attachments to people and objects.

By adulthood the memory is steeped in mental, emotional and materialistic ignorance – ignorance being the inability to see through the personal clutter and reflect on the pure mirror.

Although the pure intellect is the divine gift to humanity, it is only a mirror. A mirror must reflect what's in front of it. If the mirror surface is smeared with personal emotions, aimless thought and materialistic aspirations, that's what's reflected back.

Cleaning the Mirror

As I in inner space detach myself from personal clutter (the ignorance of wanting the inessential) I become more intelligent. I jettison some of the burden of time or past. I don't think, speculate and worry as much. My inner space is not so crowded and clamorous. I have a greater sense of absence of self – more inner space, more fulfilling peace.

Insights begin that I know are more real than my previous beliefs and opinions. My focus on the stillness of the insights leads me into a deeper absence, a deeper inner space. I begin to realise irrefutable truths and perhaps the first level of God-realisation – that I am immortal life. Whether others agree or accept my realisations is irrelevant. I *know* they are true.

What is happening in all this is that my intelligence is being speeded up enabling me to more often see *through* the individual human intellect to the deeper divine universal intellect.

So, anyone realising the deepest level of God has to have cleansed the mirror (the intellect) of the normal human clutter and clamour. They are then, relatively, pure intelligence – nothing. (Relatively because they still have a physical brain or body.) Pure intelligence is nothing. Nothing in front of the mirror reflects nothing. And so God is then realised as nothing.

Even so, the nothing is only a reflection in the intellect and therefore is not God or Source as we masters have assumed. God remains behind the intellect, behind the mirror – not in front of it!

Nevertheless the purest state possible in the inner space of existence is the reflection of pure intelligence in the purified mirror.

But most people for most of their lives reflect mostly on the clutter within. Every action is an attempt to clear the clutter. But reflection on the clutter invariably creates more clutter – even though action may dissolve a bit of it – and the fundamental ignorance remains.

The upshot of all this is that God or Self-realisation occurs in the inner space of abstract existence within the body and not elsewhere.

The Spiritual Master

The master has consciously emerged from being unconscious in existence.

57
Intelligence

I define a spiritual master as someone who has realised the reflection of God-consciousness at its deepest level within. But as God-consciousness or divine intelligence is the basis of all intelligent activity within and without, I am also speaking of everyone.

The difference is that there are many levels of consciousness before the realisation of Supreme Being, God or Source. And because supreme consciousness is potential in everybody, it can be difficult at first to accept that someone else has realised what you haven't. However, the words and presence of the master – or the individual – should indicate the depth of their realisation.

I in everybody, who am inwardly separate from the reality of existence, am undeniably intelligent in a deductive, reflective and knowing way. But I who reflect on the master-consciousness which has realised Supreme Being or the equivalent, am demonstrably far more intelligent than the normal level of massed intelligence. As such, I am able to reflect on the abstract extremity of existential intelligence – which creates the inner peace, fulfilment and equilibrium that the normal level of massed intelligence ceaselessly strives after.

So why am I in the massed sense so limited in intelligence and yet so acutely intelligent in the master? Because of what I am able to reflect on. The master has cleared his intellect and the masses have not. In the master I reflect directly onto the intellect and see straight, that is, I see 'what is' as it is. In the masses, however, I reflect for the most part on the personal clamour and clutter clouding or obscuring the intellect and receive versions of the same in return. As a result, the masses pursue the same wide but predictable range of human aspirations and fail to find the inner peace, fulfilment and equilibrium of the master.

The master has *consciously emerged* (some more, some less) from being unconscious in existence, whereas the masses have not. In the masses, I am unconscious (some more, some less) and for the most part am identified with existence. Identification means I – the id-entity – am deluded by existence. That is, I have no knowledge of the reality behind it.

Individual Consciousness

From the master perspective I can perceive the actuality of existence behind the irksome delusion of the troubled masses. In the truly en-lightened master, I can literally soar to the heights of Individual Consciousness within and to its limit – the realisation of Supreme Being or the one-and-only God, Source.

But I can go no further. This is the limit in inner space of temporary separation from sensory existence. And I – not being the immediacy of the realisation – inevitably mistake the limit for an end, when it is simply the extremity of individual conscious-ness. Certainly, in the moment of supreme realisation, individual consciousness vanishes into 'nothing' – and so do I. For I am indi-vidual consciousness; and as individual consciousness I extend from I in the chortling infant, through all the rigours and delights of living, to I who reflect on the body as it is dying. Only in death and supreme consciousness do I vanish: in death, permanently, in consciousness, temporarily.

A Perfect Whole

Any real perception of truth, life, love, death or God depends upon the swiftness of intelligence. Intelligence is speeded up beyond the normal, and even beyond the abnormal of genius in the world, by dissolving the clutter and clamour of personal attachments and considerations. This is done by an increasing inner knowledge of something within being greater than I and my intellectual speculations.

Genius in the world is certainly an example of abnormal intelli-gence. But the genius is partial. It applies only to a section of the living life. The rest of the life is invariably as personal and troublesome as it is for anyone who has not realised the only real genius, God.

Without the individual cleansing of the inner mirror of the intellect, it is impossible to see the phenomenal reality as it is. The phenomenal reality is a *whole* and the normal personal way of perceiving it is from a particular point of view – part-icular being partial, biased.

Even from the master-consciousness, the impersonal view is still from inside abstract existence – inner space – and not from inside the phenomenon itself. Inside the phenomenon is the noumenon – that which can never be known by anyone with a human brain or body.

Without attachment to personal considerations being removed I will see and interpret the outer in a prejudicial way. Instead of seeing the earth and events as they are and the intelligent scheme behind them, I will create a personalised world of effort, opinions, confusion, problems, disappointments, passing failure and partial success.

This world of my own making I will impose emotionally on the outer reality. And what is more, I'll have to contend not only with my world but with the personalised world psychically fabricated by all men and women before me.

Nonetheless, as I clear my own inner space I eventually have the speed of intelligence to outdistance the clamorous demands of the personal. This clamour presents itself as the emotional expectations of society and other people, as well as the demands of my own conscience.

The point is to be able to see straight, to see 'what is' as it is, *within* and *without.*

Once the intellect is cleared an amazing transformation in perception occurs. Inner space reflects a totally different picture of the inner and outer reality. First, both are seen to be a perfect whole. Not that they are the same. It's just that inner space when cleared doesn't exist in itself – in the same way as outer space can't be said to have any objectivity apart from the objects in it. Moreover these objects are products of the senses which again are completely subjective.

Outer space is simply a reflection of the purity of inner space. Neither is objective. Both are completely subjective. But not in the way the world regards subjectivity as in emotionality. Real subjectivity goes right back within to Source, God.

Second, it can be said that cleared inner space is nothing. Therefore the only thing extant is the objective sensory universe. But that is dependent on the mortal physical body to which we all return – after sleep, in recovering from unconsciousness and even after the most profound realisations of God.

In other words, without the awareness of the physical body there is no physical universe. No body, no physical world. And no body, no inner space. Nothing. Nothing, that is, that can be spoken of – except to say what the masters describe in realising nothing – amazement, wonder and glory.

And that's only a reflection, not the real thing.

58

The Divine Intellect

Individual consciousness continues through all levels of God-realisation up to and including the realisation of Supreme Being. There the immediate knowledge is *I am* This or Whatever. We have already seen that I do not realise, that I reappear very swiftly after – either as a memory of the event or as the personal pronoun of the realiser in the return to his body and daily life.

But something *is* realising Supreme Being, *is* being Supreme Being or being supremely nothing. As this is not I, what is it?

It is *purified* inner space. Purified inner space is the ultimate intelligence – and it is that which realises the sublime truth.

Even so, inner space cannot exist in its own right; there has to be a reality behind it. The reality is the divine intellect that makes existence possible and non-existence possible as the realisation of God or being nothing. The intellect is that nothing, *is* that purified inner space.

The name 'intellect' is only an intellectual or mental description; the word objectifies the intellect for us objectified creatures so that it has a positive meaning. But the intellect is nothing, a complete negation that's not even a negative. To call the intellect purified space – which I am doing – tests the very meaning of intelligence as we apprehend it. But space it is. And not ordinary space as we perceive space around us – but purified space, destitute of any object, including mind, thought or image. Hence the realisation of it is the realisation of nothing.

The fact that in the moment of realisation I am no longer present doesn't mean that I have *vanished*. I have merely *disappeared* – for now. I am still very much present in the realiser's memory. Even after the most exalted state of inner consciousness is realised, I will be back recalling an event to mind or remembering an address or phone number.

No matter how abstract I become, the realiser wouldn't know what he had realised if it weren't for me. For I am the existential intelligence, the knower, the recogniser, the rememberer, the be-er.

As amazing and extraordinary as the ultimate state of realisation is at the time, the intelligence of the realiser is not yet swift enough to prevent the reappearance of I. After the realisation I most certainly have the gnosis to reflect on the silent knowledge that most others don't have, but I am still there. I may even call myself different names in an endeavour to represent what has been realised. But it is I who does that. So I'm still there.

Only when I have completely vanished without return can reality be. That state is physical death.

I understand how masters and some teachers could assume from their particular realisations of God-consciousness that I have already vanished. In every case I certainly disappear in the moment. But I return – self-evidently in everyone's experience.

Phenomenal existence cannot be dismissed, disregarded or disowned – no matter how deep the realisation. To contend that the body does not exist and then to return to it is turning a blind eye to the obvious, and allowing a duality to persist.

There is of course no duality once it is realised that inner and outer form one complete existence – *the inner being simply an abstraction of the outer and the outer being simply a manifestation of the inner.*

And I'd like to add this. Every realised master knows that in saying, 'I am That' or 'Not That' (or any description at all), he is simply attempting to put the indescribable into the inadequacy of language. (As a result some masters stop talking. But I doubt if any have stopped for good. The use of writing or an abacus is not playing fair and is a form of delusion.)

No one can really question what a genuine master has realised or is being. And I'm not questioning any master who assumes he is the absolute state of consciousness. All I'm doing is gradually presenting what I know to be the ultimate truth. The absolute truth is certainly beyond that. But my point is that the absolute is impossible of realisation. And that us masters have tended to give a wrong impression of having realised absolute truth – or that absolute truth is possible of realisation – an impression that has to be called (horror of horrors) an individual one.

59

The Role of the World

Power Versus Force

One of the most important discoveries in my spiritual life is this: every deep realisation of individual consciousness *then* has to be lived out in time in appropriately challenging circumstances. The circumstances are determined by the realisation *and* the living life up to that time.

I also saw that the deeper the realisation of the consciousness of God, the longer the 'testing' period is likely to be.

All masters have climacteric realisations and lesser ones as they descend deeper into God. These combine to create a flow of circumstances. But as time in existence is far slower than the consciousness of the truly realised master, the circumstances seldom catch up to really trouble him.

This is one reason why the master is not affected by the force of circumstances as others less realised probably would be. Another reason is that such a depth of realisation provides the necessary knowledge and inner strength of *equilibrium* – which is not intimidated or overcome by circumstances.

Nevertheless every living master is in the throes of facing the test of his realisation(s) as the circumstances of his life.

A fiction exists that deeply realised masters are immediately free. Inner freedom is indeed the state of God-consciousness. But there's still the outer. By the divine order of things such a realisation marks a new beginning in the external life as the *power* of the realisation is tested against the *force* of the world.

The world exists for this purpose.

The world of course isn't there just for masters. Everything I've described about the living life of masters applies to everyone – at their particular level of consciousness. It's the very basis of evolutionary life.

Applying this broadly across existence, masters are facing the 'consequences' of their profound realisations. Spiritual teachers

196

are facing the consequences of their revelatory insights. And everyone (including masters and teachers) is facing the consequences of being attached to what they were before. In masters these emotional and mental pressures have been largely dissolved; and in true spiritual teachers considerably reduced.

By virtue of divine integrity the circumstantial line-up is never more than the individual can handle. It may appear that one individual has to face far more testing conditions than another, as, for example, when someone is driven to a radical action like suicide. But please recall that there is only one 'I' – and comparisons where I am concerned are unreal and irrelevant.

The pressure of circumstances and living is likely to be greater where materialism is the dominant interest and seemingly (to the mind) more overwhelming when the big issues strike. But because of the many distractions available in materialistic living there's a kind of respite in being able to busy oneself in other matters or by thinking about them. In anyone really living the spiritual life of negation the focus is one-pointed within, and seldom is any outer distraction able to relieve the early pain of self-dissolution.

Masters in particular in their early years must have undergone an agonising time as the inevitable ignorance of self was being burned out by the incoming divine consciousness. (If not then, then later.) The more love of the divine the shorter the period of the agony. But even so the process will have taken several years. Then the process continues in the form of 'testing' circumstances.

Supreme Consciousness

The pinnacle of my realisation of individual consciousness happened nearly forty years ago. It was during my transcendental realisation. This went on for three weeks and an extended account written down shortly afterwards is in my autobiography.

I was not asleep or in a trance. I was lying down completely awake and focused within. My physical senses were performing normally, autonomously.

In another room was the divine master-consciousness in the form of the Blessed John who had come briefly into that body from deep within the unconscious to teach me.

Suddenly I am the Supreme Being, supreme consciousness. I see existence like a tiny sphere far, far away and start physically laughing because I know that nothing in existence – no sensory effort and not even love – can reach me or be what I am. I am above all. I am all. There can be nothing apart from me.

At the time and for many years after I assumed that no deeper realisation of God was possible. I was correct in that no deeper realisation of *individual consciousness* of God is possible. But I was also wrong. What I didn't realise was the significance of existence being there at all in the realisation. The union with that knowledge took nearly three decades. Is there a deeper level of God after that? Please read on.

60

Undifferentiated Instinctual Intelligence

Looping the Loop

As my inner space becomes more emptied, the realisations of God continue. Finally, as the master-consciousness, 'the end' is realised – the realisation of Supreme Being, or equivalent, where nothing is beyond. That and that alone *is*.

In this supreme moment I disappear. But with miraculous swiftness I 'return' – as the inevitable knowing/reflection on the moment(s) before. Dormant I may have been. But while the body lives no one can escape what I am. For I am the intelligence in the body, and of the body, that makes knowing possible.

Although I am able to describe the memory of the realisation (inasmuch as it can be articulated) I can never be that original moment. This explains why I, in the master, inevitably regard the supreme realisation as 'the end'. I am just that far away from the eternal *now* that can never be described, to assume this erroneous conclusion.

As already stated, I have merely reached the end of my tether, the end of the kingdom of inner space, the extremity of *individual consciousness*.

The great magnet of outer existence, my body, now starts drawing me back. I'm like a toy ball attached by elastic to a bat. Having reached the extremity of the loop out I must now loop the loop by returning to where I began.

And what an extraordinary non-existent existence awaits me.

The journey back is through a sort of reverse set of the circumstances and situations encountered in coming out. They're the 'same' but different – like swimming against the stream and then turning round and swimming with the stream. Same stream, different dynamic.

Also, I'm now completely transformed in having the power to reflect uninterruptedly and subconsciously on God, the nothing.

Thus the journey back is not nearly as arduous or long as the journey out – even if it takes twenty years.

In both going out and coming back I draw to me others steeped more and less in ignorance. Going out I do my best to free them for I am still in relative ignorance. Most drop away after a time and new ones arrive. Most are more intelligent than those who came earlier because everyone I teach is a reflection of what I am.

As I become more intelligent, more space, more absent, so that potential is there relatively for those who are with me. Still they come and still they go. Except for those who must serve what I am and who in serving must receive. All come with me as far as they can.

The Way Back

On the way back I encounter in others the ignorance I left behind on the way out, and those whom I must serve. But now I am a totally different consciousness, more a teacher by conscious presence behind the words. Circumstances in the form of people and situations converge on me and do indeed test my equilibrium and absence of personal will. As the years pass the intensity and at times virulence of outer circumstances gradually fade. Until living finally becomes effortless with nothing to do but what is done.

The return can be measured by the remaining years of the living life. An early death in the fortieth or fiftieth year is unlikely to provide enough time to complete the return of a Supremely-realised consciousness. But it's all part of the existential game which really never ends. And the precious consciousness of God-realisation at any level is not wasted.

The Demise of Individual Consciousness

Having looped the loop by returning back through inner space, I the knower disappear into the individual physical body out of which I arose.

Undifferentiated Intelligence then reveals itself.

Undifferentiated Intelligence is the demise of individual consciousness.

Individual consciousness took the master to the extremity of inner space and back – with I the knower more or less present to provide conceptual confirmation from the memory of exalted moments.

But now such confirmation is superseded by evidence far more tangible and universal: *the external, phenomenal and circumstantial life is perfect.*

This is not to be confused with the inner space realisation that the whole of existence with its tragedies and conflicts is perfect. What I'm speaking of is the perfection of the actual outer living life.

Completion

Completion is revealed by intelligence, not consciousness. Intelligence doesn't have inner reflection. *Intelligence-beyond-knowing is revealed only in the actuality of the living phenomenal life.*

As undifferentiated intelligence cannot be known (because of the virtual absence of I), thus I am not able to say that I who write this am undifferentiated. But the evidence of undifferentiation is there. It may not be complete since I know completion is only possible at physical death. But I can report what this extraordinary moment-to-moment intelligence (which I am not) reveals.

Barry Long lives in a kind of paradise. Not only an inner paradise as any deeply realised master might say, but in an *external* paradise. My actual surroundings where I live, and wherever I happen to be, along with the moment-to-moment external circumstances, are a continual harmony.

That's not to say I don't accidentally injure my body; that apparent lacks don't occur such as running short of drinking water in the drought; or being comfortably marooned at home by temporary flooding in the wet season; or sharing the property with lethal snakes. I soon recover from the injuries, I buy in some water (because I have the money), the flooding subsides in a few days and it seems that if I'm not aggressive towards the snakes they don't have a problem with me.

Now and again spiritual thrusters with more zeal than realisation throw my teaching back at me in books and letters as their own inspiration, sometimes plagiarising whole phrases and sentences. Given the chance and inclination I endeavour to inform them of what the Blessed John once taught me, 'Always be true to the source of your inspiration'. This, when you're lifting stuff from a realised master, means clearly acknowledging that source.

Anyway such plagiarising has to be a sign that the master's becoming famous!

Then there's the odd coward who's obviously feasted on the master's divinely inspired table for years and sends unsigned disparaging emails revealing his or her own self-conscious turmoil. No problem here. The staff who work for The Barry Long Foundation are asked to destroy unsigned missives without reading and without passing them on to me, so that there's no indulgence or psychic satisfaction for the sender. I mention this because the persons in both cases will most likely be reading this book and perhaps they'll see something of value for themselves.

Then there's the fact that I have cancer along with the effects of drugs to inhibit the cancer, arthritis, jelly spots on the iris of the eye, low sustained physical stamina, hardened cushions between the vertebrae, increasing absence of short memory and most of the usual signs of ageing which end in death. But that's all a part of the actuality and by Grace I have no problem with it. Nobody who is not yet old can ever imagine what it's like to be old. Such prescience is not allowed in the divine order of things. The younger have just to get on with it and keep the world turning.

The main thing in my experience is that whatever appears as a blip or lack in the external will be sorted out and filled very shortly. This is not an expectation. It's the way life is. If the lack is serious enough my body will die. No problem. It means I don't *have* to achieve anything externally; I simply do what I do with very little reflection. Everything falls into place if *I* am out of it.

It can't even be said that I have no choice which is part of the deepening master-consciousness. To have no choice implies a subtle awareness of choice, the abstract presence of I.

The area of important relationships is where the undifferentiated intelligence continues to reveal itself. For instance, most masters have a female companion, perhaps a wife, or women with whom they are sexually intimate on a regular basis.

In the journey back the master does what he has to do. There's no choice for him in whatever he does. But the point is that such relationships put stress or strain on the people involved – including any children of the women – until everyone is in harmony with the master.

Although the master himself may remain for the most part in equilibrium, the situations are not externally harmonious. This indicates that the journey back is not yet complete. Moreover external stress and distress demand action or compromise on the master's part.

The same applies to relationships with the master's mother, father, sisters, brothers and close relatives. If they are not externally harmonious, and if ignored instead of being consciously addressed, completion is lacking.

This may be easily misconstrued by a consciousness which looks inward for the measure of harmony. But ultimately, towards the end of the journey, external existence is the only indicator. In short, how it is out there is how it is in here. The other way round of looking inward for verification introduces a subjective note – I the knower who assess by inner reflection. With the only arbiter being the external, there's no room for the subjectivity of I.

Furthermore, the external actuality cannot be manipulated. It is as it is every moment – a perfect outer mirror of undifferentiated intelligence. It may be said that I have to judge whether the external is perfect. That's a bit like saying, 'How will I know it is God when I realise God?' When God is realised there's no shadow of doubt that it's God. And there's no shadow of doubt when the external is harmonious. Everybody's natural intelligence reveals that. So there's no doubt when the harmony is just about complete *in every respect.* How could there be when I am no longer there to judge? The fact is I disappear in the face of natural intelligence.

When the loop is nearing completion inner space virtually vanishes. And along with it vanishes what before were reflections of peace, nothing, or equilibrium. When those aspects of the reflected reality have been realised there's no longer any need of them. They merge and vanish into an absent state of undifferentiated, unreflected intelligence – along with *the end of the compulsive need of inner space.*

That's the reality behind realisations. With the inner reflection virtually gone, only the external remains. Perhaps this marks the convergence that ends in no inner and no outer – to speak of?

The Dawning

How do I now describe, in my own experience, the seeing of completion in the actuality?

It was a dawning, not a moment of realisation. I can't pinpoint it in time. Like any dawn there's no distinct moment of light. The light just keeps coming with no immediate recognition. Suddenly the fact is there. The actuality, *'your'* actuality is 'perfect'. Nothing is missing. The delay in recognition is simply due to the time it takes for the light that can't be measured to penetrate the brain.

I know that the delayed recognition of 'what was always there' is characteristic of the realisation of God at any level. But completion is not something of inner cognition. Completion is only evident in the actual 'perfection' of the outer living life *now.* The work-life is perfect. The love-life is perfect. The companion is perfect. The physical surroundings are perfect. Every aspect of the existential life is perfect. Nevertheless, it must be remembered that only God is perfect; that perfection here is always relative and always only now. So of course it is only perfect for me – now. And anyway who's speaking other than I, an impulse of imperfection? Even so, any normally intelligent observer would be able to see that BL's living life is … well … near perfect.

61

The Ultimate Truth

The ultimate truth is the complete absence of any knowing individual existence. This is impossible while even the deepest realised master is alive. In other words the ultimate truth is only in physical death, the end of the physical brain.

Even then there is nothing to discover.

To use a reasonable analogy, all that happens is that the truth of the realised master is merged in complete union with the beauty and creativity *inside* existence. In short, the truth realised while alive unites with the wonder and mystery of universal nature in all its power and glory. This is undifferentiated instinctual intelligence *inside* existence. It is present in all living things and demonstrated in human experience as the unfathomable swiftness and intelligence of instinct in the body.

It is not a case of I or the individual consciousness being instinctual intelligence. That would mean it could be known or described. And the knower or describer is always outside existence – even if deepest inner space has been realised.

Deepest inner space is only an abstract extension of the play of existence. If it were the actuality of existence, everyone, not just masters, would have realised it or be it. But that's not the case with undifferentiated instinctual intelligence. *Undifferentiated instinctual intelligence is universal and therefore not the property of any man or woman no matter how deeply realised.*

In undifferentiated intelligence, I have vanished, not just disappeared as I do in God or Self-realisation.

But I must add that the depth of anybody's reality – that of any 'ordinary' man or woman – cannot be judged or assessed while a physical brain exists. Everybody at any moment is a light – and that current light in existence is not necessarily the full shining of the light beyond the brain. Nonetheless, a master's demonstrated realisation of divine consciousness is a certain indication of the purity of that light.

Instinctual intelligence being universal is in everybody's living experience. It's in your body, my body and the body of every living thing. It determines where the roots of the plant go, how animals find water and how we do this and not that. To know and really perceive it requires an acuity of reflection beyond the normal hurried glance. It needs frequent inner and outer conscious studying in the moment and not through books or other people's concepts. Being universal it's always present.

In the play of our unique self-consciousness, the instinctual intelligence is so incredibly in control that it employs, and actually determines for the good of all, our fluctuating likes and dislikes. Thus does it ensure actions that are right for us, even if not good for us in our opinion. Instinctual intelligence is pure and simply God, the all-knowing, all-present and all-powerful unnameable.

No one can say where instinctual intelligence really is. The positional mind will give it a place. This I have done by saying it is inside the body. But I hasten to deny this place as a reality. Because in the absence of a brain – an absence approximated in deep dreamless sleep – all existence and all positions disappear, as I and my body do.

Where does that leave us?

It leaves only the idea of reality before I came in, before the so-called Big Bang, before self-consciousness, before consciousness, before *any thing.*

'*Sic transit gloria mundi*' – so passes away the glory of the world.

Tantra

Without the profound recognition of God as woman, and the selfless love and service of that, it's not tantra.

FROM HERE TO REALITY

62
Tantric Love and the Master

Years ago I announced publicly and widely that 'I am a tantric master'. I explained that the sole purpose of tantric lovemaking was to bring the women involved to a greater knowledge of the love of God. I said tantra was a God-given power and that every master was not necessarily a tantric master.

What's the difference between BL and other masters in the tantric sense?

When I say that the power of tantra is God-given I'm speaking from the outer as well as the inner. The outer is my living service and devotion to woman as God over nearly four decades. The inner power originates from the God-given vision of woman being the indescribable Lord which is free of gender.

The power of tantra is potential in every man and woman because the basis of human sexuality is pure love, and pure love is the love of God. But tantra has to be lived as a complete way of life, not just in making love. Without the profound recognition of God as woman, and the selfless love and service of that, it's not tantra.

The difference between tantric love with a master and non-tantric love is threefold. First, at an early stage the women involved are introduced to each other by the master, who emphasises that in tantric love there can be no secrets, therefore no fear, and that honesty is paramount. Second, the women themselves are united in a mystical bond of love that is neither social nor attached; a sistership that comes from recognition of the uniqueness of each other from having shared together their lowest and highest moments with the master. Third, any jealousy and competition between the women is gradually dissolved in the mutual knowledge that something holy is being done and being confirmed in their own deepening inner experience of the meaning of real love.

While a genuine master is sexually intimate with women, he encounters all the ignorance and unhappiness that sex causes in woman. He's not causing it; it's already there. He has the power to gradually reduce or perhaps remove the acquired unhappiness from the women. The power of his love continues long after the physically intimate association has ended.

I was making love to five women on a regular basis and after three years told each to go her separate way. Once a tantric master has taken a woman on and affirmed in her a deep level of the love of God, she must re-enter the world of man and relationships. The love of God is not an end in this existence. It must be applied and expressed as action in the external.

Having discovered the real love within, the woman's experience in the world inevitably teaches her that she must always put her love of God before her love of man – or frustration and disillusionment will follow. Man is woman's only external love – and her only problem. Putting him first is the fundamental cause of every woman's unhappiness.

In the process of tantric love the master may be largely unaffected within. But the point remains he is *doing* something (to bring about a result); and nearing completion there's nothing to do. Eventually the master will be removed from 'having to do'.

The sexually active master may mistake having no choice for completion. To consciously have no choice is certainly a state approaching completion. And a master who makes real love because he has no choice is contributing to the need of love, or God, on this sex-driven planet.

Even so he is still doing for a purpose – no matter how worthy, noble or self-sacrificing it may be. It is simply another stage in the long haul of closing the loop. Nearing completion there's no more purpose; everything that was *needed* to be done has been done. The living life is almost complete.

All that I've said above about masters and love can be assumed by lesser men. But physical love made without the unwavering knowledge of higher purpose is done for self-satisfaction and that's not holy. As well, there can be an intellectual assumption 'I have no choice' which is perilous for every woman concerned.

A Mystical Union

Although I no longer practise tantra, I continue to have the power of tantric presence and communication. Even more so now.

With the exception of Sara, my lovemaking with the last of the other four women ended in 1995. Today each loves what I am as the outer embodiment of her unwavering love of God within. This is spontaneously reaffirmed when we speak on the phone, meet, or they write to me. I suspect it will not change.

The miracle of the tantric master's love is that the individual woman sees her inner love reflected in the purity and selflessness of the master's love of her and his love of God. For her an unquestionable mystical union of the inner and outer love has occurred. In no way does she see BL as God. She simply sees God's love of her reflected in his embodiment.

Each woman says she is eternally grateful. And I love each with a love beyond all understanding. That's the love she sees and knows she's united with.

But no one should get the impression that these women are different to others. They are different deep within but unless someone sees that, they'll appear pretty ordinary although... I can't say any more that can be understood. Except that they are not paragons, for anyone.

63
When You're Old Enough to Die

Woman and the Ideal

I'm now seventy-six. For six years I've been living intimately with one of the women, Sara, in a divine union of love and harmony. My work, such as writing this and speaking to the people, is effortless and undemanding, a continuous pleasure. My whole life is problem-free. But then that's what happens when you've nearly closed the loop and you're old enough to die.

I always knew that my active tantra days had to end, but not the power of tantra which never ends. As tantra was the practical expression of my love of God, I also knew that tantra meant honesty, no hiding and no self-consideration. True tantra will always end with one woman. She is the end of the journey of true love. She embodies the love of every other woman who has been loved. She is none other than God in existence in female form.

Nonetheless that's the ideal.

In this outer separative existence where everything is done by living, there is no ideal – only the pursuit of it. The paradox is that the ideal can't be pursued to an end; you can only be it. And then it can't be known apart from what is revealed in the actuality. Pursuit of the ideal – and everybody is engaged in it in some form or other – is a preparation.

No Perfection

Nothing in existence is perfect. Man is not perfect because his nature is to have something to do – and all doing contributes to imperfection somewhere.

Woman's essential nature is to love and be loved. In that she has nothing to do and is more perfect than man. What makes her do against her essential nature is that she neither loves suffi-ciently nor is loved sufficiently. This translates as: she neither loves God sufficiently nor realises that God's love of her is sufficient. And invariably she looks for man's love first. And so her cyclic world of problems keeps on turning.

As no other body can be blamed for any body's deficiency, woman's lack of love and of being loved is because she loses sight of her essential nature and essential love. Once restored by the love of God, and the putting of God before any man or any thing, she, like the realised master, simply does what she does. She can't cease to do externally because the world of bodies is a place of doing. But in real love within, and with its reflection without, the living as the doing ceases to be problematical.

Harmony

I've said I live in a union of love and harmony with Sara. I have not known such completion within and without before. There's very little that we don't do together; we're seldom apart except for brief practical periods. We enjoy nothing more than being together.

She amuses me, delights me, cares for me and loves me with a devotion that would astound me except that I know it is the love of God. My love of her is the same. She frequently says she can't believe it, not because she doubts it, but because such love as we enjoy is beyond the mind and emotions and therefore beyond belief.

> This love beyond world space and time
> Whispers in the heart
> Though unpossessed
> You are forever mine.
> (from BL's audio recording, *Songs of Life*)

I hasten to add that if Sara left me for another man or for any reason, I would continue to love her without interruption. I've announced this publicly at my meetings. For it is not Sara as such whom I love, or BL as such whom she loves, but the love of God that each of us reveals to the other and in which we are both immersed by Grace.

64

The Alien

Woman's Cosmic Affliction

That being said, there is still the alien, the spoiler. The alien is a natural effect in every woman of child-bearing age – the monthly undergoing of menstruation.

Undergoing is certainly the right word to describe it. As a mere male observer it seems to me that menstruation – especially premenstrual tension (PMT) – is a sort of natural affliction of woman, ranging from perhaps minimal disturbance to severe, and sometimes debilitating, physical pain. In all cases in my experience there is a distinct alteration in perception which stops when the period comes. As the condition is widely recognised as tension before the period, the indication is that it's abnormal compared with the usual state of most women.

Menstruation has been called 'the curse', which probably originates from the male-dominated Judaic-Christian religious myth of the 'fall', and may be wrongly construed as a mythic form of retribution for woman. It's not a curse on woman; it's a curse for her – even though she may accept it by getting used to it.

I've endeavoured to find a cause for this affliction of woman. Years ago I described it as the body's natural way of discharging the material symbol of woman's unhappiness in not being loved. She certainly seems to find more tranquillity in her body when pregnant. And doctors tell women who suffer severe pain in menstruation that the difficulty is likely to diminish or disappear if they have a baby. Perhaps being pregnant and having a baby is associated with a deeper love in the female. But nothing being perfect, pain in one form or another has to follow.

Menstruation clearly is a cosmic, meaning a profoundly inexplicable and unavoidable, thing. Localised effects don't explain the cause of it. It could be said it's as natural as breathing. But breathing, unless impaired, doesn't cause pain or distress. Is it some sort of cosmic impairment that's been foisted on womankind? The best I can discover so far is that woman's whole system is impaired by lack of love.

Cosmic Love

Many men and women have loved each other as couples. But I haven't heard that that love reduces PMT or the pain, except perhaps early in the association. So what's the answer, what's the indication?

In my experience the love that starts to reduce menstrual problems is the cosmic love of the cosmic God. By cosmic here I mean something greater and more selfless than human love and far surpassing any human concept or understanding of God.

That's a pretty awe-inspiring love. It has to be cosmic. To my perception the menstrual affliction of woman has a cosmic source. And the solution lies in a great power of love over-whelming a great force of doubt, discomfort and aggravation. But it must be said, of course, that the individual woman is not at fault. This is a mighty confrontation beyond human intervention.

Power is cosmic because it comes from God. Cosmic love is only potential in human affairs. It's not here until it is lived and then only to the degree that it *is* lived. Force, on the other hand, is always in existence or of existence. It's not potential as power is; force is already here and it certainly demonstrates that in the menstrual affliction of woman.

Self-doubt: Symptom of the Alien

The incoming force associated with menstruation is alien. It's an alien invasion from deep in the cosmic unconscious – from deep in cosmic space within. The alien slips in by taking advantage of a temporarily weakening natural body function.

In most women in my externalised experience the hormonal imposition appears to obscure inner vision. The effect of this seems to be mainly self-doubt combined with a compensating reaction of 'wilful independence'. Self-doubt for woman means doubting her essential nature which is love. Uncertainty about being loved also dominates, except for brief moments of clarity. As in all wilfulness, the woman herself is certain that her doubts, fears and independence are justified.

Where there is deep self-knowledge and love of God the woman knows for the most part that the negativity is a surface reaction. The disturbance then is perhaps brief and in some months absent. After the hormonal tension abates the woman is usually as mystified by the negativity as the man.

However, in these separate bodies it *seems* that the criteria for enlightenment in love or truth or both, is a *constant* state of inner equilibrium and surrender of any position; this expressing itself as light or joy in the eyes, stillness and harmony in the flesh and a knowledge that all is well. To me that's all we can go by. It might be different when we die. But for now that's how it is, since everybody on earth seeks harmony. And yet we sensory creatures can never dismiss the indescribable anguish of deep physical pain.

Of course the range of periodic change varies in all women, but the fundamental doubt and the compensating reactions are the norm. For example, the change may manifest as a desire to be more alone, silent or to retreat into some sort of isolation. Other women may have a burst of physical activity before the period starts. There can be crankiness, short temperedness and irritation with chat, particularly with man and his structured ways.

In menstruation intense pain can also cause psychological dis-orientation. Some women may have a minimum of physical pain but the altered condition of mind and emotions is probably always there, though perhaps not expressed.

But there are always exceptions and I have to say that at least one woman has written and said she enjoys her periods and has no pain. That is indeed a Godsend. And without doubting the woman's own experience I would still be inclined to ask the partner.

65

The Alien in Man

The Drive of Sex

What about man? Does he have a cosmic affliction, the effect of an alien, unavoidable invading force?

He certainly does. His affliction is the sexual imperative. He cannot resist thinking about woman, imagining her female parts, slyly being a voyeur and generally working himself up into a foment of desire which usually culminates in masturbation or orgasm.

The sexual imperative is every man's torment either because he has no woman, or his woman won't indulge his sexual appetite, or because of the disastrous material and mental situations sex drives him into, or because he can never have any real peace while it's there.

Practically everything I've described about the effect of menstruation on woman, can be applied to the effect on man of his sexual drive. His salvation too, in time, is the love of God – together with the love of God in woman.

Woman is not driven by sex. Her drive is the desire for love. But like all drives it ends in disaster, disappointment, heartbreak or disillusionment. Her force collides with man's force and the result is sex – for the most part with not enough love.

Frustration is man's main problem in his sexual affliction. Even with a loving full-time woman partner he is often frustrated – which is caused by seeing himself in a one-to-one sort of cage. His natural drive is to fancy being with different women – which is a deep unresolved affliction. Cultural concepts of monogamy and religion add to his frustration and often a sense of being trapped.

Man's sexual drive – and the global frustration it produces – is responsible for all wars, cruelty and violence. Such destructive collective frustration is so deeply subconscious that it boils over

into politics, corporate affairs, the law – and practically every
level of the attempt at civilisation.

It is not only man's affliction. The frustration afflicts every
living thing. But in a male-dominated, sexually driven, unconscious society, the ubiquitous violence, cruelty, greed, and
exploitation of others and nature is excused as normal.

What can a man do? He has to master his own unconscious
sexual drive by making it conscious and gradually transforming
it into love. The sexual drive is only unconscious when the goal
is satisfaction – and not fulfilment. How does he do this?

He begins by loving woman, the focus of his fundamental
hormonal drive. Although man can temporarily bury his maleness
in religion, good deeds, political affray, international confrontation, compromise, institutionalised sport or boozing nights with
the boys, his thoughts soon turn to woman. There the transformation must begin. Otherwise, in whatever he does, there will be an
element of concealment, dishonesty and self-deception – the
norm.

Is woman blameless? Of course not. Throughout history she
has fed man's sexuality and surrendered her innate power of
love. This power can change man. But it's not a power that
woman can wield for her own satisfaction, like feminine flirta-
tiousness. The power comes from her love of love – her own
original nature. And that is her love of God, the unknown, her
own largely forgotten fundamental focus.

When woman is once again in possession of this divinely intelligent power she no longer competes with man or tries to change
him. In a loving relationship she puts God or love first, refusing
(despite her love of the man) to serve his sexual drive or her
feminine tendency to give in to him. She doesn't try to change
him. She just refuses to have sex without love. And gradually
where the man has sufficient love and sensitivity, he will get the
idea and change himself simply by being with her. A rare phenomenon, but possible.

In using woman for sex and satisfaction man has passed on to
her some of his sexual aggression and frustration. In many cases
she has become more man than woman, reflecting masculine

attitudes, militancy and confrontational self-assertiveness. This makes her emotional, hard and usually unattractive to man. Since she can't be responsible for her own love – her love of God – man will love her and leave her, compromise with her, or be dishonest in his avowed love of her. In short, both must put love, or God, before the other.

FROM HERE TO REALITY

Summing Up – Midway

Pausing after reading and letting questions be until answered by revelation is far more effective than trying to find answers with the mind.

66

Existence

Existence is the only reality. That's the crux of it. There's nothing beyond existence. But what precisely is existence?

In the first place, existence is the actual phenomenal world now – what is, freed of interpretation, consideration, speculation and description. In the second place, existence also consists of the extension of inner space where the above interpretive reasoning takes place. Together, the two make up the whole of human existence.

But how far 'back' as inner space does existence go? Clearly, from the descriptions of realised masters it goes back to the extremity of individual consciousness which is 'nothing'. And without exception this 'nothing' is instantly recognised as God.

Can it be said then that God is within the human brain, since every realised master still has a brain? It certainly seems so. And do all the incredible mystical experiences and spiritual moments that so many 'ordinary' people have, also happen in the brain? Again it would appear so. No one without the presence of a brain has ever said differently. Wherever there's a brain there's existence and wherever there's existence there's a brain.

But perhaps there's no brain. Perhaps what we call the brain is the universal intellect. Maybe this explains why so many living forms don't have a brain. Perhaps the brain is a fabrication of the mind whose ceaseless activity obscures the truth of the intellect.

Perhaps there's no mind either, and the pure intellect is reflecting the whole of 'what is' without the troublesome complications of the brain/mind.

From all this we seem trapped in a combination of an outer sensory materialistic existence and an inner reflective world of psychological images and reactions. Although the images and reactions disappear in glimpses and realisations of the enlightened state, that living moment of exaltation fails to persist, other than in the memory or as gnosis.

External space is only comprehensible because of the objects in it. Similarly, inner space exists only because of what's in it. Remove all objects and we end up with nothing – the truth of the divine intellect.

Letting questions be until answered by revelation is far more effective than trying to find answers with the mind.

Now

Outer and inner existence is always *now*.

However in this now nothing can be known because I – the knower – have disappeared. But only for now. As long as the body is alive I return to intellectually differentiate existence into objects of time. And the world of ignorance, pain and suffering continues.

Inner space is the mirror of the universal divine intellect. When nothing is in front of the mirror it reflects nothing. And so in Supreme God-realisation when I, the last differentiation of existence disappear, there's the reflection of nothing – which every deeply realised master knows in his own experience.

Inner space at every level diligently reflects what I bring to it. If I bring material aspirations such as present science does, inner space will reflect back a flow of materialistic possibilities – but always leading towards nothing. As a result science finds less and less substance and more space.

For science to keep hold of the material and theoretical basis of its inquiry (not to mention the theoretical sanity of the scientist) science invents discrete forces and invisible particles. These (unbeknown to science) are actually units of time intellectualised by the scientific mind. As I the scientist work in time, and not now in the appreciation of the nothing, I never run out of time or 'things' to discover and name. (Except when the scientist is dying.)

When massed humanity presents its problems and troubles to inner space, the mirror assiduously reflects the disturbances back as worry – but again always moving things on towards a temporary solution in time, which creates more space or some respite, for a time.

When I (motivated by the incomprehensible Will) *now* turn and focus more and more on inner space itself I realise different levels of God, each reflecting more 'nothing' and therefore less presence of I or time than the level before. Until finally, I am *now* next to nothing and realise the reflection of the one and only timeless Supreme Being as unlimited space.

The Integrity

To reflect such lofty and exalted realisations, the mirror of inner space must have integrity. The integrity is that inner space is the *reflector* of the undifferentiated God inside the actuality. As such the mirror is a perfect mirror. It holds nothing for itself. And when nothing is there (nothing arising) it reflects nothing. Nothing in the mirror is a reflection of the undifferentiated God. But only a reflection.

Graciously and generously the perfect mirror of inner space gives back what is put in front of it; along with a moving touch of reflected reality which is nothing, absence or non-existence.

Graciously and compassionately the descent into inner space is gradual. I, myself, who am all ignorance to begin with, am progressively purged and purified so as not to be overwhelmed by the fear of extinction that accompanies the realisation of being nothing and the sense of being alone in the midst of differentiated existence.

Consciousness and Intelligence

In every body I begin as a baby with likes and dislikes. Simultaneously I grow in awareness of sense 'reception' and make mental connections to bring the different impressions into a memorable whole. This becomes my unreliable world. My intelligence is mental, a reactive response to the environment.

With increasing experience the mental facility extends to the ability to reason. In reasoning (stringing concepts together) I discover more significance in my impressions of the environment. I begin to 'know' the effects of sex, satisfaction, excitement and depression. After many years of the stress and strain of that, and the passing celebrations of temporary successes, there perhaps arises a yearning for love or something that doesn't fade, waver, give up, or disappear into another episode of experience.

I am still identified with existence, the actuality. So for the most part I'm still a mentally reasoning, unconscious, materially orientated creature. I can, and may, achieve great heights in the unconscious world that I have created and am unknowingly creating. But I'm neither conscious nor really intelligent.

When I begin to question my living life as a reality I start to focus more or less on inner space. In inner space I'm confronted with all my misplaced assumptions, beliefs and opinions – the result of my material worldly drives and fluctuating certainties.

The pain of detaching (more or less) from these creates more inner space and I become more conscious. Just what being conscious is I'm not sure. I only know that I have a deepening inner knowledge within of something I can't describe. And I see the meanings of things that my most mentally quick friends and acquaintances don't seem to see.

Inner space proceeds to reveal more absence within and I am likely to realise aspects of God, or reality.

When that happens I am consciousness – consciousness being an advance on intellectuality. As the journey in consciousness – the journey into inner space – continues over the years I realise more of the incredible, the indescribable.

Finally I reach the realisation of the intelligence of Supreme Being, the end of individual consciousness. I can go no further. I've completed the loop out. Now I must loop the loop by completing the journey back.

I am now immeasurably more intelligent than I was before but am not yet undifferentiated intelligence. For that I must return whence I came, thus completing through existence the amazing journey out and back. Then intelligence itself will reveal just what undifferentiated intelligence means.

No I

Once a deep level of inner space has been realised as the reflection of God, every level closer up towards the physical may be accessed at any time. This is because the deeper level is as 'nothing' and the level above is always more of 'something'. Nothing can access something; but something can't access nothing.

We see this demonstrated in a psychic sense when seriously ill people 'see' non-physical figures beside the bed which they apprehend as loving, healing or helpful influences. And thus the genuine reports of 'angels'. The fact is that these psychic influences or entities are aspects of deeper disembodied intelligence. They are free to 'enter' the physical realm of the brain similarly to how the realised master, without being contaminated, 'enters' the troubled or confused mental and emotional world of the people.

As the deeply God-realised master-consciousness 'leaves' the profundity of 'nothing' to teach in the surface world (which he must while he has a body) I the knower is autonomously resurrected because anywhere above 'nothing' is 'something' and where I am and most people live. I serve the master by remembering where he left his car keys or where he lives, or even aspects of his realisations that I have conceptualised and remembered. For really, I am the power of the memory.

Thus do I enable this book to be written – while at all times surrendered and serving the flow of original knowledge or undifferentiated intelligence that is beyond my reflective capability. If I were not surrendered to this amazing power and source I would get in the way with my knowing and pollute or block the new.

But am I actual? Or at this deepest stage of God-realisation is there only the *reflective function* and no I?

Yes. There is no I and in its absence only the reflection on outer existence and the purely practical memory within. Thus in truth there's no I and never was. I is not needed in pure reflection at the level of God-consciousness. Although God-consciousness is a state of freedom through the utter surrender of I, the personal pronoun is used as a means of communication.

For understandable reasons some masters as they go deep into God-consciousness endeavour to avoid using the word 'I'. If you've realised that you are all of life how can such a state be encompassed by a small and insignificant word such as I? To me, however, avoidance of the word 'I' is a refined form of self-consciousness. I as Barry Long have no difficulty in that regard. I am what I am at every level right down into existence. And so are you – once you've truly realised and accepted what I (you) *really* are – nothing!

Nor do I hesitate to refer to BL as a master, which has upset other masters. I simply 'know' or am what I am. To me all divine knowledge depends on the depth that God has been realised – and on the state of undifferentiated intelligence beyond that.

The Spiritual Life

At the psychic level adjoining the physical where the masses live, the troublesome self pirates the intelligence of pure reflection and gives it substantiveness and momentum in the form of 'I'. I (or self) then begins reflecting on its own creation – mental confusion, emotional clamour, discontent and unhappiness. Thus is the simplicity of inner space extended to accommodate thousands of years of human emotional clamour and mental clutter – the psychic.

Out of this chaos was born the spiritual life. The spiritual life is the attempt by individual intelligence to dissolve the clamour and clutter befouling the psychic that was once pure psyche. In other words, the spiritual life is a kind of collective battle to win back precious territory in the fourth kingdom of reflected intelligence.

If there was no rubbish smearing the intellect there'd be no spiritual life and no need of it.

Just Another Day

The sun rises daily on everyone's difficulties and problems – and sets at night after most of the daily effort is expended. The sun is like a relentless timekeeper that won't let humanity rest – for more than a few hours.

The same unrelenting sun rose behind the clouds on Napoleon's final rain-soaked battlefield and lit the effort of his dreams – until all was over at sunset. The same sun rose and set on Hitler's final day and all his psychological effort to muster the strength to take his own life. The same sun rises on everyone's day of effort to be free of... what? And sets with nothing really done or achieved because tomorrow is just another day of sunrise, sunset and doing.

The Bigger Picture

FROM HERE TO REALITY

The Inner Light of Intelligence

*Within every man and woman an inner ethereal light shines
according to the individual's accumulated self-knowledge.*

67

'My' Own Experience

For most of our lives we depend on others' experience to communicate. For instance, not many of us have been in the midst of war with bombs and guns going off all around and the immediate possibility of physical injury or death. We rely on what we've read or seen on TV, or at the movies – on someone else's experience. From this we assume we've got the idea and are able to converse about it. But our words and opinions lack the reality of our own experience.

The word to 'converse' derives from to 'convert' which means to turn around or transform. So most of our conversations and talk consists of converting other people's experience – what we've read or heard – into words, and saying what we think. But what we think is another world away from the real thing – what we ourselves have experienced. No one can successfully tell us the smell of a rose, the taste of a banana or the sensation of an orgasm. The reality is only in our own experience.

And when we speak from our own experience there's no room, or little room, for doubt. When the experience is truly intimate no one can convince us differently. It is the truth to us. If the person we are speaking with has had a similar experience there will be no argument or opinions – just an easy and fulfilling communication beyond the normal, behind the words.

When people don't speak from their own experience they tend to waffle, mixing up some of their own experience with what they've heard, read, or imagined. Before speaking in public they are understandably nervous and then require a written script or an auto-cue. But when you speak from you own experience you speak with authority. Your words are validated by your having participated in objective truth. The reality of the moment of the experience is always there inside you and is not dependent on memory.

Your own experience is a kind of imprinted passion, an immediacy of knowledge that comes from 'having been there'. Of course, if you convert this into a moral or cultural argument you are then in danger of inciting the bias and prejudice of others – as well as your self. From such a mix of truth and untruth arises demagoguery and fanaticism.

Your own experience is the precious element of self-knowledge distilled from each living life. Most of our outer and inner life is like rubble discarded from a gold mine. The gold, the value of the life, is self-knowledge and this, as described in another essay, is what 'goes on' after physical death. While you live, this precious essence of intelligence is identifiable as your own experience.

Self-knowledge

How deep does my own experience or self-knowledge go?

It extends back into the mists of time, since your intelligence is the intelligence of life on earth which, given an existential time-scale, represents 2000 million years of experience. Somewhere within the psyche this is accessible as your own experience, but not through your mortal flesh-and-blood brain which itself is the product of organic life on earth. Looking through the brain/mind for immortal knowledge is like standing in a bucket and trying to lift yourself up by the handle. All you get is stress, strain and frustration.

It is undeniable, however, that many people have received intimations of other times on earth. This is due to a sudden flash of self-knowledge which, due to its speed, passes unregistered through the brain like X-rays (swifter light) pass through flesh and reveal the bony structure underneath. Self-knowledge is always here, stored in the individuated life that has animated the Self's many, many, recurrent bodies, including the body reading these words now: same life, same Self, different body, different time. Much of this book and *The Origins of Man and the Universe* are examples of self-knowledge.

Why is convincing self-knowledge of other times so rare? Why is there not more evidence?

The purpose of this particular life is to get on with it, to do what we have to do, wherever that may take us. In that sense, our living lives are quite superficial. What we don't realise is the profundity going on behind the scenes: that whatever we do is an attempt to find the truth, either of ourselves or of life itself, and that the activities pursued, along with the circumstances and conditions accompanying them, are determined by our self-knowledge intent on revealing more self-knowledge.

The Light of Intelligence

At this point we have to appreciate the broader, universal meaning of intelligence. In short, what is the effect of intelligence wherever it appears? The answer is: intelligence is *light*. This means that within every man and woman an inner ethereal light glows or shines according to the individual's accumulated self-knowledge. Not everyone is going to see this light but those who love you or respect you do. It's the light that causes such responses, although the mind, which is generally blind to the light, will invariably come up with other explanations.

Intelligence also sheds light. In your experience of the world you can see there's a recognition of this. People speak of 'seeing the light' as a metaphor for sudden understanding and also to describe spiritual insight. En-light-enment is the ultimate goal of Buddhism and Taoism, clearly referring to a quality or essence of intelligence far beyond the norm.

Even in the intellectual world there are the Ages of En-light-enment referring to the dawning of a relatively brighter light of intelligence in human affairs; a renaissance, a rebirth of cultural, artistic, or intellectual freedom from the preceding darkness. The light of intelligence in every context means clearer vision. But we are concerned here with clearer inner vision – an inner light – which automatically confers an ability to see through the often confusing and contending outer appearance of things.

68

Every Body a Light

Every body alive is a light. Thus the true nature, the inherent character of every living body, is light.

This arises from the fact that every body is a projection from the 'Father (or God) of Lights' within, the divine intellect which contains every idea (every light) that ever can be. The projected divine light is undifferentiated. But in passing up through the various prisms of abstract existence (inner space) the one light becomes many to finally manifest as the innumerable physical bodies (lights) that cover the earth.

The Missing Kingdom

Natural objects are commonly classified into several kingdoms or primary divisions – animal, plant, or geologic. Each kingdom has a glow or light of its own, and within the glow the light of each form varies. Thus the light of any form in any kingdom is not quite the same – although retaining the common group glow.

In people, the primary light common to all animal forms varies infinitely due to our self-consciousness. In the unself-conscious animals the basic light is slightly different and the multiplicity of variations is reduced. In plants the basic character of light is different again and the variations are much less distinct from the whole. In the geologic kingdom the difference in basic glow is stepped down further and the variations considerably reduced.

The self-conscious intelligence of people is unique among the animal bodies of the earth. As a result we have a unique existence. That's not to say that the existence of the other animals is not unique in its own way. All we can know or be is the intelligence we are. And that intelligence has an enormous range and the potential which finally allows the individual to realise something in inner space that we call God, Life or Supreme Being.

Presumably, from a reasonable point of view, humanity is the 'highest' expression of intelligence in all the natural kingdoms of the earth. We are the only ones, apparently, who have an exterior/inner perspective. Moreover, our physical body is made up of all the fundamental elements of the animal, plant and geologic kingdoms. In short, we are that which we eat, drink and absorb of the earth. We are products of the earth.

Yet we are also something else. That's because there is another natural kingdom not included in the common classification of natural objects. This is the cosmic kingdom of the galactic heavens which surrounds the earth and the earth's kingdoms. The cosmic kingdom is allied with the microscopic kingdom of force and energy in matter. Both cosmic and microscopic are clearly natural sensory objects projected by the human brain and defined by the mind – as are the other three primary divisions.

As we are the result of the fusion of all four natural kingdoms, the 'missing' cosmic kingdom is responsible for our superior and unique reflective intelligence. That's not to imply we are superior. We're simply an extension of life on earth. One day perhaps the individual man or woman will realise that the intelligence they really are within is the centre of all life, all brainy intelligence and all earthly existence.

The cosmic element of our make-up – our brainy intelligence – is simultaneously purely physical and abstracted as inner space, just as our perception of the cosmic starry heavens is purely a sensory result of having a human brain-body. As the human brain-body is a product of the earth and the four kingdoms, all that we see, interpret, and presume as our existence, is simply an extension of the physical – the body or the brain. Without a brain-body, the entire projection of existence vanishes. The question then is: does any element remain? And the answer is: yes. What remains is the pure intelligence that was always *within* and *behind* the existence of the four kingdoms.

At this stage of the book we have reached a climacteric, a crucial crossover from the mortal to the reality of intelligence behind the brain-body. This brings us back to the light within every body and every thing, as mentioned at the beginning of this essay.

69
The God of Lights

The potential of human intelligence is spread over various and vast levels of the divine psyche within. The realisation of any level determines the speed of intelligence and the power of the individual light. Thus the collective lights of the people of the earth – due to our widely varying self-conscious intelligence – have a far greater range of illumination than in the unself-conscious species.

However, the mass of human lights is not complete in itself. Combined with the lights of the four natural kingdoms, the result is one divine expression of the essence of intelligence – the God of Lights or the Celestial One (celestial from the Sanskrit meaning, 'bright'). In other words, beyond the brain *the whole of the material earth – its living biological lights and the surrounding cosmos – forms a phantasmagoria of scintillating light beyond any imagining.*

The sparkling brilliance of the light, its ceaseless turbulent magnificence, is caused by the continuous birth and death of all living things and the moment-to-moment passing, changing and erosion of all material things – a divine movement of life and Will orchestrated by the inscrutable intelligence beyond all.

Notwithstanding the splendour of the divine light, it is colourless. (Colour is a reaction in the human brain to sunlight or starlight.) The light of intelligence consists of such a play of radiant splendour that the most beautiful colours are as nothing by comparison. Our three primary colours and their innumerable combinations in nature and human art are only made possible by the reality of the ceaseless inner radiance.

We humans, as the perceivers of all life on earth, the geological formations, and the extraterrestrial vastness of the universe, are the most important link with the God of Lights. As we see existence, is how it is. And since each person and individual interprets existence differently, there are mighty variations in the human lights that at death merge with the Father, or Source, of all light and lights. But it must be kept in mind that the Father of Lights is the whole divine psyche and that at death our individual light gravitates to a commensurate level of light. Even so, in the act of merging, each light becomes part of the whole. And all self-conscious distinction vanishes.

The entire existential system – birth and death, change and evolution – is controlled by the incomprehensible intelligence of the Source. The Source is purpose, as well as omniscience, omnipresence and omnipotence. It is God, the ultimate (the Absolute God being still beyond).

From 'outside' existence the God of Lights purposely directs every event, condition, life and death for the benefit of the whole. Nothing and no one is spared the necessity to contribute. To the divine intelligence, a lifetime in human terms is equivalent to the blink of an eye, and time as we know it is simply the tool of purpose.

So the God of Lights in effect works through existence, its manifest creation, to increase the essential purity of its own light. It does this through the seven levels, or heavens, of the psyche down to the lowest level of the psychic. As the psychic is the level of human corruption or ignorance of God, the divine intelligence is forced by purpose to begin there.

Recurrence

By virtue of its omniscience, omnipotence and omnipresence, the God of Lights sustains a continuous cycle of recurrence. Every child born is imbued with an appropriate share of corruption left behind in the psychic by the dead. The child's lot in the living life ahead is to face in circumstances the recurrence of this unrealised ignorance. But at the same time the child is imbued with the divine light of intelligence which will enable it (more or less) to face and dissolve the inner psychic distortion – and help restore the psychic to pure psyche.

It is not the child's person that recurs, as the doctrine of reincarnation implies, nor the failings of the child in a previous life.

The only recurrence is of the impersonal ignorance of humanity – justly and omnisciently apportioned among every body for the betterment of the whole.

70

The Divine Imprint

Although after death nothing remains of the individual to recur, there is a divine imprint, an imprimatur, implicit in the light of pure intelligence born with each body. This may be termed a mystical identification or identity – mystical meaning having a reality neither apparent to the senses, nor obvious to normal intelligence.

The divine imprimatur is why you don't wake up in somebody else's body. It is your indelible imprint of self-knowledge that has accrued from many thousands of recurrent lives including this life. The imprint is part of the vast divine memory, which records every moment at every level of existence.

Through the agency of the divine light – of which we are all a part – people can have extraordinary insights into mystical states. These range from flashes of clarity related to heaven, the cosmos, and God, to lucid glimpses of past events that suggest previous lives of the individual. However, as nothing remains of any person or individual after death, the answer is far more profound than this personalised conclusion.

The divine imprint in each body has layers of significance, again exceeding our normal power to rationalise. For example, in the unself-conscious animals and plants there are group lights. Each animal shares the same fundamental light. And the birth, living, and death of the particular animal or plant contributes infinitesimally to the illumination of the group light.

Due to this progression, generations of animals and plants can be seen over time to adapt to changes in the environment. We rationalise it as adaptation without explaining why or how. But the power of any organism to adapt is due to an increase in intelligence, or glow, within the group form. As humans we say adaptation follows experience – again failing to see the full significance. Because of the increase in the inner light, all animals and plants become used to, or better able to cope with, environmental changes – as we see in their altered behavioural patterns.

The bodies or *forms* of all the species are only the means. The virtue behind the forms is in the basic light which remains as long as the particular species continues. When a species is extinct it is not a disaster from a mystical viewpoint.

It simply means that that light is complete and has merged to contribute to all the group animal lights. The principle is similar on a descending and indefinable scale when applied to geological matter – remembering that all things consist of the mystery that is matter.

Soul Mates

Human lights also form groups. But due to our evidently unique self-consciousness, single lights in a human group can merge consciously with the Source, the inner reflection of the God of Lights, while the individual is alive. From this the whole group gains in quality of intelligence – and lights in other groups move imperceptibly closer to the same ultimate union with God.

People may be in the same group of light all their lives but never meet. On the other hand, when two do meet, a mystical (meaning inexplicably faint) recognition will occur. There may also be a particular affinity with someone beyond the usual drive and attraction of sex. Out of these subtle irrational recognitions arises the sense of soul mates. It could be said that any two lights in the same group are soul mates – arising out of the same group soul – but the test is whether the two bodies ever meet. And having met, they may never meet again. The reality is that the sense of oneness or love, while it lasts, is an indication of the proximity of two immortal lights that may move on, without the physical bodies necessarily changing position.

Since nothing in the divine creation of lights is permanently fixed and all is a fluid psycho-spiritual-mystical expression, blendings and overlappings occur at different levels. This can bewilder people who, through no fault of their own, are still physically orientated and hopeful. The physical dies but the lights go on 'forever'.

Blendings and overlappings account for many seemingly weird experiences and perceptions, often wrongly dismissed as imagination or naivety. For example, people can have a rare attunement with certain animals – and even plants or rocks. And in the zodiac it is not that uncommon for a body born in a particular astrological sign to evince, behaviourally and psychologically, the characteristics of the sign, and at times even to physically resemble an aspect of the glyph or animal symbol.

Inner light, as divine intelligence, is infinite. No matter how the world population of human bodies soars, there's no depletion of inner light. The divine creation is without limit and certainly beyond any rational interpretation or explanation. It indicates nothing more than the amazing and astonishing non-personalised intelligence and integrity of the God of Lights, Creator of All. All you can do is get the idea. Any attempt to analyse or rationalise the idea will result in error, confusion and frustration.

The Human Brain

The whole purpose of the divine idea of existence was (is) to create a living system capable of realising – making real as knowledge – the divine intelligence in and behind existence.

71

A Superlative Living Machine

From an existential point of view the human brain is a living mechanical organism. It's a one-way – inner – system of division and projection.

As a prism divides colourless sunlight into the seven colours of the rainbow, the living matter of the brain divides the divine light (shining from behind) into our various physical senses. Then, still energised by the effortless power of the incoming light, the brain projects the physical world *as we see it* through the senses.

The common human perception is that the senses register a physical world that's 'out there'. The truth is the reverse. And of course the seven colours mentioned above are purely sensory.

The source of the brain's data is the constant, undivided supreme light of pure intelligence behind the brain. With compounding prismatic complexity the brain projects the endless and unlimited stream of images and impressions that form sensory existence. The divine intelligence never enters the world, never really enters the brain. Its mere presence is a constant pressure on the brain. From this the brain forms impressions of what is in the light and projects the impressions.

The brain possesses no self-knowledge. It has no inkling of the intelligence behind it, the reality and Source of life. The brain is purely a projective function, a superlative living machine that manifests everything in sense. Initially, the brain stores no data, has no memory. Only in the brain's lower levels do memory and self-reflection begin.

The explanation for the different levels is this. First, the brain is divisive by nature and its function is to divide. This is the result of the brain's structural formation out of the elements of the four kingdoms – the geologic, plant, animal, and cosmic (reflective intelligence). These are also the Ages of the brain and they form its four basic levels – distinct and separate layers of substantive past extending back to time immemorial.

Each kingdom or Age forms a discrete group of brain cells. The four groups will always be there since they form the actual physical structure of the brain. However, the *contents* of some cells in each group are virtually expunged once their purpose has been served. Examples of this are the dinosaur cells and all the extinct forms of life in the skeletal chain leading up to the human brain. The emptied cells, through the process of time and experience, are then more conducive to developing self-reflective intelligence.

In people today brain cells are continuously being partially expunged. Old data is replaced by new data, due to the enormous inflow of electronic information via TV, the internet, mobile phones, and so on. The most recent data shuffles the older data further back into the reflective group cell – which forms the memory. Traumas and emotional crises in the normal life are signs of expurgation. In living the spiritual life, where self-knowledge has reached an intense level of inner reflection, it is possible in my experience to hear the old cells dying (explained in detail in my autobiography).

Self-reflective human intelligence is a far cry from the originating pure intelligence at the deepest level of the brain. Ascending from the deepest level, the intelligence is weakened and degraded threefold by passing through the primordial and primeval Ages of the brain; and finally surfacing as the human mind.

72

The Latecomer – the Story of the Brain

The brain is a latecomer to existence. It wasn't always here. Here is the story of its development.

Before the human brain the four natural kingdoms – geologic, plant, animal and cosmic – were potential in the divine light of intelligence. Contrary to the historical concept of evolution, *the development of the four kingdoms was complete in the divine potential – though not in physical manifestation.*

The explanation is this: first, there was nothing for existence to appear in, and second, there was no reflective consciousness – no mind as man or woman – to perceive it. Without a reflective mind, none of the four natural kingdoms exist – even now.

The physical manifestation was instantaneous. There was no interval – no time – involved. But today, to the backward-looking human mind reflecting on the fossilised and geological evidence, the conclusion is of a periodic appearance of each kingdom. But I say again, there was no delay and no appearance on earth or cosmically. *All four kingdoms appeared simultaneously* – but only with the first self-reflective, self-conscious human brain.

The evolution of the brain's perceptions – from the simple, to the complex, to the complicated – was the only delay. And the delay was due to the nature of existence – time.

Long before life's appearance in existence, life's function had already been completed in the divine potential. Life (before existence) vitalised the most elementary forms and continued to vitalise, and then animate more complex forms until, as a natural progression, the potential of a complex animal brain was produced out of the skeletal ladder of all previous life forms and brains.

Simultaneously (still before existence) the animal brains developed into more complex formations until finally the self-reflective, self-conscious, human brain manifested as mankind. Only in that moment did existence start appearing as it is – inasmuch as man could perceive it.

Man is not man as such. He is a brain that creates every thing, including the distinction of he and she, male and female. The brain is the only existential means.

Remembering that the brain is actually made up of physical elements of the four natural kingdoms – animal, plant, geologic and cosmic – and recalling that the last element, the cosmic, is what provides the human brain with its unique reflective intelligence, it is easy to appreciate our intelligent love of the starry heavens and sky – and of the rocks, flora and fauna of the earth.

The whole process of existence over immemorial time has had only one purpose – to construct a physical brain through which the intelligence implicit in the process could at last return home.

First, the intelligence had to spend aeons of time in geologic seismic material. As this formation started breaking up and eroding into various mineral fragments, the life-force potential in the intelligence was released and took hold in the form of bacteria and micro-organisms. Development – due to the divine purpose – then led to the mutually dependent plant and animal kingdoms. But always the development proceeded towards the creation of a brain which could in a sense govern and organise the survival of the form. Until this was accomplished the entire process was directed from within. (The means is described in my book, *The Origins of Man and the Universe*.)

The different brains of every animal species were a gradual advancement towards the manifestation of the self-reflective human brain. Even though that has now been achieved, the human brain/mind remains resistant to the ongoing and ingoing process of intelligence. Through negation and physical death, the intelligence is still moving through the brain/mind and eroding the fixations in the individual. The brain/mind's response is the attempt to compensate and maintain its position through the momentum of progress.

The mind, as the intellectual force behind material science and physics, may have advanced a theory of evolution based on survival of the fittest forms but a theory is not the truth. The theory, being purely material or sensory, lacks the profundity of inner knowledge. (The word 'theory' derives from the Latin 'to look at' as a 'spectator'. Since everything science stands for is based on assumptions and speculations it has the good sense not to use the word 'truth'.)

Divine intelligence – the source of all intelligence – is behind the brain and shines as pristine light into the brain. The brain converts the light into sensory matter and different forms, and simultaneously converts the intelligence into *the limited reflective capability of the human mind.* But knowledge of the initiating and uncorrupted pristine light escapes the conceptualising mind.

With its restricted intelligence the mind has deduced the plausible but necessarily inferior *historically* based evolution theory as the explanation for the process of life on earth. As popularly expressed, the theory concerns the evolution of the species through survival of the fittest. Yet the idea of the theory clearly is applicable to the whole of existence – from language to science, and social attitudes to every single daily development – in one word, progress. Everything in the world of the brain/mind, including the entire universe, is evolving, becoming. But the obvious broader view seems to have escaped notice – possibly because it is closer to the truth.

Evolution is not the truth. Truth is *now* and does not evolve. Evolution is deduced by the mind from *past* observations of existence. Truth is the pristine original light of intelligence behind the brain/mind's formal and intellectual assumptions. Truth or pure intelligence is the sole power behind existence. Truth created the brain. Truth, therefore, is responsible for everything in existence. Truth or pure intelligence is always present – but remains unknowable by the brain and its agency, the mind.

Due to the historical and reflective nature of the brain/mind, every concept of truth is only a *reflection* of truth. This reflective intelligence enables us to know anything, to work out anything and to be anything. Where there's no knowing there's no inter-pretation and no being as we know it. If such a state as this were possible, it would not be possible to be anything – to even know (or want to know) you exist. Even so, while there is a sensory brain existence continues.

The unknowing state is the reflection in the mirror of inner space of the purity of divine intelligence – before the intelligence is mediated and conditioned by the mind.

Nonetheless, as I've said, the divine intelligence is the cause of existence inasmuch as it created the brain which then projects the sense/body. The sense/body then projects the outer appearance of objects. The mind then inwardly records impressions of the objects and conditions on the memory and reflects on these – thus forming a complete existential circuit.

73

The Gunas and the Brain

Anyone familiar with the three gunas of the Hindu mystical tradition will see something of their origin in the first three kingdoms of nature – the geologic, plant and animal – described in the previous essay. The gunas, according to the ancient Sankhya system, are said to represent the three primal qualities or elements of matter – tamas (density, dullness, mass or inertia), rajas (force or drive), sattvic (space, power of divine intelligence). These in the BL system of knowledge equate with the passage of divine intelligence through the first three kingdoms.

Tamas is the intelligence trapped in, or identified with, the material density of the geologic Age. Rajas is the intelligence freed of dense matter and driving into organic matter with the force of life (first into plants and then into animals). Sattvic is the intelligence still in organic animal matter but no longer fully identified. Reduced identification with matter (or materialism) creates more absence, space, divine intelligence – the sattvic state of mind.

Note that the Sankhya system combines the plant and animal kingdoms into one. But the two are distinctly different Ages: one through which the intelligence has passed and the second, the animal Age, which it is passing through now – hence we humans are still basically animals. Note also that the Hindu system fails to identify the cosmic fourth kingdom, the source of the reflective intelligence, which makes possible any organised system of thought or knowledge.

The gunas are said to determine humanity's ever-changing moods. Like the four Ages of man the gunas themselves are constantly being divided by the brain so that each moment is one of the rapidly changing divisions – thus providing the ultimate sense of *now* in which everything is different from the moment before.

However, at the lumbering speed of the human mind, one guna or Age can seem to endure in the person for hours or even days – or perhaps even for a lifetime. For instance, tamas or stone is the mood of depression, indolence or denseness; rajas equates in the mind with the inner conflict of unfulfilled *wanting*, and with the action of driving into the world and sattvic is the spiritually introspective state of mind.

The true living of the spiritual life – by negation of selfishness – speeds up the intelligence. In relation to the gunas this means that the three moods come and go more swiftly at a continually increasing rate. Finally the sequence reaches the equivalence of Supreme Realisation in which there is no more movement – only equilibrium.

Perspective

The omissions in the Sankhya system described above are not due to a lack of intelligence in the founding consciousness. In fact the intelligence and self-knowledge revealed is amazing by our modern standards of thought. The omissions are merely a matter of perspective. Perspective has to be understood in relation to the passage of time. For instance, in the epoch of the Sankhya system dating from before the Christian Era it was not possible to have our modern perspective of the earth and moon viewed from a spaceship.

Although intelligence is not limited in itself, it is limited by human perspective. In other words, human intelligence where self-knowledge is concerned (knowledge of Cause) is intrinsically linked with progress in existence. As an example, the profound intricacies of perception in this book could not, and were not, possible of expression in earlier times.

Of course, no expression is important in God-realisation. The moment is enough, is all. But by the way of things, every man or woman who realises God will be moved to endeavour to express that inexpressible truth in some form of language that is meaningful to others. Even so, language is always inferior to the moment, though certainly an aspect of it.

God-the-cause-of-all may have been realised by the founder of the Sankhya system, but the perspective – the breadth of common living experience – was not there as it is today. Even the experience of a refrigerator or hair dryer changes the inner reflective dynamic. Thus does science or progress provide a divinely organised broadness to the mind which makes possible more accurate and profoundly intelligent descriptions of life on earth – without resort to scientific theory. But let me say that science or progress alone – without the focus of self-knowledge – merely creates more science and progress.

In the moment where the divine light of intelligence meets the brain it is always *now*. Neither now nor intelligence moves. But the presence of intelligence agitates the brain which then makes the mind and every thing in existence appear to move. This creates time.

Movement means space, space means distance and distance means time.

Anything that moves is evolving in time. And that's everything. The closest state to now in existence that does not move is the uninterrupted stillness of the mind and emotions – signified by the master-consciousness – in either woman or man who has realised God or Supreme Being. Even so, there is still participation in the apparent movement of existence, and the reflection of that in the surface mind.

However, God-consciousness is not realised without having earlier in the living life been involved in the normal movement of the human mind and emotions – despite claims by some individuals that they have always been realised. Such knowledge comes *after* the realisation, not before. And the test of the profundity of the realisation is that the resultant knowledge and inner peace are not interrupted by circumstances for the rest of the living life.

It all comes down to swiftness of intelligence. On rare occasions individuals – and not necessarily masters or overtly 'spiritual people' – slip momentarily into states of extreme intelligence. Matter loses its tight cohesive form and begins to waver or shimmer with a soft beauteous and tremulous light. An example is Wordsworth's famous poem describing such a moment when he looked upon a field of daffodils. The point is that this radical state of intelligence is just behind our usual human perception.

Electronic devices, such as the electron microscope, also demonstrate the insubstantiality of matter. Although artificial forms of intelligence, they show that the reality is there even though, for the most part, it is beyond present human capacity to realise. Electron microscopes utilise the speed of light and the speed of light symbolises the swiftest intelligence we current humans can relate to.

74

The Human Mind

The human mind is completely dependent on memory. Memory is all in the past. Thus the human mind is purely a reaction to the past which by synthesis and assumption it then projects as the future. Assisted by innumerable individual minds that make up the world of the human mind, a future is created that does not exist except as a reaction in the mind.

Without attachment to memory, the problematical human mind is neutralised and the intelligence of 'what is' prevails.

The human mind is the final projection of intelligence by the brain. But the mind is only relatively intelligent. It is reliant on the past and unable to sustain itself, being wholly dependent on perceived relationships between external objects and inner impressions of its own making. No relationships, no mind.

The mind's limited intelligence is due to it being many Ages away from the original divine light of intelligence informing the human brain. By the time the divine light becomes the human mind, it has passed through the tardy and degenerative densities of the four kingdoms which make up the physical constitution of the human brain. From being the cause and source of all, the divine intelligence is now reduced to an unconscious, completely reflective, deductive, self-conscious, self-centred function – human intelligence.

The human mind's limited intelligence is perhaps best illustrated by its futile ongoing attempt to *make sense* of sense. Without the mind, sense is what is. In attempting the impossible, the mind remains in a basic condition of fluctuating uncertainty and confusion. This, however, is tolerably relieved by the mind identifying with the steadying momentum of the brain's ceaseless projection of sensory existence.

This in turn keeps the mind continuously busy trying to *understand* what's going on outside, and to match that against its impressions inside – another activity as futile as trying to reason the sense of sense. The mind's intelligence is so minimal (because of its distance from the divine intelligence) that any interruption in the momentum of its focus throws it back on its own resources. As its only resources are the memory and emotions, the mind starts thinking aimlessly about past events, or more earnestly, by reflecting on its stored emotions to the point of distress or despair.

Any stillness or silence due to accidental, or induced, reflection on the source of itself, terrifies the mind. Drug substances often induce disorientating images of no sense thrown up by cellular residues of the brain's past – due to the brain being composed of elements of the mineral, plant and animal kingdoms.

Mind and Matter

The human mind assumes it is independent of any cause apart, perhaps, from its hazy concept of the brain. Thus do scientists, atheists, and all materialists identified with the mind fail to recognise the supreme intelligence behind their own limited intelligence. From all this arises two things: first, the perennial philosophic and spiritual debate on the source of duality; and second, the perennial confusion regarding mind and matter.

Everyone who starts to question existence believes they have a physical brain or mind. In other words they believe in the reality of the physical world or in the mind in which they continuously think, reason and plan. Or, in the case of mystics and masters, the belief is in the reality of inner space in which God is realised.

None of it is the truth. Closely examined the three cases are examples of duality, as subtle as that may be in the case of mystics or masters (who still eat and breathe). The duality of inner and outer, and mind and matter, is a concept of the human mind. It may be said, mindfully, to be due to the divisive nature of the living brain behind the mind. The brain refracts (bends into two appearances) the inflow of divine light with the result that in every area of living there is a fundamental division – negative and positive, hot and cold, up and down. To this the personalising mind adds love and hate, boredom and excitement, sex and love, for and against, Conservative and Labour, Republican and Democrat, winner and loser, and so on to infinity – the whole caboodle being the continuous play of opposites in the mind.

The truth remains that there is only what is. And what is cannot be divided, interpreted, or conceived of, because it is identical with the original divine light behind the human brain.

Human activity is the endeavour to unite the opposites and bring peace or fulfilment into existence. A vain exercise while you still believe in the truth of the mind's reasoning.

While inner and outer remains, you can be sure you have a mind and a brain.

But when you're dead, perhaps you'll discover you never did.

75

Negation

Negation is the means by which we return to the pristine state of intelligence that was present before we were born. We humans can't conceive of the pre-natal state as being intelligence – let alone intelligent – because we define intelligence in relation to sensory or worldly experience. And the pre-natal intelligence, of course, is devoid of experience.

For example, we call animals intelligent that respond and behave like humans. An ape is more intelligent than other monkeys because it's been observed to have used a stick as a tool – just like man who is scientifically defined as being 'a tool-using animal'. A sheepdog responds to command signals – just like man. A racehorse, heavily under the whip, 'enjoys' winning because man enjoys winning. Animals behave intelligently for man because he feeds them. And porpoises learn to do intelligent tricks for a (fishy) pleasurable reward, just like man.

When we examine human intelligence we see that it is based on a mental-emotional relationship to objects, as well as conditions between objects. We like some things and we don't like others – which is our human intelligence expressing itself as personal feelings or emotions. We follow an established line of enquiry, as in science, religion and philosophy, building mentally on areas of information already laid down by the selective intelligence of others. From all this nothing really original eventuates; just an endless personal building on the past.

And where does it all end up? In the grave – with all the other hopes and wishes of human intelligence.

Only the False Can Be Destroyed

Negation means negating what we believe in. What we believe in is what we've heard from somewhere in the past. And our human intelligence has become attached – fastened emotionally

– to that particular object or position. Especially persuasive is faith or belief in religious and political precepts. That's not to deny that such feelings can be intense and carry great conviction. But that's the nature of emotion. Emotion is convinced it's right on the basis of its own intensity. But it is still personal and therefore not true.

Sometimes the love of God is mixed up with the emotion of belief. And there is only one way to find out which is which and that is: to negate the belief, to give up all practices, relationships and thoughts associated with it. What remains will be true. For in truth, only the false can be destroyed.

The most universal, misleading and deceptive belief is the personal conviction that you have a right to be angry, moody or resentful – and the right to express any other negative emotion when the reaction seizes you. In other words, that you have a right to be unhappy.

Negating in yourself the emotional momentum of anger is the beginning of the end of anger. When the negation is complete, an amazing stillness replaces the anger. Similarly, the negation of any emotion, or attachment to any belief or opinion, results in stillness. When the entire rag-bag of the emotional self is negated, there is the sublime stillness of the pre-natal pristine intelligence – which was always present beneath the clutter and clamour of attachment to human intelligence.

Negation works only when the emotion is *intelligently* faced in the moment it arises. This requires a certain speed of intelligence. This speed is reached when, with practice, the emotion is perceived to be destructive of harmony in yourself and in relation to others. Such an act of consciousness obviates the tendency of the mind to suppress the emotion. Suppression means that the force of the emotion will rise elsewhere in the experiential life and again disturb your equilibrium.

Negation itself does not move. What moves is the emotional and mental identification on top of it. As more stillness comes, the remaining misidentification still moves, but not with the same distracting momentum.

Negation should not be confused with negative. Negative and positive are two poles responsible for existence – both inner and outer. But negation is the reflection of pure intelligence, the unmoving reflection of God that is always within. To the world, negation or the intelligence of God, *is* negative because it is continuously drawing everything back to Source. Thus death and the passing of everything in existence is simply the ending of movement; while birth and progress are simply the beginning and continuation of movement – ceaseless evolution or becoming.

Because the masses are identified with the world of movement, the world cannot end while one unrealised brain lives. Thus discontent and unhappiness will always exceed stillness. But when negation begins in the individual a separation from the world starts to occur. This marks the beginning of the *conscious* spiritual or mystical life.

FROM HERE TO REALITY

Right Words

Anything universal is common to everyone (like the human body) and as God-realisation is not universal it cannot be regarded as universal truth.

76
Keys to Knowledge

This essay defines and illustrates some of the key words used in the book; such words as personal, individual, universal, cosmic, ultimate, absolute. When used correctly these words are right words – harking back to Job's famous Old Testament comment, 'How forcible are right words'.

To begin with we largely gloss over and mix up the words we use to describe anything really meaningful. We accept words like those I mention as generalities and abstractions, instead of specific pointers to the mystery of life on earth. In other words, right words rightly seen can answer all our questions.

Right words refer to a reality of knowledge that is inside everybody underneath their beliefs and opinions. Right words resonate with significance and meaning to individuals who have cleared sufficient inner space to listen and apply the words *in their own experience*. The reality of knowledge is in my own experience.

The Personal

Every master by his realisation has dissolved the personal that controls most people's lives. The personal life is governed by feelings: self-consideration, the fear of what people will say, of inner secrets being exposed and the dread of death. The master-consciousness is above these. Truth alone, not self, is the master's main concern. But he will still enter the personal awareness of people and endeavours to erode their attachments to the personal by imparting an individual perspective. Personal is not individual.

Individual

God-realisation (or Self-realisation) is *individual*. It's individual because it is not *universal*. Anything universal is common

262

to everyone (like the human body) and it is clear that everyone is not God-realised. God-realisation may be potential in every body but we can't assume that. Anyway, potential means not yet actual and only a possibility.

Does the fact that everyone has a body make the human body a universal truth? Obviously so – if the true meaning of the word (and the significance of the body) is seen. No one has ever realised God or Self without a body – is that not significant?

Universal

Universal implies something within the awareness of every body *without exception.* God-realisation can't be a universal truth because there are probably close to six billion exceptions on earth. Only when and if God is realised in every body as uninterrupted knowledge can it ever be regarded as universal.

So God-realisation is not a universal truth but purely an individual truth, occurring randomly wherever it does.

Such statements, of course, imply that the way we *brainy* humans see or imagine things is vastly different to the way things really are. For example, the word 'universal' and its significance clearly tells us that living on earth is an amazing process of indefinite, perhaps everlasting, inner and outer being. Death is universal. Birth is universal. And life is universal. All represent one universal truth. Therefore death, birth and life are one universal process – common to every body.

This is so even for those who have realised the extremity of individual consciousness, God-consciousness. No one is exempt from existence. What that means in its profundity I trust will be clear by the end of this book.

Cosmos

As there are no synonyms in the English language, we can go further with this consideration of significant words. What's the difference between cosmos and universe?

Cosmos is from the language used by the Greeks from pre-historic times. It is founded on a unique perception of the *whole*, which the word 'cosmos' means. To these most ancient of ancients, the whole contained no division between inner and outer – something beyond our modern comprehension.

We moderns of the West (which has subsumed and misinterpreted the original wisdom of the East that has now gone West) favour the divided word 'universe'. Universe is of the later Latin deriving from uni: entire, plus versus which means turned towards, with the ad-vers-arial corollary of against. According to the dictionary, versus, in the context of universe, means turned towards 'the whole body of things and phenomena' which pretty well describes the materialistic outer focus and adversarial culture of the West.

Cosmos is used by the Slavic nations of Central Europe (Russian, Czech, Polish, Ukrainian and so on), and universe is used by the West. Today, of course, both words refer generally to outer space and particularly to starry outer space. For their space pioneers, the West pinches cosmo-nauts from the Russian kosmo-naut while sometimes using astro-naut, a reference only to the outer stars. (Are there inner stars?)

The Ultimate

Ultimate is from the Latin and means, last, final, furthest – to come to an end. Last, final and coming to an end clearly refer to existence, as perceived by the mind, for everything here erodes, passes or dies. Beyond the ultimate no further existence is possible. But there's another word overlooked and ill-defined in the escalation of right words...

The Absolute

Absolute is from the Latin, to set free. There is only one thing to be set free of and that is the inevitable pain and suffering of existence. As death, the ultimate, is demonstrably the compassionate means of this, so the word 'absolute' points to 'something' indescribable beyond the ultimate and including or greater than the compassion implicit in death. In our language and to our brainy comprehension, this 'whatever' is a completely different and unique state.

To us, something indescribable is tantamount to nothing. And the only way the absolute state can be apprehended by us who are still alive is 'as nothing'. This, of course, explains the fundamental reality in God-realisation: that it, or the realiser, is nothing. Beyond that, there is no going until death.

Absolute also means free from imperfection: perfect.

From absolute derives absolve which in the original Latin means to loosen – another pointer to the meaning of death. However, the Roman Catholic faith has seized on the noun 'absolution' to mean the remission of sins pronounced by a priest as in the act of penance.

This of course is outrageous. First, because there is no sin; second, because only *continuous* inner devotion or love of God, the nothing, can absolve, loosen or free a man or woman from attachment to existence – the place of pain, disease, old age and suffering. And third, for someone to claim they act on behalf of God, the absolute, is a grotesque travesty of universal intelligence and truth – priest or no priest.

FROM HERE TO REALITY

After Death

The only real evidence is provided by the masters or mystics who have realised the informal God – God being the reality of death and certainly not any historical personage.

77

A Glimpse

Really, we cannot speak of after death. The only death we know of is the death of someone else's body. Never our own. If we presume we are dead and see our body, obviously we are not dead.

Of course there are psychic visions of the dead. But they are meaningless to the person who has died – as far as I, the observer, can know. Perhaps the visions are no more real or important than our shadows are to us. I can only know the effect of the visions on me. Sometimes the effect is fear, sometimes prophetic symbolism, sometimes even elation. But all those reactions occur in the observer who is alive.

To those who have received them, there is no denying psychic communications from the dead. But that only confirms the presence of a psychic world within us *who are alive.* We don't have to be dead to experience psychic phenomena. But what it is to be *not alive* remains the eternal mystery.

Nevertheless, a master who has realised the reflection of Supreme Being or Self in inner space can perhaps lead us into an area where we get the idea of what it is to be dead. Perhaps.

The realisation of God in every case results in the knowledge that the greatest truth is nothing. In other words, that God or the ultimate state of consciousness or intelligence is no-thing, no condition, no me – a complete and utter non. Because of this knowledge it is not uncommon for masters to say that they are already dead – something of a mystifying statement for people who regard death as a dead body.

The key obviously is in the word 'knowledge', the master's realised knowledge. This, as we've seen, dismisses the mind's knowing as having no real validity. Of course the master still has a reflective mind that knows and recalls things. But, having gone beyond attachment to knowing in the extremity of inner space, he now sees that identification with the human mind with its opinions, concepts, theories and interpretations, is the only obstacle to pure knowledge of truth or God.

So what has brought the master to this knowledge? Like most people he once was trapped in the mind and its knowing. But somehow he was pulled through the mind or out of the mind far quicker than most by – what? And why?

No one knows. Not even the master himself, if you ask him to describe it in rational or reasonable terms. But he can tell you from his knowledge which is neither rational nor reasonable. He will say that it was God, or Self, or That, or It, or the Unknown or the reality – which really will not satisfy anyone who hasn't realised nothing as an uninterrupted state of inner knowledge and is still a slave of the mind. Such inner knowledge can't be thought about. Once realised it *is*.

The wonder is that the master can bring the knowledge, let us say, up through the mind which then objectifies it into conceptual language that can be related to by some people, but not everyone. The great mass of humanity is fixed on understanding which is the limit of the mind. But people able to hear the master are those who have an inward bent and are able, more or less, to get the idea without trying to understand.

What pulls people to the master?

The same magnet of knowledge beyond knowing which brought the master to the truth. The physical master, having realised the truth, is then a conduit for the truth. It is not him; it is the other, the unknowable. So what is the unknowable that enlightened the master?

Grace. But what is that? Grace is that which is beyond all subjectivity, even the realisation of Supreme Being. Is it absolute? No. While the mystery remains of death of the physical body, nothing that is realised in inner space while alive can be said to be absolute.

To the living, death alone is absolute.

Absolute is universal. Anything not absolute is personal or individual, something not common to all. Death happens to all. But death is not really absolute; death is simply an inevitable process. Absolute is that which is behind death, as it must be behind birth and life – behind everything.

The absolute behind death is what drew the master consciousness out of the man and what draws the people to the master. For the master is as dead as death gets here. But he is not yet really dead, is he?

From the foregoing it would seem that physical death is a state of knowledge in which there is no knowing. This means I cannot know that I am dead. If I can't know it, or know anything about it, how can it be meaningful to me, or how can I enjoy it?

I can't. Because, as when the master realises God, I disappear. There is then nothing – which means no reflecting or knowing capability.

So what's there to look forward to in death? Or put a better way, what's the benign truth of death that can be demonstrated from the evidence we have here before death? What is that evidence?

The only real evidence, as I've said, is that provided by the masters or mystics who have realised God – God being the reality of death. In an earlier essay I described God-realisation as wonderment, amazement and glory; as an incredible state of freedom; as being nothing (since I and the past disappear).

Although the masters have only realised the *reflection* of God in the mirror of inner space, it is a purified reflection. So perhaps there's an indication, a glimpse of death, in what the masters describe.

First-hand Evidence

The following are excerpts from the letter of a man after he had recently realised God. He writes:

'I am the now. The still point. Never moving, still. Existence moves, I do not. I cannot be touched, changed or affected. I am the unwavering light.

Nothing in existence can leave existence. The void is too pure, it cannot be penetrated. There are no words out of existence. God is not perfect, for perfection implies a pinnacle reached, an end. There is no ending; no beginning. A mystery.

I once said I had been given a gift. This implies worthiness etc. God does not gift. It simply is. It is always there. With God there is no reason, purpose or understanding or anything that can be conceived. Always beyond, always beyond reach. That place is my Home, yet to the mind it would be utterly alien.

Beyond there is no journey for I never move.

So I am "enlightened" but *unaware*. There is the ever-unfolding of what I already am. Where God is nothing else is. God extinguishes all. I the "Shining One" is far greater than I realised. Of course there is no comparison with God. Comparison doesn't exist there. How strange it is, for we are Shining Ones whether we want it or not (if I can put it this way). Again it simply is.

There are other things I cannot express like the vastness of the Nothing. Here again vast is wrong. It is beyond. No centre, no boundaries, no form. Things keep arising. No understanding needed or possible.

Amazing Grace! Everything is done by Grace. I cannot say there is a God for that gives a name and a limitation. It is beyond vast, beauty, magnificence. It is beyond, beyond beyond... No use writing any more. PS. Am I going mad?'

If we look at all this we can perhaps get a glimpse, a slight idea, of what awaits in the mystery of physical death.

FROM HERE TO REALITY

Nature

Speaking mythically we brought the external nature with us –
or it was provided – to remind us of the impersonal beauty and
stillness from whence we came.

78

Our Re-creation

Nature is the *work* of God's mind inspired by the pure and utterly still idea of the earth in God's intellect.

Most people enjoy nature because in truth it is our real nature. But being progressive historical creatures we have devised and burdened ourselves with a human nature. Human nature is the cause of our increasing loss of contact with nature.

Our physical body is a part of nature, as is every other living and inert thing. Nature includes the entire substance of the earth (out of which everything is made), as well as its clouds, rain, seas, air and all that appears in the starry firmament. We see the stars and appreciate them through an earth-made brain, something that our studied intellectuality overlooks.

All things of the earth's nature delight us. Even the busiest of human beings enjoy the *re-creation* of being in nature, walking through it, swimming in it, or just observing it. Not surprisingly most of the earth's natural elements are in our body. That's how we resonate with nature and enjoy an affinity, even though it is external to us. We relate inwardly.

Even if we see something beautiful, it's not the eyes that register the beauty, it's the knowledge of beauty inside us. It's really a recognition, a *re-cognition* of a reality we have known before, the place where our *essential intelligence* came from and which is forever behind our projected living life. Speaking myth-ically (which is the only way to describe the truth of our beginnings) we brought the external nature with us – or it was provided – to remind us of the impersonal beauty and stillness from whence we came.

It would be an intolerable shock to come into the dense substance of these bodies, and the even denser mental and psy-chological condition through which we are forced to perceive and communicate, but thanks to the modifying levels of the psyche we are let down gradually. Even so, we are born into the world of matter with an understandable squeal, although the mater, the mother, bears the pain for us. We adapt fairly quickly, although the child may have to live in two worlds for a time as we've discussed – and possibly be scolded for it.

The fact is that our psychological being is entombed in matter here until the death of the body; or until through experience (and Grace) I am able to realise the reflection of pure intelligence within. Then I realise that I, whatever I may be, have always been free.

79

Dream or Illusion? – Neither

The extraordinary freedom I've described that comes from realising the potential of pure intelligence is hardly meaningful for men and women still entombed in matter and suffering from the ignorance of self. Nevertheless, some people who have realised a degree of this freedom refer to existence as a dream or an illusion. But to me, anyone who says that, has not realised the ultimate reflection of truth.

Pure intelligence, being potential in this matter of existence, implies the presence of divine compassion beyond such dismissive labels of the human condition. To tell a mother whose child has just died that it's a dream or an illusion is an awful act of ignorance and self-fixation – an admission of having failed to realise the divine *purpose* of existence. Remembering may be an act of ignorance; but not forgetting your former pain and ignorance is the source of divine compassion.

'No one needs help,' the partially realised individual may say.

Then what are you doing here?

'Just being,' may be the answer.

Not likely. You're still driven to move from one place to another, to endeavour to disabuse others of their ignorance as far as your knowledge permits, to do something or many things until the body dies. It's true that it just happens, but it still happens. And still you say, 'I', exhibiting a quality of intelligence, or purpose, behind your actions.

So what *is* the purpose? For these people it's to realise the source of compassion, the missing knowledge that has caused a great deal of confusion among followers of Eastern-based religions.

Maybe such a realiser will love a woman, although he may say he's beyond such love. I wouldn't count on that. Matter is mater, mate, She who is in charge of matter, and I suggest he waits until his body dies before assuming he's free of Her.

Such individuals conveniently forget that they were once also steeped in ignorance and self-made pain; and that it was a long hike out to freedom. I trust that if any of these chaps read this far that they'll be true and stop eating because the hunger is an illusion; and let their body excrete wherever it is because it's only a dream – and who's to care?

Mostly these people are followers of a tradition, an historical Eastern religion whose core tenet is non-duality. To call existence an illusion without explaining who's being deluded and who's behind the illusion is evasion – and that's duality. Non-duality, as I've explained, is God being everything and ignorance arising only from God not having realised God, and, once God is realised, God then having the freedom to be, right in the midst of the world with the people, without being moved by it, and at the same time, right in the midst of God-consciousness, in the reflected reality.

80
The World and the Earth

From Natural to Normal

The world is not the earth. The world is made by man. The earth is made by God, the supreme creative intelligence behind all that exists – including you and me – and all that does not exist.

The world is superimposed on the earth. The world has been developing since the beginning of time when man first appeared. It is now an enormous psychic superstructure living off the goodness of the earth and gradually choking the life out of the earth's nature. And for us people, the world is stealthily destroying the quality of life.

The world consists of man's inventions and their evolution. It also consists of the emotional and mental unhappiness that man's inventions have caused. For example, man discovered gunpowder and invented guns that for 500 years have been killing people with ever-increasing effectiveness – and leaving their loved ones suffering, mystified and angry.

It wasn't the earth that killed the people. It was man. Certainly, the ingredients of gunpowder, aeroplanes, cars and all the other lethal-for-someone inventions, were in the earth and therefore made by God. But they're not to blame. It's the unenlightened intention behind the invention, and then behind its use, that causes all the mayhem and suffering – in other words, the state of mind, or state of ignorance, out of which all intentions arise. Astoundingly, man in our time prefers to concentrate on developing artificial intelligence and robot mechanisms, instead of improving his own robotic intelligence. Predictably, his robots – promoted as harmless substitutes for tedious work – will be used to kill people.

Man No Longer Natural

Everything is provided for man in and on the earth. His body came out of earth-woman and is sustained by the air of the earth, its food, its water. Everything that naturally comes out of the earth is good. Good means having purpose. In nature the purpose of everything made by God is to sustain the life of something else that's good. Usually this is by the sacrifice of a living body, as in the case of insects being the food of birds, and larger animals living off the death of smaller or more vulnerable animals. All this happens in a perfect impersonal harmony – perfect because it is not driven by intention. It's just natural.

Man has substituted what he has made normal for natural. So his life is normal which means he's constantly looking for something to lift him out of the boring ordinary to provide some zest and relish, something that might be called the spice of life – that which is natural.

But at the same time he's afraid of what's natural, he's afraid of love, to really love. He's afraid to sacrifice himself, his self-made inner body of troublesome intent, for the sake of others and inner harmony. And he's afraid of death – death being the most natural thing on earth. So man lives in continual conflict and subconscious fear. This he projects as his drive into the world, making the world so often a conflictual, violent and fearful place.

Nonetheless, he often seeks the relief and reassurance of the great natural nature of the earth made by God. He walks in nature, holidays in it and plays in it, breathing in its pure calming delight, but only briefly, before once again being forced to drive into the purposeless progressive world created by his intentions, good and otherwise.

Purposeless?

Yes. He's going to die. And whatever he achieves, will be lost.

Can man live without intentions?

Perhaps not, until he is free of fear. But he can live more naturally, not by eating organic produce, but by starting to reduce the time he spends thinking and worrying instead of focusing on facts and action.

Is that all?
Of course not. But it's a start.

81

The Greatest Movie – Now Showing

As I mentioned earlier, existence is a projection – just like in a cinema where the frames of film are projected singly and rapidly onto a screen by an intense focus of light behind the film.

Each image on the 'film' of existence is a minute part of the whole idea of existence held in God's unmoving intellect.

The screen is an indefinable substance or material called sensory matter.

The intensity of light carrying the image to the screen is God's supreme light of intelligence, the inner sun behind all.

And the apparent movement of the images on the screen is due to the speed of the projecting mechanism – God's mind.

Thus does God's stationary intellect, through God's ever-moving mind, present the unending drama, romance and mystery of the earth and everything on it – certainly the greatest movie ever made, and always showing.

The impulse in everyone and everything is to return to the source, to get back to the divine light from which we are all projected. And the great unending movie of existence is that infinitely slow process happening in timeless time.

'

Absolute God

Everything done is part of the great living process designed, initiated and sustained by the incomprehensible creative intelligence of Absolute God.

82

Beyond All Superlatives

Absolute God is so far beyond our comprehension and apprehension that it cannot be called intelligent, or labelled meaningfully with any superlative. In other words, absolute God is too 'intelligent' to be called intelligent and too 'creative' to be called creative.

Absolute God is simply Absolute God. And loving it – without image, expectation, or feelings – is the only recognition within our power. Absolute God at Source is an indescribable radiance of (for want of a better word) spirit. Spirit, you'll recall, is the source of psyche. And psyche is the source of the brain and sensory existence. The incomparable power of Absolute God is affirmed by the relatively inferior force of the cosmos, whose fiery galaxies and collapsing suns are shielded from the naked eye by thousands of light years of perceived space.

To convey the idea of Absolute God's protective blessing which makes life on earth possible, the best analogy I can use is the solar system, itself a lesser model of the cosmos. If the earth were the next planet to the sun there would be no life as we know it. But in the divine scheme of existence, the earth is safely distanced and cocooned from the initial intensity of the mighty sun. Similarly, on an unimaginably vaster scale, life on earth is nourished by, and at the same time protected from, the unspeakable radiant power of Absolute God.

In the solar model, the initial intensity of the sun is broken down many times before the modified rays hit the earth. First there's the distance the rays must travel across 93 million miles (150 million kilometres); then the imperceptible resistance of space; the variable bending of space due to the gravitational force of the intervening planets; the dampening effect of the earth's magnetic field; the resistance of the earth's atmosphere; the resistance of the material structures of the brain, and finally, the resistance of the human mind. This does not take into account the reduction in intensity of the sun's rays at source, due to the enormous gravitational pull of the solar mass itself.

In a similar way is the incomprehensible power of Absolute God broken down and modified for us by the increasing densities of the multiple levels of the psyche, then by the psychic, then by the three material structures of the brain through to the final density of the mind.

However, all intervening levels between the Absolute God and humanity can be instantly traversed by love or recognition of the Absolute God, bearing in mind that love without an object is the ultimate communication. Although the physical remains due to sensory existence, it is not necessarily a hindrance. Any seeming duality vanishes to the degree that love of the Absolute is a continuous subconscious focus.

Love Is Not a Feeling

What needs to be explained here is the preceding reference to love of the Absolute being 'without image, expectation or *feelings*'. Feelings are emotional, whereas feeling in the singular refers to the physical body – a feeling like hunger, cold or physical pain. But love of the Absolute is neither feelings nor a feeling. Such love is pure knowledge, pure knowledge being spontaneous inner joy, or love without conversion into feelings.

The mind emotionalises inner joy and love. The mind does this because it can't understand love or joy that does not have an object, or the perception of winning. Pure knowledge, however, is 'as nothing' to the mind and completely beyond the mind's register. So to make 'something' of this extraordinary unimagineable inner reality, the mind converts it into a familiar emotional feeling – and thus obscures the reality.

Self-knowledge alone is able to appreciate the non-feeling of divine love or joy. It has (is) the fineness and subtlety necessary to reflect on the greater reality behind the physical senses. That reality is the brilliantly scintillating divine sense-centre.

Sufficient self-knowledge resonates with this ceaselessly radiant inner sense-cluster and enables it to be beheld. The impression of the centre being a cluster is due to its many faceted diamond-like reflections of the divine light of intelligence. Converted into sense by the brain, the reflections become the five familiar senses of sight, sound, touch-feeling, taste and smell and the more abstract senses of heat and cold, balance and so on.

Gloria! Gloria! The Light! The Light!

83
Divine Intelligence

Divine Intelligence is far beneath Absolute God but far superior to our own intelligence. However Divine Intelligence is well and truly in our own experience – and this essay will demonstrate its many aspects.

Divine Intelligence is pure and universal. It is there for us to perceive as instinctual intelligence in our own physical body, and in the natural existence of every other living thing. This is another gracious divine gift to us. And its divine origin is unmistakable in the simple selfless beauty of the animal.

The gift is not exclusive, not dependent on individual realisations as all the masters have had, which are clearly not universal and therefore are not of the divine itself. The divine gives direct to all – not just to a selected realised few, no matter how purified they may have been in the mirror of inner space.

Evolution of Intelligence

Even the rabbit and bird are involved in the amazing instinctual procession of intelligence. Each must live out the life as rabbit or bird. At the end of the life each creature will have contributed to the increasing intelligence of succeeding generations of rabbit or bird in the just as amazing, inexplicably slow, progress of evolution or becoming. It's not the evolution of the form of the animal, rabbit, or bird that's going on. That's been done. It's a deepening of the great intelligence of *all* life on earth to which every form contributes in living and passing.

Instinctual evolution is a process of adaptability – each species adapting to the inexorable changes in the environment mostly caused today by man-made progress. *In order to adapt and survive the changes, all animals – including man – require more instinctual intelligence.* For example, man's chemical pollution of the environment began several hundred years ago. The instinctual intelligence, which is the immediate God that knows all and is behind all, anticipated this. Concurrent with the start of man's polluting activities, the species, including man, began developing an inner chemical body.

The chemical body acts like a sieve that sifts, strains, or screens out the most harmful pollutants. The chemical sieve is kept at manageable levels by the constant, conscious, cleansing flow of intelligence or life through the system (in a similar way to how a smoker's lungs are partially cleared of the daily ingestion of nicotine). With the pollutants held in substantive suspension, they are more easily located, dissolved, and excreted in the waste matter of the natural body. Today our atmosphere is so polluted that if Julius Caesar were to suddenly appear in his physical body, he'd be clutching his throat, unable to breathe, and within a few seconds would drop down dead.

Another 'induced' body that has recently begun forming in the species and man is the nuclear body. Due to man's irrepressible irresponsibility as the medium for indiscriminate progress, the nuclear waste from bomb testing, nuclear accidents and the like, has long since passed into the food chain. We would all be dead but for these extraordinary natural additions to our systems.

Of course the earth's own necessary volcanic activity, forest fires and other natural phenomena have released untold quantities of pollutants into the atmosphere and environment since time began. But these contaminants all tend to serve the living nature of the earth. In fact, elements of them comprise much of our physical constitution.

Unstoppable Progress

The profundity of instinctual intelligence is too immense and awesome to be even imagined. Thus does the true master know 'nothing' and desires to know nothing; for he has realised the inner reflection of the unknowable immensity behind all.

However, despite all the masters' realisations of God, they can't halt the amazing and mostly destructive outer evolution that is progress. Buddha couldn't, Jesus and Mohammed couldn't, and all the innumerable others like them couldn't. This is because all is controlled absolutely by the universal, instinctual intelligence, which, in theistic terms, is referred to as the spirit that 'blows where it wills'. Only this spirit is not theistic and doesn't blow or come and go like the wind. The spirit of God's intelligence doesn't move. It's always there to be seen in every living creature.

84

No Outer, No Inner

A Brainy Production

The starry heavens that we see at night, and the people and things that appear around us in outer space, are all productions of the brain. Similarly, the thoughts and feelings that appear in inner space are also productions of the brain. As the inner and outer objects are produced by the brain, so is the space in which both appear. In short, everything that exists – space and all – happens inside the brain. There is no outer or inner. The whole of existence is a closed-circuit brainy production.

But what about the brain itself? As the brain is part of existence, does the brain make the brain? Can the brain produce itself? Can anything produce itself?

Or is there a fundamental cause beyond the brain?

Science, being the foremost example of the rational deductive human mind, cannot see, let alone admit of, a fundamental cause. The closest science gets is to theorise about a 'Big Bang' beginning of the universe as the start of time. Scientists see that the Bang came out nothing – the timeless – but blindly ignore the timeless cause in order to persevere with the obviously flawed material model.

The scientific model is a prime example of reductionism: for example, if I look at an apple and reduce its existence to the tree, and the tree to the earth, and the earth to the universe, I can deduce my way back to a supposed first moment in time – the Big Bang Theory. This is simplistic and terribly misleading for anyone seeking the fundamental cause, the truth.

In biological science, and in the popular imagination, which depends mostly on scientific thinking, the fundamental cause is perhaps called life – without any attempt to say what the cause of life is. Can anything be its own cause?

Atheists are no help at all in answering the question. Philosophers confuse issues. Religions are mutually exclusive and from that restricted position postulate different concepts of God that depend on a belief system called, in the Christian religion, faith or inner experience, such as, 'God spoke to me'.

But was it God that spoke? This is not to deny anyone's experience of what they know to be God. But since all experience, outer and inner, happens in the brain, (which itself is an experience otherwise how would you know you have a brain?), can credibility be given to the projections of a brain that is ignorant of the cause of its own existence? At least the fact that so many people experience God, points to some inner cause that's not wholly brainy or materialistic.

Anyway, how do I know I have a brain?

I don't. If I hadn't been told, or seen some other body's brain, I wouldn't have known.

85

One Cause, Countless Effects

So What Caused the Big Bang? – Silence

It is logically impossible to argue that anything can be the cause of itself.

So how can Absolute God be intelligently presented as the cause of all? Such a proposition immediately raises the question, 'Well, who or what caused God?'

That, anyway, is the deductive argument, deduction being the normal rational and scientific method of proceeding from the many to the one, from the several pieces of evidence to the supposed single cause. The method invariably arrives at a past event as the cause.

The error in this is that God, the cause of all, is not past. God is now, immediate. Anything that proceeds from God, the cause now, is an effect. And every effect is clearly in the past since it comes after the cause which is now.

The best example of deductive reasoning is the scientific theory of the Big Bang beginning of space, matter and time – the material universe. The theory proceeds by reductionism from the assumed current positions of the galaxies (the many) back through fifteen or twenty billion years of assumed past to the supposed first (single) micro-second in time – the Big Bang event.

The scientific conclusion is called a theory because it leaves the logical question unanswered: Well, what caused the Big Bang?

No matter how the scientific minds manipulate their calculations they can't get closer than a micro-second to the answer – the timeless state (which they know is there) *before* the Bang. The timeless obviously is nothing – nothing at any rate to speak of, or that can be deduced or calculated. But because the scientific mind is rational and not yet logical – incapable of putting first thing first – it puts second thing first. Instead of science seeing from its own calculations that nothing is the answer, it continues searching for *something*.

On the scientific evidence itself the timeless truth is only a micro-second away from the reasoning deductive mind. But as the old saying goes, an inch is as good as a mile off, and a micro-second from the truth is as good as forever off.

From the above it's clear that we can't think or rationalise about God-the-timeless-cause because all thinking and rational-ising involves the past and the memory – time itself. But what we can do is clear the intellect, which is inner space, and gradually the timeless causal state – the nothing (to speak of) – will shine through. In other words the intelligence can be speeded up suf-ficiently to approximate the speed of now and reveal the truth or God behind existence.

Every Cause an Effect

It is not generally realised that there are no causes in existence. Every apparent cause is an effect of some other effect. *The whole of existence – in every particular – is an effect of a previous effect.*

Humanity lives in a world of effects without cause. When the individual man or woman is sufficiently jaded from being an unconscious effect caught up in an unconscious stream of effects, they turn within. Why? To find the cause. But any belief proffered by organised religion or an historical system is not going to lead to the cause, although it may indeed reduce some of the inner clutter and clamour.

The point is that all beliefs and systems are effects of ignorance. The ignorance is not necessarily in the religions and systems themselves founded by a master, but in the individual who believes and follows them. Ignorance is always in the follower or they wouldn't be following.

What is followed or believed in is irrelevant where cause is concerned. It's all a distraction. But then all of living is a distrac-tion because everyone is following and believing in something. And yet the whole living process engaging everyone is the only thing that eventually leads to the truth, cause. What is done doesn't matter. Everything done is part of the great living process designed, initiated and sustained by the incomprehensible creative intelligence of Absolute God.

Inevitably, for us self-conscious creatures, living leads to a procession of disappointments and disillusionments until finally, perhaps, there is an awakening to the futility of existing and, perhaps, release.

Living is the only 'Way'. And everyone's living life is unique to them. No two lives are the same. The outer activity may be similar but the unique living life is within. And the inner life determines the situations and circumstances – favourable and unfavourable – that encompass the person from birth to death.

The unique inner life can be equated with what Hinduism calls karma – the consequences of the past repeating themselves as recurrent existences. Then comes the popular and misleading bit that when the past is eliminated, liberation from rebirth occurs. Misleading, because, when the past is eliminated, there's no one to know.

The karmic motive power behind life and death is not personal, but is deduced to be, and thus gives rise to the personal doctrine of reincarnation. As I've explained, the past and the consequences thereof refer to the actions in thought, word and deed of the whole of humankind and at birth each individual is invested with a portion of this sum total of ignorance left behind unresolved by the dead.

One living life is not enough. Many, many living lives are necessary. But each living life contributes to the inner light of intelligence beyond the physical brain. This intelligence, although neither personal nor individual, carries the distinctive divine imprimatur of the life beyond. In one living life the light may seem obscured. But to the light beyond the brain one living life is merely a split second.

Existence – God Thinking

Every micro-second God's mind is recreating and re-projecting every single thing in existence.

86

God's Mind

We live in God's mind. Every object, person and condition in the world around us and in ourselves is in God's mind.

You can see the movement of God's mind around you now and throughout your living life. You see it in the many species of animals, plants, fish, birds, the infinite variety of human beings; the incessant to-ing and fro-ing of all humanity and all the things that are changing, including your body; the imperceptible process of ageing; the wind moving the trees; the fury of the violent storm; the gentle rain; in other words, the entire world of objects – plus the coming and going of birth and death.

If God is God, the all-powerful, the all-present and the all-intelligent, could the truth be otherwise?

If what I've said is not the truth, then there is no God, no Source of all. And we might as well tear up this book and finish our lives. But we can't – because God is in charge and responsible for what is in God's mind.

Our difficulty in grasping the vastness and profundity of God is due to the dominant human perception that our living life now is *our* life. It's not. Our present living life is only Life that is living *for now*. The life that we are is so much vaster and profoundly unlimited that it can't possibly be visualised or conceptualised (concepts being the basis of the way we think).

The chief limitation for us is that we die. In time our bodies live and in time our bodies die. Time is the great limiter of existence, the tyrant, not of age, but of ageing. Everything is ageing, even the newborn. And ageing ends in the death of this life.

The Source of Time

God's mind is not in time but it is the actual source of time. Time is the process of God thinking the endless procession of

God's thoughts. Recall that God's thoughts comprise all the objects and conditions we see constantly moving and changing around us. And time is what strings them together, just as time strings our thoughts together in what we call 'time to think' or time to do anything.

All that you see from where you're sitting now is God thinking at the incredible speed of now. Because such swift intelligence is beyond human comprehension, the scene from wherever you are appears to be perfectly knit together in a perfectly comprehensible – but inexplicable – equilibrium of continuity.

God's Intellect

However, God's mind and thoughts are not God – any more than your thought-full mind is what you are. Just as something acutely intelligent is behind our mind, so God is behind God's mind.

Where do God's thoughts come from? From God's *intellect*. God's intellect is deep behind God's mind, just as the human intellect is behind the human mind and the source of most of our thoughts. Even so, God's intellect is still not God.

God remains far, far beyond – as your reality does.

87

The Earth Idea

The earth is one complete *idea* in God's intellect. The idea contains all life that has ever been on earth or will be, and every condition and circumstance that can apply to life here. Every thing and every body is a distinct part of the one earth idea, each a pristine potential of perfection within perfection. Your reality, the light of your individual consciousness, is there, within the idea.

God's mind seizes the earth idea and projects the component parts as a continuous moving train of thought. The result is existence – the ever-changing physical world of nature, people and things; along with the ceaseless mutation and evolution of every thing, as each form comes and goes eternally in physical time towards the perfection of its own idea.

Nothing in the earth idea is separate. All is one. Each thing is an intrinsic part of the whole. And in truth the part can't be separated from the whole. In God or Self-realisation the part realises the whole, while at the same time realising identity with the whole!

It would be an error of the human mind to presume that when man travels to the planets he leaves the earth idea; or to think that the wider universe he sees is not part of the earth idea. Whatever he sees in his cosmic travels will be seen through the earth brain-body. While he has a body he cannot leave the earth idea.

Are there other ideas in God's intellect?

Not really. The idea of the earth contains everything. There is no other existence but the existence of man, wherever he is –– even after death. Many years ago in writing and speaking of UFOs I said that their source was us in another time. That still stands. There's nothing else but what is 'here' now. Now, of course, is ever-moving and with it moves 'here'.

The earth idea also contains the idea of God and all the aspects of God. So God's intellect is filled with numerous divine ideas that together make up the spiritual or radiant energetic earth – the ethereality – behind the physical earth.

God's ideas never change or modify. They are eternal. That's because the divine intellect doesn't move – in contrast to God's mind which is in perpetual motion in matter. The divine intellect is absolutely stilled by the supreme intelligence of the almighty indescribable God way behind it – which, paradoxically, is again part of the earth idea.

No Brown Cows

In God's intellect there is no mixing or blending of the earth ideas. Each idea remains completely separate and pristine from any other idea. For instance, cow is cow. Brown is brown. Neither is definable outside the single idea. Never do the two parts mix or combine.

But due to the movement of God's mind in matter, the indefinable idea of cow manifests on earth as a mixture of the idea of brown and cow. Hence, brown cows. Then tree – green tree, fig tree, apple tree, fir tree and so on throughout the whole projected existence.

Plato saw this. But from what we have of his perceptions he didn't explain it very thoroughly.

88

The Futility of God's Thinking

We think because God thinks. But the fact remains that all thinking is futile because it can never lead to love, truth or God. Even God's thinking which manifests as the continuity of the whole of existence is simply a distraction from the truth for the human mind. To the human mind human thinking seems to have purpose. Yet all that thinking does is perpetuate thinking. Similarly, God's thinking perpetuates existence.

To God's mind God's thinking also seems to have purpose. That purpose is the attempt to reproduce, in sense and time, the whole idea of life on earth in one complete and final divine thought. But that's impossible here in time, just as it's impossible for our mind to express everything we know in one complete thought. And just as God's mind never gives up trying and failing, neither do we – by expressing endless streams of meaningless thoughts (concepts) about the mystery of existence, and our own personal existence.

The reason for the failure is that both lines of thought – God's and ours – occur in sluggish physical time. The idea may be clear, but the projection into existence is broken up by time into a long succession of objects or thoughts. Time is the distance between each object and thought. So time translates into distance; and, as everyone knows, the time it takes to cover any distance determines the speed. In truth, an emotional mind is too cluttered and slow to receive a clearly communicated idea; whereas to a clear spiritual mind comprehension is immediate.

The Intelligence and Power of God – No-thing

Time, I repeat, is *not* in God's mind, nor is time a component of the earth idea. Time arises in existence as the imperceptible interval between the divine mind's projection of the world, and our interpretive human thoughts. On the very rare occasions when anyone stops thinking – stops interpreting what is – time stops momentarily for that individual. And if ever he or she gets into God's mind behind the projection, existence as it is commonly perceived, is radically transformed.

The explanation is that in every micro-second God's mind is recreating and re-projecting every single thing in existence. In short, existence is a continuously interrupted *re-production* and only a seeming continuity when strung together by the human mind. The micro-intervals between the projections are blank, a state of no-thing. This no-thing is the intelligence or power of God behind the apparent movement of projection. When individual intelligence is resonating at a speed of self-knowledge equivalent to the micro-interval of nothing, God or Self is realised. The stream of existence remains exactly as it is, but the significance or meaning changes.

The upshot of all this is that the human mind, like God's mind, is pure intelligence behind the mental, emotional and psychological projections. In other words, any personal sense or reasoned interpretation of existence pollutes the mind and distracts it by thinking.

The micro-interval between existence and non-existence is represented here by the incomprehensible swiftness of now. Human nature is so busy with the objects and conditions of existence that it fails to register that everything occurs and exists in the 'timeless succession' of now. Now is the power of God's mind. Now is the boundary that separates existence from the state of no-thing. Now is so swift that it is still. Now is an all-present mystery, the very means of existence.

89
The Human Intellect – No Ideas,
All Concepts

Just as God's mind is a moving reflection of the ideas in God's intellect and produces the amazing physical world, so our mind reflects off the inferior human intellect and produces the troublesome and hostile aspects of existence.

The human intellect is relatively close to the earth and symbolised by the orbit of the moon. The divine intellect is way, way out in deep solar space. It is possible for us humans to reflect on or off the divine intellect and share in the wonder and beauty beyond the mind. But this requires a speed of intelligence expressed as self-knowledge beyond the common threshold. Without sufficient speed we can't get through the human intellect. Our thoughts bounce back to us, at best with short-term answers but no overall solutions.

As described in the previous essays, there are no ideas in the human intellect – ideas are the exclusive province of the divine intellect. The human intellect, on the other hand, consists of innumerable *conceptual substitutes* for the pure ideas behind existence. Everyone ever born has contributed their personal notions and beliefs, making the human intellect a ragbag of opinions, speculation and little lasting wisdom. The persistent concepts are those popularly modified along certain lines until outdated, or discarded by fashion or usage of the times.

While the ideas in God's intellect are kept separate by the divine intelligence of detachment, concepts in the human intellect are held together by emotional identification with objects and conditions in the ever-moving sensory world of God's thinking. When your mind thinks, the original thought bounces back off a succession of the closest-matching concepts in the human intellect. You then form your own synthesised version from the synthesised concepts that have been put there by others in similar circumstances!

The combination of God's mind thinking the ceaseless thoughts of existence, and humanity continually thinking synthesised thoughts, results in changes in popular concepts such as fashions, styles, designs, sayings and popular music. Synthesis is the actual basis of deductive reasoning, which proceeds from the past to reach a conclusion in the present. Synthesis is responsible for many of the errors in human affairs.

In contrast to human thought, the swiftness of intelligence implicit in God-realisation passes effortlessly back through the human intellect and reflects directly onto the divine intellect. This reveals knowledge of eternal truth or the idea of God.

By Grace, impulses from the divine intellect frequently flow down through the back of the human intellect and into the minds of men and women. This inevitably means a refreshing injection of new knowledge, a new idea, a new direction in the common conceptual and linear human way of looking at things. Such brilliant ideas from a deep vertical place within, never fail to set a new course in science, medicine, archaeology, biology, technology, art, industry, and so on. Sometimes the same brilliant idea is realised by different people in different parts of the world. Hence the old adage, 'great minds think alike'.

Evolution and Involution

The earth idea, of course, contains the notion of evolution but the evolution of things is not the prime purpose. The prime purpose behind the earth idea is *involution* of the individual's consciousness. The realisation of the earth idea or God is not a result of evolution.

Evolution goes forward in existence while simultaneously involution goes back within. Evolution is progress, involution is withdrawal – the gradual withdrawal of intelligence from identification with God's thinking; in other words, withdrawal from attachment to existence. God-realisation follows after the individual gives up personalised thinking and then gives up attachment to God's mind: in short, by not only giving up attachment to every thing in existence, but also to the need to exist.

This can only happen as an uninterrupted state when the individual has suffered enough from existence and existing – and loves the wonder behind it all.

Awareness

Human awareness through the senses produces existence. But awareness is beneath consciousness. To an individual detached or detaching from existence – becoming more conscious – awareness and the human mind certainly continue. But the intelligence no longer reflects unnecessarily on the inferior human intellect. The result is a reduction in aimless thought, aimless activities and worry.

90
Humanity

In the realm of consciousness beyond the personal aspirations of men and women, the great body of humanity is seen for what it is. Consciousness sufficiently realised can view the human intellect from the divine side, the opposite side to the human mind.

This reveals that humanity is not a divine idea. It's a concept in the human intellect. And everyone is a cell in that great conceptual body in the sense that each one is contributing to the evolution and extension of the concept. Although the concept is motivating human affairs through the basic energy of conflict and tension, the concept is not real.

The only real 'thing' is the pristine idea of each individual consciousness in the divine intellect. No bodies or persons are in that; there is no collective forming a mass, as in the concept of humanity. The ideas form a whole, a whole idea of pure intelligence or light(s) paradoxically consisting of ever-changing individual pinpoints of consciousness. In other words, there is finally no individual consciousness in the whole, only the pure consciousness of the idea of – in the absence of any better word – God.

Progress

The concept of humanity is identical with the concept of progress. Without one there can't be the other. Neither is real. Both occur only in the presumptions of the human mind.

For instance, at *near* death I presume that those who survive me survive. This is a continuation of the mind's entrenched concept of the progress of humanity. But clearly it is nonsense to presume that the physical world goes on in the same way as when I had a physical brain. I presume this mainly from concern for those I've loved, or assumed responsibility for, and now, by force, am leaving behind. But for the same reason I can't say that either. Perhaps it's only I that's being left behind to perish with the brain, and that I'm still trying to cling to the continuity I've known?

There's another angle to this as well: my concern for the vulnerable loved ones – such as young children – who will be left behind. Presumptions are based on probability, the notoriously unreliable aspect of human thought. The indisputable fact is that everyone left behind – including young children – are looked after by a more reliable power than the person who's dying. The person, who can die at any time, can hardly be reliable for any beloved 'survivor'.

The question for every body still alive is: have I ever known anyone left behind who was not looked after? The answer is no, because even the very rare extremity of death is a compassionate gift from life or God for the truly bereaved. And on the more impersonal level, it could be asked, is the death of someone we love the chance or opportunity – mostly overlooked or lost – for us to discover the divine idea behind death?

Persons survive in a projected personalised world of concepts and impressions divorced from the actuality of what is. Purified consciousness sees through the projection and knows it is not real. It can't be real because every body dies. What is real never dies, never moves and never passes away.

That is not to say that the actuality is real or not real. What is not real is I, the knower, who puts anything at all on what is. What's real can't be known.

A Summation

To sum up: I the person live in a fabricated world of impressions, interpretations and concepts of an imagined ideal. That world is within a more real world made by the futile attempts of God's mind to recreate the divine idea behind all things. Even that is not real. It's all world within world.

Humanity and progress have been developing in the human intellect since time began. They began as a couple of hazy amorphous notions. With the gradual increase in world population, more people started to think and affirm the concept of other people unseen – the start of the concept of humanity.

Simultaneously the ever-increasing swiftness of communication with others unseen – now the global village notion – affirmed the concept of progress. So a world of humanity and progress are now the commonly accepted concepts – a combination of presumptions by the mind and utter fabrication.

The only truth within is in consciousness sufficiently realised. Before consciousness can be realised to any real degree the person must die to their self. This is behind the saying attributed to Jesus that unless a man loses his life (his person) while alive he cannot find (the reality of) Life.

FROM HERE TO REALITY

The Ideal

Any deliberate attempt by man to bring an idea in God's intellect into physical existence becomes a futile ideal.

91
God Save Us from Idealists

Nothing is more doomed to failure in human affairs than the ideal. Idealists throughout history have caused untold pain and suffering – and much ruinous confusion and doubt about the goodness or rightness of God or reality. The trouble is that ideals sound so good and right at the time. But they fail because they're invariably proposed or initiated by the enthusiasms of personal minds.

Examples of the destructive nature of idealism are legion. A few examples are: Marxism, which ended in the vicious and brutal suppression of a whole nation's liberty, along with the tyrannical destruction of millions of people; Christian ideals which led to the unspeakable cruelties of the Inquisition, and the wars to 'regain' the 'Holy Land' occupied by another people; Hitler's ideal of a super-race entailing the programmed elimination of millions of Jews.

The list of barbaric and wretched failures goes on and on – and will continue while idealists are able to impose their biased vision of the good on human affairs.

Ideals appeal to followers (not to originators) for two reasons: one, the idea behind the ideal is an aspect of supreme good, an eternal idea in God's intellect, the source of all good – and therefore an attribute of our higher being. And two: people trust that such a clearly desirable ideal will work for good in their lives and the lives of others.

The Spiritual Ideal

People continually attempt to attain, or manifest, an ideal through external means and psychic manipulation. The spiritual ideal is a common example. The spiritual ideal in every case is gathered from the precepts of others, and in particular, from the inspiration of a founder back in the ancient past. By the time the original inspiration gets to the present, it has been misconstrued, embellished, exaggerated and otherwise corrupted by a huge succession of conditioned and biased tampering minds and emotions.

And so arise the ideals of nirvana, the bodhisattva, enlightenment, heaven, sainthood, unity with God, Moksha, paradise etc, along with numerous ideal 'ways' of attainment. The ways of the Buddhists, the Hindus, the Christians, the Islamics, the Jews, the Taoists, the Advaitists and the whatevers, are all different. If any of their ideals or ideal ways were real, it would be universally obvious to everyone. That has yet to happen. And being impossible, it won't.

The nature of the human mind is to convert an apparently 'good moral ideal' into concepts and thought. This, allied with the mind trying to manifest the ideal in physical time, finally degenerates into frustration, confusion or doubt in those who attempt it, or are party to it – despite random and varying realisations of the reflection of God, Self or the unknown.

The Purpose in Failure

Even so, as the divine idea is behind every impossible ideal, there is purpose in this universal failure. Through such failures the individual consciousness is slowly being purified, until perhaps the point is reached within of such abysmal personal failure that all ideal notions and efforts are realised to be vain and empty rubbish. This state, when lasting, is humility. Humility is only to God the unknowable and does not comply with the ideals and expectations of the world.

Such an enduring moment of utter personal powerlessness is inevitable in any deep realisation of God. I am reminded of such a happening reported in the later life of the revered medieval Christian saint, Thomas Aquinas (1221-1274). Thomas wrote scores of volumes, and his writings are the basis of much of today's orthodox Roman Catholicism. Before he died, he stopped writing, leaving his greatest work, *Summa Theologica,* forever unfinished, because he said it had been granted to him 'to experience such things as made all he had ever written seem to him to be of straw'.

But the Church did not hear.

Virtue

God's mind, of course, is far more divinely powerful and pure than the human mind. So what chance has our inferior human mind got of presenting an idea and thereby attaining the ideal? None. No chance at all. Even so, we humans still hanker after the ideal and keep trying through every action to present it, do it, achieve it, or be it.

Pursuing the ideal is natural for us, actually an imperative. We can't help it. What the divine mind does, we do, more or less. But in our minds, pursuit of the unattainable ideal produces subconscious frustration, tension and an inner sense of failure, which leads to self-judgment. From this arises the thought, I'm not good enough, not worthy, or perhaps, that I've even failed my destiny or God.

Despite the futility of pursuing ideals, there is virtue (divine worthiness) in our efforts. Each individual, even after a world-first sporting record, invention, or achievement still strives on to do, be or attain the impossible – the ideal. In continually trying to improve our productions and performances we are perceptibly (and mainly imperceptibly) extending the limits of human achievement that once was thought impossible.

Take sport. Take human endurance. Take the increasing efficiency of our machines, mechanisms and electronics. In every field that which would be called the equivalent of a new record is being established somewhere every day. But there is nothing personal in all this. It is one single seemingly mighty endeavour by a living entity called humanity to improve itself, to shuffle, albeit uncertainly but inexorably, towards an undefined and unknown ideal.

As we humans are personal people we enjoy, and are entertained by, the personal exploits and achievements of individuals within this great movement. We make heroes of them, award knighthoods, congressional medals, titles and other personalised symbols of recognition. These honours are, of course, well-earned in most instances – but not all. Personal influence, the self-interest of others, and exploitation, are sometimes the deciding factors in who gets what and who doesn't.

FROM HERE TO REALITY

Negation

No positive, no negative, no middle way, no way.

92
The Simplicity of 'Hereness'

One extraordinary faculty alone – a principle at our intelligent disposal – can bring about the complete 'hereness' of the divine idea behind the visible and invisible totality of existence. That principle is negation.

Hereness is always here. But in no way is it associated with I who might say at this moment, 'I am here'. That is I speaking, the same reflective I that in Descartes announced, 'I think (reflect), therefore I am', or in St Augustine who said, 'I think (reflect), therefore God is'. Without the complication of I, hereness simply is.

In sleep and unconsciousness, I disappear, but hereness continues. Hereness is beyond our comprehension because we cannot comprehend or understand anything without the knowing reflection of I. Hereness is immediate – now, free of discrimination, distinction, comparison or difference. In short, hereness cannot be known.

What is this that can't be known? How can it be?

Hereness is the original state of intelligence before I, the namer, interpreter and knower, arose in man. Before I, hereness is.

I am ageless. I was in man and woman before recorded history, and then in succeeding generations of Persians, Egyptians, Greeks, Romans, Barbarians, Mongols, Moors, Arabs – the lot, up to and including the present-day population of the planet. The domain of I is the immeasurable accumulation of what the world calls experience and information – which ends with the personal memory.

The World 'Idea'

By comparing and naming down through the ages, I have fabricated an intellectual *world idea* of existence. Although man-made and not really an idea, it is a vast and cumulative mental and emotional structure – added to by everyone in every generation. I, who am always in existence, and always have been, have projected my spurious world picture onto the hereness of what is. In my ignorance I rule the world of my ignorance – and so cannot enter hereness.

Because the problematical world fantasy arises with I in every body born, it carries the irresistible conviction of being real. To question its reality is to question the sanity of everyone, including the questioner. The only possible universally acceptable exception is religious belief. In religion, you can pretty safely believe in anything, as long as it relates to the invisible, the apparent non-existent.

Down through the ages religion has been the overriding influence in human affairs. It is older than every other activity and enquiry – preceding, by thousands of years, politics, commerce, science and philosophy. *Religion is the ideal foundation of the world idea.* Clearly then, religious belief is the place to start negation.

Negation however is not self-denial. It is true that due to religious convictions men and women practising self-denial have managed to give up some aspirations and ambitions connected with worldly activities, as well as some negative reactions. But no one has yet *intelligently* suggested giving up the pervasive religious ideal itself because it is the basis on which the vast troublesome world has been constructed. This does not refer to any particular religion. It refers to the whole notion of religion as being a way to reality.

Psyche and Spirit

Undeniably people involved in religions have had deep, life-changing spiritual insights, and enduring realisations of truth or love. But all occur in the psyche, and therefore are not really of the spirit. Despite the psyche's descending ramp of fineness and subtlety, it has a limit. And although forming the invisible part of existence accessible to human intelligence, the psyche never crosses over into spirit, even in the deepest spiritual realisations. Spiritual (meaning of the spirit) may be the impression; but spiritual is not spirit. *Spiritual and spirit, like psyche and spirit, are absolutely separate.*

Negation is Hereness

Negation is the intelligent elimination of every mental, intellectual and emotional construction put by man on the original sublime absence inherent in hereness. All spiritual or psychic realisations are accompanied by a presence, a very subtle sense of participation or 'being there'. This may seem to be an absence of I, or a knower. But it is not the absence essential to negation because it occurs in inner space. Hereness occurs only in phenomenal sensory space – here, now. There is no presence, no participation, nothing but hereness.

Negation requires intelligence which has no form, no participant, no place beyond 'here'. The practice can only be effective after a considerable degree of self-knowledge has accrued. The self-knowledge then powers the intelligence to a frequency beyond normal understanding and beyond even the superior intelligence of God-realisation. Without this power of radical discrimination, attempts at negation become the usual effort of trying to live according to some spiritual teaching, ethic or code of morality.

Negation also presupposes that the individual has been intelligent enough to get his or her external life right, so that no area is disturbing. This requires considerable discrimination since it is normal to gloss over such difficult areas because of fear of the consequences of taking right action to eliminate the problem.

Negation will make sense to anyone of reasonable intelligence. But the power and strength to live negation as a way of life depends as mentioned on the degree of self-knowledge. Without that level of self-knowledge negation will merely make intellectual sense. But it must be said that many individuals are practising partial negation due to different degrees of self-knowledge.

Negation makes sense because it is concerned only with eliminating the problems in the life. This is everyone's aspiration, anyway. But it seems that no one has ever described the right practice of negation without giving it a *positive* value which it certainly does not have. Spiritual paths, ways and ideals all fall into this category. Anything positive attracts a negative. And so even the most altruistic and moral teachings presenting a positive way of living unavoidably introduce the negative that abounds in all moralistic codes of behaviour. And of course, all spiritual teachings, from the eight-fold path of the Buddhists, through Christian love, to the doctrines and practices of Islam, Judaism and Hinduism, are divergent – and inevitably their adherents have a record of fighting and killing each other.

Beginning Negation

The reality of negation begins by discontinuing efforts to follow or conform to any spiritual teaching. And then negating or dissolving mental reference to concepts associated with a spiritual path or emotional identification with such feelings. These manifest as what should be done and shouldn't be done, instead of simply doing as you do.

The reality behind such negation is obvious in everyone's living experience. Trying to follow or conform to expectations – either your own or someone else's, be it those of lover, partner, parents or children – is one of the main causes of discontent and unhappiness in everyone's life. Spiritual expectations are no exception. The spiritual expectation (promoted by Christian dogma) is that suffering is good or holy when it is obvious that suffering can never be intelligently regarded as good. The only right suffering in the natural life is in dissolving *attachment* to your own and others' expectations, trying to live according to another's rules. When the negation is complete, no more troublesome thoughts or emotions arise. And in the resultant stillness there is the clear perception of the divine reality, or idea, behind life on earth and your assumed existence – hereness.

In hereness there is no participant, no being, no reference – just the pure intelligence of 'what is'.

FROM HERE TO REALITY

The Great Cycle of Life and Death

You are life, the vital immortal life animating your body and all living things at this moment, now.

93

Without End or Beginning

What is it that pushes sap up the trunks of trees? What makes the birds fly, the grass grow, the plants flower, the animals and us develop and mate? What is it that makes every body move – human, animal and insect? What's behind the constant motion of all things, even the dazzling force of the scientist's atom?

Life.

Life is the pressure behind it all, behind all life on earth. Life drives irresistibly into existence. No one and nothing can withstand its amazing power to be, and to live.

Firstly, where is life? Where does it come from with such astonishing constancy and effect?

Life is within. If life were not there, you would be dead. Life enables you to live. Until life withdraws from within, your body goes on living. Life animates your brain. Your brain produces the senses that allow you to register the world. When life withdraws, as in death, it withdraws from your brain. The world and life in the senses then vanish. In sleep, life reduces its animating pressure so that the physical mechanism can rest temporarily in the stillness of life and be vitally restored for further action. Life is behind your brain.

Secondly, how does life grow everything and move everything outside you?

Through the stupendous inner pressure and power of all life that has died in form before – and which is compelled to strive to live again.

The Process

When you are dead and the vital life has withdrawn, the world of the senses vanishes. No senses, no world.

But doesn't the world continue for those who survive?

When you're dead and have no brain-body, such a question

clearly is meaningless. While you are alive it is possible to speculate that the world continues. But that's unfounded speculation, or wishful thinking: you are assuming that death is the same as physical existence, which is clearly an error.

The key is that you are not only life but evolving *consciousness*. Both life and consciousness are autonomous, meaning real in their own right and the two ultimately are distinct or unconnected elements of what you are. Life, however, is secondary to consciousness. Consciousness extends from the physical world to the deepest extremity of the abstract psyche, whereas life is found only in physical existence and next to the physical.

Life, in fact, is the vehicle of consciousness. As consciousness you can't exist in the flesh without the presence of life. Consciousness makes life meaningful. You can be alive but unconscious – due to anaesthetic or injury – and life will have no meaning. When your body dies and you are no longer the lifeform you appear to be here, the only reality is the consciousness you are 'then'.

You are not the body, not the brain, not the mind or emotions: you are immortal life imbued with an ongoing divine light of individual consciousness – the imprimatur of self-knowledge.

As you've probably surmised by now, the whole arrangement from being born into living and withdrawing at death, is a mighty, divinely-initiated and sustained process – culminating in the vital life and individual consciousness being freed of form, and soaring to an unimaginable height of fullness and delight.

But sooner or later, after a further mysterious process, the individual consciousness separates from life. Consciousness 'goes on' proceeding deeper *inwardly* towards reality, while the life vehicle joins the *outward-going* urge to live again by animating the conception of another human embryo.

The Ethereal Double

The great unending cycle of life and death is controlled by the divine imprimatur – the ethereal double. In German this is called the doppelgänger – 'doppel' for double, plus 'gänger' for goer, demonstrating an ancient perception in the German psyche of the 'going on' I'm speaking of. In my *The Origins of Man and the Universe*, published in 1982, I refer to it as the psychic double. But since then I've realised the ethereal world, or ethereality, behind human existence. This is far deeper and more comprehensive than the 'psychic', and better able to be conveyed as the dazzling mystery or idea it must always remain behind the words.

You'll recall that the imprimatur is the initial divine imprint on the life which makes the consciousness in everyone individual. In the human mind, life and consciousness are assumed to be one, but as the previous section shows, life is merely the vehicle of consciousness: life occurs only in sensory existence, and in the first degrees of the psyche closest to existence. The deeper the consciousness descends into the psyche after death so the sense of life – feeling or sentience – reduces and fades until finally, as described in the last section, consciousness separates completely and 'goes on', while life returns to conceive another human embryo. Wherever there is life there is feeling or sentience. Feeling or sentience show attachment to earth existence and the degree of it determines how 'soon' the recurrence.

The ethereal double is responsible for the look of your body, its psychological make-up, gender, dispositions, and the circumstances of its birth and death in each living life. It is your immediate reality – as close as the life and intelligence empowering the body – yet completely ethereal. It is you, yours and why you don't wake up in someone else's body.

The ethereal double consists of your unique self-knowledge – your individual consciousness – accruing from uncountable recurrences. Although 'yours', it is not accessible by the surface mind. It is like a key that fits only the lock made for it or by it. And as will become clearer as we approach a greater appreciation of the ethereality, the impersonal individual consciousness is simply another essential light in that blazing total light of intelligence behind human existence – God, the Will.

The ethereal double also contains your potential of consciousness, that which draws you on to become more intelligent through the highs and lows of living experience.

Uniqueness

Self-knowledge arises from experience. Just as in this life your experience is uniquely different to that of any other individual, the same uniqueness applies to all the lives your consciousness has ever lived. Moreover, the range of human experience is infinitely variable and made more variable by the fact that previous experience colours the way current experience is registered. So the uniqueness of self-knowledge keeps growing.

But what is self-knowledge the knowledge of? Clearly, self – as in personal ignorance and selfishness. But what is self in relation to the greater picture of many living lives? Self is every possible experience of life from living to dying, to death to being born, all of it.

In each particular life self starts off as the relationship between your body-mind and the environment, the world. The common error is in assuming the body-mind is your self and that the world isn't. Many, many living lives gradually reduce this distance of duality until the world and body-mind are realised as one – as within, so without.

Then there's dying, death and being born. One living life can't register all the experiences of dying; there are too many ways of dying – but only one reality called death; likewise in being born – many ways but only one reality. In each case the experiences are multiple and different but the end result is the same – you are either dead or born. To be the fullness of death and the meaning of birth beyond the many experiences of both, results in the knowledge 'I am this … this is my self,' in other words, 'the entire cycle of life and death is what I am without the duality of I and it'.

The ethereal double is responsible for the circumstances and situations that must be faced from birth to death. It is the equivalent of God in the first instance, determining what is necessary for the individual to grow in self-knowledge, as well as providing the innate intelligence to cope with, or overcome, the many challenges inherent in physical existence. Self-knowledge always relates to the good of the whole, but this is unlikely to be evident to the person in times of stress and pressure.

The First Heaven

At death, the immortal life and individual consciousness of everyone, freed of the laborious burden of the body-brain, wakes up in the first level of the abstract psyche. This is the first level of pure intelligence, the level of vital life itself, a place of joyous release and revelation, and may be termed the first heaven. Without the presence of individual consciousness there would be nothing to register the amazing fullness of life here since life itself, being instinctive or *immediate*, has no reflective capability. The individual consciousness, however, is reflective, enabling it to reflect direct on the wonder of life and register that self-knowledge.

In the first heaven, the consciousness has not yet separated from the vehicle of life and spends time immersed in the pure delight of vital life. How long is determined by how quickly arises the urge to live again. With sufficient detachment from earth experience the consciousness will resist the initial urges of recurrence and descend deeper into the psyche. Consciousness either 'goes on' or is drawn back into existence.

Returning to earth from the first heaven is not unlike being on holiday on earth and after a time realising that despite the enjoyments it's time to go home. 'Going on' marks the gradual separation of consciousness from life, until life and the earth no longer hold any attraction, except perhaps as in service to those still closer to the earth.

The New Embryo

The vehicle of life carrying the individual consciousness will now empower the new embryo with life and intelligence, investing it with a pattern of the life to be lived and the means of accruing more self-knowledge. The pattern consists of one tiny share of human ignorance left behind at death by uncountable generations of men and women after the vital consciousness separated from the former person. In all of us the person is the embodiment of ignorance, the troublesome self, until transformed into love and self-knowledge through the living process. As few people manage this before they die, a residue of ignorance is left behind.

The new person developing with the baby body will be forced to face its share of ignorance in the form of all the circumstances of the life, good, bad and indifferent – and hopefully transform some of it, bolstered by the potential consciousness of the ethereal double. Thus, by success and failure, does life on earth evolve towards a purely hypothetical perfection. But also in this way does the individual behind the person evolve at death into a greater potential of intelligence.

Forms of Life

Life has no form of its own. All forms of life are part of the earth idea in the divine intellect projected into existence by God's mind. And the eager, untiring wonder of pure life animates all living things. The length of life in any form is determined by the Will, which also empowers the movement of God's mind.

Some lives must end early, some well into old age, some by accident, some by disease. But all forms eventually must die to sustain the great cyclic movement of life and death – and the divine miracle of the never-ending transformation of ignorance and consciousness.

94
Your Life

Your life is not just this present living life. Your present living life is a kind of sideshow from the main event. It lasts, perhaps, seventy or ninety years in physical time, the slowest time there is. It's not the living life that's tedious; it's the time it takes and the person it makes.

The blessing is that the time ends – and the slow and cumbersome physical body, made by this most laborious time, dies. But the life you are never dies, never ends. None of this is to suggest that what you are reincarnates. What you are *not* – your negativity – is all that reincarnates. However, there is recurrence which I've mentioned earlier and which I'll endeavour to clarify more in this essay.

The immortal life in each man and woman has a unique divine imprimatur or stamp. The imprimatur is eternal and serves to 'identify' the same life in the countless successions of recurrences. The quality of the imprimatur mutates or changes infinitesimally as a result of each living life. The catalyst of this ongoing enhancement is virtue – virtue being the divine worthiness of the life that's been lived. Thus the imprimatur is the register of the total virtue of all recurrences.

Divine worthiness or virtue can't be assessed by us here. The closest we can get to understanding it in our own living life is possibly as stalwartness, fortitude and self-denial in the face of adversity, and humility, surrender and gratitude to the unknown.

So there it is. The only reality is the *life* that's being lived, the life that makes the living possible. The common sense demonstration of this is that when the life withdraws from what is living, the living ends. But this obvious fact is shrouded in everyone's hazy hope of living again in some other form or realm, or in the just as foggy belief that nothing is immortal. The result is that the focus is on the living thing that's going to die, instead of being on the immortal life behind which makes the living possible.

The divine imprimatur at any moment reflects the accumulated virtue of the human race. But of itself – in its own reality – the imprimatur is self-luminous, shining with the incomprehensible brilliance of absolute goodness and rightness and may be called the perfect body of light – God. As the magnet that keeps all lives moving towards the impossible ideal, it is completely uninvolved.

The statement in the Christian New Testament, 'Every good and perfect gift comes from the father (the perfect body) of lights' would have arisen from a realisation of the truth of the imprimatur within. The more modern term of spiritual or intellectual *enlightenment* is also a dim echo of the state.

The divine imprimatur is also the centre of each of the other species (although our self-reflective consciousness adds another perspective). The death of each form within a particular species enhances minutely the light of the centre, while at the same time contributing to the inscrutable divine purpose behind the existence of that species. In this way the imprimatur acts as the group centre of all lives.

Another word for virtue is pure intelligence – the greater the virtue, the purer or swifter the intelligence. The imprimatur is the stamp of ultimate divine intelligence, or virtue. As a potential, it is the intelligence or purity that all the living lives are endeavouring to unite with.

95
The Processes of Death and Recurrence

At death the body decomposes. The sustaining vital life has withdrawn and the remaining trace elements of the body, essential to its physiology, return to the earth from whence they came.

Several other processes are involved in death. First, the negativity that developed and expressed itself through the body throughout the living life does not decompose. It is psychic and therefore immortal. There is no good in it; its selfishness would not sustain anything except its self.

The negativity joins the other negative emotions in the psychic, reinforcing, to a minute degree, the collective negativity left there at death by those who have died before. In the same way as the impersonal elements of goodness in the body return to the earth to nourish living organisms, so the personal negativity returns to the psychic to nourish selfishness in the world.

The negativity will be reborn to some degree in a new physical baby body. But there will be no remembering of the person(s) who left it. All remembering will have been removed in the dying process.

At death the life or light that 'goes on' adds more or less to the shining of the imprimatur. Less means that if the light is dim it tends to diffuse and dim the surrounding 'cells' of light but without reducing the shining of the whole. Even dimness is still light. This is similar to how the health of our physical body is affected by a relatively malfunctioning cell without reducing the overall wellbeing. If the new light is bright it adds to the overall shining.

To us, the perfect body of God's intelligence can only remain potential. In itself it is potent and all-powerful – potent meaning active and no longer potential. As such it determines the course of every living life.

Wherever there is living matter there is divine intelligence of life. We call it instinct, the seemingly unconscious intelligence in every living thing. As conception requires the union of living sperm and ovum, intelligence is already present. This is the divine impersonal intelligence every baby is born with.

At the moment of physical conception another unsuspected pregnancy occurs – a divine pregnancy initiated by the perfect body. This impregnates the embryo with an outline of the life ahead – in the form of a tiny share of the total human negativity in the psychic. The negativity only exists because the circumstances and situations that produced it were not faced rightly, which means righteously, before the person died. Righteously means acting or being with the knowledge that something greater than your self is in control. The negativity will manifest as the testing circumstances and conditions of the life. Even so, the life will be assisted by the innate divine intelligence providing favourable situations, along with the saving grace that everyone experiences at some time.

So the baby is born with the testing circumstances of its life already determined – and the good that underlies appearances. These include even the type of parents, other family members, the circumstances in the home (if there is a home), the situation where the birth takes place and every other influence.

What we're speaking of here is the Will of God, that which is in charge of every life from before birth to beyond death, an incomprehensible power that can only be approached through love.

Yet the life is not fixed. The element to change circumstances and situations is always present. That element is the consciousness or divine intelligence within – the imprimatur of self-knowledge accruing from all recurrences. The consciousness is not personal and is what we can call in the first instance the intelligence of God. It is available more or less in every situation that the child as an adult must face.

In growing up, the child grows in experience and out of that develops a person. The person is purely materialistic and selfish, meaning self-fixated. It is concerned with manipulating situations and people to provide it with pleasure (what it likes), and with avoiding situations that don't please it, or don't give it pleasure (what it doesn't like). Too much of anything in between it calls boredom. Boredom then drives the person to find some kind of excitement – what it likes.

But excitement has an unseen downside. It creates either more boredom (because the excitement has ended) or circumstances that the person doesn't like. This see-sawing goes on until death. Or until the intelligence of the adult starts to predominate by realising that the pleasure of heightened experiences – such as drugs, alcohol, sex, imagining, wishing, daydreaming and self-indulgence – is not worth the consequences, the pain.

As the intelligence speeds up (hence the 'quick and the dead') it starts to perceive that the life as it is, is more fulfilling than the unstable and fluctuating life of trying to satisfy the person. This results in some purposeful action – compared to the person's constantly shifting and mainly aimless lifestyle. The intelligence is moved to get the life right, to be rid of things that the person has become addicted or attached to and which are causing ongoing unhappiness in the life.

The person cannot see this, let alone initiate meaningful action. The person is inclined to let things drift and put up with the emotional pain and discontent. The pain and discontent are negative expressions of excitement and to the person trapped in an habitually boring situation, the negative and its unhappy emotions give a sort of buzz-feeling of being alive. It settles for that.

96
Spiritual Awakening

By the mid-adult years an individual is supposed to have reached a substantive degree of maturity. This, acting on the store of self-knowledge in the unconscious, may trigger a spiritual awakening.

Everybody has degrees of self-knowledge – real intelligence – which can make the living life easier. But in most cases it is not enough to cause a radical psychological transformation, so most people's lives go on much as usual. On occasions, however, the ongoing accumulation of self-knowledge through experience reaches a critical point; it bursts like a light into the mind and changes the whole psychological perspective and outlook.

This is likely to be termed the moment of awakening, enlightenment, or realisation. There are many different degrees of this change.

The most common in man occurs in his late thirties, forties and perhaps fifties. At a critical point, the impersonal intelligence of self-knowledge shines through to the surface mind. The mind is then able to survey the life as a whole and sees that decisions and initiatives taken by his person in the younger years are now the obligations that make living tedious and unfulfilling. This initiates a revolt against past structures and is commonly termed the mid-life crisis. Sometimes it leads to a complete change in the lifestyle. But often the Will in the intelligence is not sufficient – consideration of personal security and fear of change wins – and the individual tries to settle down midst the intermittent frustration and discomfort of compromise.

Woman, of course, may also experience this form of awakening, but not so widely as man, it seems. Woman's natural mid-life change is associated more with the menopause. In this she endures a usually extended series of psycho-physical symptoms, the physiological being stressful and unpleasant. But supported by sufficient self-knowledge these years of change culminate in her emergence as a woman of wisdom and peace.

The varying depths of awakening and liberation in different individuals have to 'mature' by being lived out in time against the resistance and opposition of the world. It takes years to come to full requital. Although an incredible inner transformation has occurred, the circumstances of the life also have to be transformed into a similar *external* living harmony. That takes time and unflagging one-pointedness.

Fundamental change is always accompanied by an external trigger which may be difficult to discern. The more obvious triggers are those associated with the irresistible love of a new man or woman, the death of someone, or an enforced termination of a successful career. These occurrences are, of course, common but those leading to fundamental change have a mystical element that defies rational explanation – and endures as a knowledge of love or life beyond the ordinary.

Such an event can be the recognition of a woman or man of the opposite gender as the Lord immanent, which initiates a love of the other so intense that the love is realised to be not only holy, but also the reflection of the living love of God or truth. All previous loves are as husks compared to it. Again, such an amazingly real event has to be lived through in the circumstances of the life. These may not threaten the divine knowledge or love but they will be testing if considered from a normal viewpoint.

In any of the above crises where the Will initiates radical life-changing action there is no going back. Any return to the old way of life is unthinkable. Close associates are likely to be made unhappy and fail to grasp the truth of the matter. But if they have sufficient self-knowledge to see, 'it's time, it's right' (perhaps after an initial period of emotional outbursts), there is the chance of their innate intelligence being speeded up, along with the opportunity and Will for them also to change their habitual lifestyle.

Eventually the individual consciousness reaches the speed of intelligence that was always there buried under the addictions and attachments to past concepts and structures. The new consciousness then provides the unshakeable knowledge that God was always in charge; that even the earlier life based on ignorance was also God's Will – and simply due to insufficient self-knowledge.

Sometimes people believe that a kind of spiritual awakening is taking place in humanity; that humanity is growing in compassion for the earth and for the people of the earth; parallelling this is a seemingly widening recognition of the spiritual life as in New Age philosophies and activities. But little of it is true. Any spiritual improvement in the masses can be ascribed to a burgeoning increase in the human population which has the effect of spreading the intelligence wider, while diminishing its power and effectiveness.

FROM HERE TO REALITY

God and the Lord

*The Lord is not God. The Lord is God's aspect in
sensory existence.*

97
The Lord

Most religions and religious people speak of God and the Lord as though they were interchangeable. This includes the Christians who enjoy calling the man Jesus, the Lord. The man Jesus, whoever he was, certainly had realised the reflected consciousness of God. Jesus, apart from always remaining a man in human form, and therefore being subject to the vagaries of his humanity, was one with the consciousness he had realised.

Many men before Jesus had realised the consciousness of God and many men have since. But the error is to refer to any man as God or the Lord. I know of two men in the experience of my short long life who would have to be called the Lord according to the Christian ethic. The difference is that no one (so far) has been around to record and mythologise either man and the 'miracles' he worked.

To realise the consciousness of God is to realise you are nothing in the face of such power and goodness, a point made by Jesus the man when he turned on someone who called him good and said, 'Don't call me good; only God is good'.

There's nothing like time, history and churchianity to make something out of nothing when the man in question is well and truly dead. (Christian saints have to be dead a long time before getting the official nod.) But there is, of course, a great truth behind the Christian worship of Jesus as the Lord. The truth is that what is being loved and worshipped by the sincerely devoted individual Christian is God. And Jesus, who was not a Christian but a simple Jewish man, knew this. He spoke of God alone being worthy of worship.

How do you worship something or nothing, anyway? – by simply loving it. Not by loving the churchified ceremonies devised throughout history by unenlightened pious priests. Jesus made the point: 'Love God with all your heart, with all your strength and with all your spirit.' That's love. That's one-pointedness. And that's the simplicity of worship.

Not everyone can love God with such selfless fervour. Why they can't is because of organised religions whose priests have put themselves, their beliefs and ceremonies, between the individual and God. In the case of Christians it's 'the Lord Jesus'. You can only come to salvation (whatever that means) through Jesus. God help the Hindus, the Muslims, the Shintoists, the Buddhists and all the other billions of non-Christians on earth. And of course God does help them, since Jesus can't.

The Lord is an aspect of God, God immanent. But the Lord is not God. The Lord is God's aspect in sensory existence. The Lord is in every single thing animate and inanimate, but is not any particular man, woman or thing.

The distinction is that the Lord has no attributes. To have no attributes is to be as nothing to our cognition. And yet recognition of the Lord is immediate for those blessed enough to have had this divine revelation of another physical form. The body in which the Lord appears is irrelevant other than as a medium.

The Vision

My own vision of the Lord happened as a result of extreme love. If you love a man or woman with a self-consuming, self-obliterating intensity equal to your love of God, the Lord may appear briefly *within* that form. That is what happened to me. I saw the Lord, spoke to the Lord and the Lord spoke to me. And because I have no religious belief, only my realised knowledge of God as being the indescribable nothing, the Lord separated from the image in the vision and 'appeared' to me and spoke to me as nothing.

It happened in 1964. I had an enormous love of God that had been literally killing me, killing my self over a period of several years. I loved the woman as God. I knew she was the manifestation of my love of God. But of course I couldn't tell anyone that.

It was daylight. Suddenly I saw an image of the woman walking towards me. Something fell away from her. And immediately I exclaimed with wondrous amazement, 'It is the Lord!'

The Lord replied, somewhat indignantly (as though I shouldn't have been amazed), 'Of course it is I. There is no Ann.'

It was true. Ann had completely disappeared although her image was still standing in front of me. I was speaking to the image but there was nothing I recognised in it. I was looking at nothing and nothing was speaking to me. All I knew with absolute, perfect conviction was that this incredible 'nothing' was the Lord.

The Lord continued, 'I will not reveal this to anyone else in the world. Nor will you be able to tell anyone. In this way will I have my way.'

I said, 'Please may I see your beautiful face again?'

And the Lord showed me a close-up of Ann's beautified face.

The significance of the vision and what the Lord said is central to everybody's existence. There is no us. There is only God the Lord.

Although I've endeavoured ever since to communicate this truth through my teaching, I know I can't tell anyone. I suppose that's because each individual has to realise the Lord for themselves.

But I keep trying.

And I suppose that's the way the Lord has its way.

98
The Embodiment of God

Near the beginning of time when the population of the world was minimal, the deity (God) embodied itself consciously in an extremely tiny proportion of human forms. That proportion is unalterably fixed for all time by the Will. With the continuous increase in population the proportion remained constant. This meant there were necessarily more men with the consciousness of God among the world population. But the presence of more people meant a dilution in the power of the embodied God-consciousness. Spread more thinly the consciousness was not as pure: God was not quite as present. From that emerged different 'paths and ways' of realising the Godhead within.

Today the ratio of the tiny original proportion applied to a world population of six billion has spawned a proliferation not only of ways and paths but also teachers of ways and paths. The truth remains, however, that all the ways and paths are historical and not the truth. They may certainly be true, like two-times-two equals four – but two-times-two equals four is a fact, not the truth. Facts are not the truth when you're in deep dreamless sleep, or when you're unconscious or dead. The truth then is nothing, and to us historical creatures the embodiment of God is the embodiment of nothing – to speak of.

Demigods

The world population in the ancient of ancient days comprised the inhabitants of all the tribes. But there was little knowledge of other peoples in other continents; each tribe or clan was more or less a nation, or world, to itself. The presence of Godmen among the various tribes of the world is well-recorded in the myths of the ancients. The most notable that demonstrate the point in my experience are the myths of Hinduism. Foremost of these is the *Mahabharata,* a long epic poem describing events said to have occurred 5000 years before the Christian Era.

Maha means 'great' and Bharata is a family or clan name. Hindu, it seems to me, would have originated with the clan that occupied the far western region of India near the (H) Indus river. Thus the poem tells the great history óf the Hindus, one of the most ancient of ancient nations.

The *Mahabharata* introduces us to many demigods. Demigods are mythological beings with more power than a mortal but less than a god. (Mythological means before provable recorded history.) One of the central characters in the *Mahabharata* is Krishna. But Krishna arrives late in the ancestral story of the Hindus. Before Krishna were the gods Shiva, Brahma and Vishnu. In our story these can be said to be the near-original pure embodiments of God. But the bodies were not at all substantial in our terms. Embodiment at the beginning of time meant that the deity appeared in a distinct but shapeless misty form of psyche. The bodies of the people of the time were also composed more of psyche than substance. They didn't have the same physical limitations that we have today. Only with the corrupting passage of time did the bodies of their descendants degenerate into physical forms. Everything gradually became hard, hardened and harder. Our bodies today are the hardest and most substantial that bodies have ever been. And in the predictable future of evolution they will become willingly subordinate to even harder machines – as has already begun to happen.

Krishna was on the scene long after Shiva, Brahma and Vishnu. But he was still considered by many – due to his superhuman feats and powers – to be one of the earthly reincarnations of Vishnu, in other words, the deity. Krishna in the myth is also a man: he tires, ages and reveals the emotions of distress and surprise at things that happen, and finally he dies. Of course he dies. Because he occupies an incipient human body. He is not perfect. But perfection is still consciously within him.

Krishna's inner perfection is shown to us in the *Bhagavad-Gita*, which is a part of the *Mahabharata*, and means *The Song of the Lord*. In the Gita Krishna is the chariot driver of Arjuna, the son of Queen Kunti and the god, Indra, King of Heaven. Arjuna is a royal warrior and the finest archer in the world. Arjuna is about to lead an army into an internecine battle and at the last moment throws down his weapons in despair at the thought of having to kill his kinsmen – indicating that the world at that time for the Hindus was a composite of relatives.

Krishna lectures Arjuna on his duty as a noble warrior (noble in those days meaning the son of two embodiments of God) stating that it is not the acts that bind but the selfish intentions behind them. It is Arjuna's duty to kill without any self-interest in the consequences of the acts.

Finally, Krishna, being conscious of his reality, reveals himself as the Supreme God and grants Arjuna a vision of this divine being which (of course) in the purity of those most ancient of ancient days 'blazes like a thousand suns'. Arjuna, 'his heart trembling with fear' at such a sight, successfully pleads to be again shown Krishna's 'friendly human form'.

Thus for us today does this mythic story affirm the truth of the embodiment of God near the beginning of time and the world.

Myth and Truth

The myths describe the evolution of humanity with a far greater authenticity than anything devised by the materialistic sciences. But all the mythic stories are still centred on externals: the effects in existence of the presence of Godmen. Although illustrating our own divine beginnings in the world, the mythic stories are still about the world. Superhuman deeds, feats and miracles all relate to the world. And as true as the myths are as the history of humanity, they are not the truth.

The truth is the inner instinctual reality that can never enter existence but is always there to be appreciated as the intelligence responsible for the natural beauty of any thing, and the coherence of everything. We as living creatures live our lives intimately with 'This'. But mostly we have divorced ourselves from This by our need to know or be other things – including the inner reflection of This which we call God-realisation, the temporary absence of I.

Maybe in physical death we will be This and join all life and beauty – as This now gives life and beauty to us.

Maybe.

I would let you know if I could as it's likely I'll be dead before you. But I who wrote that die with the brain, the body – unless I am an instrument of truth through which the reality communicates. Then in death I shall be changed, changed into something even vaster than This.

99
The Matrix

The physical universe and our whole sensory existence, including the great psycho-spiritual cycle of life and death, is a tiny cocoon of mind-stuff in the vast Matrix of reality.

The dictionary defines matrix as a surrounding or pervading element in which something else originates, takes form or develops. It is from the Latin, mater, meaning mother – and not surprisingly refers to the womb.

In the context of this book the Matrix is the origin of every-thing conceivable and inconceivable, the invisible and visible, the extant and non-extant. It is utterly impersonal yet supremely just. For us, over the great cycle of life and death, it balances the scales of consequences for every thought, word, and deed, with unerring justice.

The Matrix is immeasurably greater than 'This' mentioned in the previous essay. Yet it is the source of This, and all such attempts to describe the indescribable.

The best I can do to perhaps give a better idea of the Matrix is to describe it as an infinite network of irresistible power and intelligence beyond any comparison with the immensity and mystery of the cosmos. The Matrix *is* the mystery.

Even so, the Matrix pervades the cosmos, and the entire cocoon of existence, determining what happens 'there' and what happens 'here' every moment in a perfect genius of complete inter-relatedness. Every minute change in the starry galaxies causes an infinitesimal change or mutation on earth and throughout the inconceivable extent and profundity of the all-pervading, all-encompassing Matrix.

In the same way does the Matrix control the fate and evolution of the world and its people. It does this with such infinite fineness and delicacy that every word, thought and action has an effect or consequence elsewhere. Because the Matrix is immediate and timeless and our existence is a product of time, there is a constant build-up on earth of consequences, good and otherwise. These unfold in time as the waves of circumstances, situations and conditions that people as a whole, and individually, are seeing and facing in this ever-moving moment of now – all the result of time and past.

The Matrix is too unique even to be called God, the Eternal, Source or any word or words denoting the exalted knowledge of divine realisation. Of course the Matrix is all that those words stand for. But all words are mind-stuff, the product of the cocoon of existence. So is 'Matrix'. But I trust that in using and describing this unusual word I've managed to convey something of the reality behind the idea of it.

Anyway, that's the end for now of all Barry Long can say about the matter, the mater and matrix.

Approaching Reality

*The truth is that God, the power behind everything, is the core
essence of man – his reality.*

100
The Inscrutable Divine Will

The inscrutable divine will is 'what is' – everything as it is now at this moment. And the ability to *really* appreciate the meaning of this depends on the degree of surrender to the divine will, now and every moment of the living life.

The key word is inscrutable, meaning incapable of being investigated and understood. The usual error is that people use their understanding to grasp what is. Understanding, however, is based on rational inquiry and mental investigation which glosses over the parts that aren't understood, and draws assumptions and conclusions without those parts. The result is partiality and a missing link.

What is, is far beyond understanding. And it's far easier to see the whole of what is than trying to understand all the parts – as, for example, most of us had difficulties in understanding all the different subjects at school. School, and our whole educated interpretation of the world of subjects, is based on learning – learning to understand. So, due to our learned conditioning, and no fault of our own, we are ill-fitted to see what is – although well-fitted to argue, dispute and debate all that I've said here.

But you can't argue about what is – because what is, is the *whole* at any moment and has no parts. It is the intelligent inner awareness of the source of the outer phenomenon which the physical senses are revealing now – without consideration of what is happening or being perceived. It also requires a state of emptiedness within, that is, a continuous freedom from identification with any personalised thought or emotion.

The inner state of emptiedness is really what allows the unmoving perception of the outer phenomenon of what is. The merging of outer and inner is the divine realisation of peace that passes understanding.

The mechanics of it are simple, once the need to understand is put aside. The whole phenomenon of the physical senses is a complete mirror. In its entirety it reflects the source of the intelligence that is looking into it. The source, of course, is the reality, God, or Self that is inside every body and behind every thing. To focus on one part of what's in the mirror – as people usually do – is to miss the whole. Then arises the need to understand which causes a subtle disturbance within that provokes more inquiry. So no peace.

It is not uncommon for people to assume that their emotional disturbances are a part of what is. This is because they have not grasped, or perhaps been told, that emotional disturbance is a sign of something arising within and an unquestionable indication of lack of emptiedness.

101
Religion and Religions

Religion is the recognition of a higher, unseen power having control of the man or woman's destiny. That's first.

Second, if the recognition is deep enough, the higher power is acknowledged throughout the living life with reverence, worship, and obedient surrender to its inscrutable will.

And third, knowledge then arises that the higher power is an inexplicable inner, intimate mystery and that simply to love it without question, expectation, imagery, thought or feeling, is to be one with it.

As a total moment-to-moment way of life these three stages of divine knowledge unite to reveal reality -- and that union *is* reality.

Few human beings can live this way. But why is that? Is there no integrity in the higher power that ensures reality is accessible to all?

The answer is, yes, there is that integrity. But the obstacles are all man-made. The main source of hindrance is man's need to believe in something and to idolise his belief. Humanity as a whole shares a common psyche. And the accumulated psychic pressure to believe and idolise, generated by innumerable past generations, and swirling deep in the subconscious of everyone, is virtually irresistible until neutralised by the logic and power of self-knowledge.

Idols

In our historical epoch the main purveyors of beliefs and idols are the established and organised world religions. The most dominant of these in evident order of antiquity are: Hinduism, Judaism, Buddhism, Christianity and Islam. And each one has its idol or idols, even though idols were evidently banned by Mohammed of Islam, and Buddha (the man, Gautama) of Buddhism.

The Jewish idol is the Ark of the Covenant, or in its absence a cabinet in the synagogue enshrining the sacred scrolls; the Islamic idol is Mecca to which due homage is paid five times a day; the thousands of Buddhist idols are stylised statues with no relation to the founder, or reality; Hindu idols are statues and shrines representing the Brahmanic pantheon; and the Christian idols include the horrifying figure of a man nailed to a cross, draped altars, innumerable pretty statues and stained-glass windows of so-called saints.

The above list of the five world religions does not mention the many sects that have broken away from each of them – some hostile to each other – nor the well-organised pagan or multiple gods of the religions of ancient Greece, Egypt and Rome, all with their priestly hierarchy and idolatrous statues.

Nothing external can represent the inner source of all. The closest is the *whole* of existence which cannot be encompassed anyway, by the human mind.

Belief in the Past

All religions are based on the past. It is rational and usual, but not logical, for humanity to assume that good comes out of the past. Also that there was a greater accessible truth then than now, and that one needs precepts laid down by past mentors, teachers or gurus to be free – freedom meaning to realise God or reality as an enduring and uninterrupted state of intelligence. This is not demonstrated in the living life of anyone still involved in a religion.

The past cannot be now. Within every religion and religious belief there is a holding on to the past, whether it be to scriptures or oral traditions, the worshipping of a past human figure or representational statues, or the *unconscious* faith that the past as given in the present is true.

Then, in each of the religions without exception, there has been the inevitable building on the original inspirational source in the form of priestly interpretations, and then interpretations of the interpretations without end or limit. So the original succinct inspirational message is lost under a welter of imaginative and psychic distractions.

What I'm saying in no way denies that many people involved in established religions have had varying realisations of God, love, the Lord, enlightenment, or reality. But the integral point is that without the prescribed religious involvement the realisations would still have happened – and much earlier or sooner. Not only in the life of these people, but in the lives of all people.

Ordinary people do have realisations and insights of truth. But because of global fixation on, and idolising of, the material world and material interests, the person invariably dismisses any subtle glimpses of reality as imagination, mental aberration, or possibly as a sign of psychiatric disorder – since no one seriously speaks of such things in the normal world. As a result, the compulsion is to cover up, say nothing and so avoid the possibility of ridicule.

Followers of religions, however, get together and swap their extraordinary stories. As well, they are indoctrinated with all the miraculous and psychic stuffing in the teachings, mixed up with bits of truth here and there. In short, they are subconsciously prepared for extraordinary subtle inner happenings should they occur. That's about the only advantage of being with a religion.

However, to *not* believe in the stuff of organised religions is fundamentally the same as believing. It is simply an intellectual or reasoned rejection, which is then a belief – all belief being a belief because it has not been subjected to sufficient intelligent scrutiny. Non-belief in anything does not erase the unsuspected conditioning of childhood deep down in the subconscious. Everyone on earth has been conditioned in childhood by some sort of scary religious belief, even if it's the bogey-man, the devil, eternal damnation, or the feared bunyip of Australian Aboriginal culture.

The Failure of Religions

The important thing for us to see is how quickly religions, particularly those with legendary historical human founders, become debased and sources of dissension, argument and sheer cloud-cuckoo-land mythologising – giving rise to an edifice of belief, which if presented in any other context, would be dismissed as absurd invention.

In Buddhism and Christianity there is no firm historical evidence of the life or death of either founder. All the scriptural testimonies are based on the anecdotal and pious embellishments of oral accounts by people who had neither met the founder, nor were even his contemporaries.

In the case of Gautama, later called Buddha, nothing was set down in writing for 300 years. And the stories of Jesus, called the Gospels, did not begin to be written down for at least fifty years after his death. Both scriptural traditions represent incredibly fanciful assumptions based on hearsay, and the usual liberal religious sprinklings of miraculous events that defy both logic and normal intelligence.

To make sense of this we have to understand that everything in existence is becoming – moving on in relation to where it was or what it was the moment before. A good example is the process of getting older, an imperceptible action of becoming. As it is with all things, so it is with religions. The original idea is built on by people who come after, this in time leading to a variety of opinions, and inevitably, to different branches of belief, or breakaway sects. Although the sects of a religion pay lip-service to the overall founding belief, each in effect goes its own way about expressing, ceremonialising and sermonising the agreed doctrine and dogma.

In Judaism and Christianity there are orthodox and unorthodox churches, each believing that its way is the right way: the Roman Catholics idolise a living human figure called the papal 'holy father', while Protestants, Baptists, Methodists, Presbyterians and a host of offshoot variations on the Christian theme ridicule the papacy.

In Buddhism, immediately after the death of Gautama in the sixth century BCE, his monks found it necessary to convene a council to try to settle the already divergent oral canon of the teaching, as well as the rules of discipline of the monastic order he'd left behind. If the teaching had been clear of beliefs and opinions, this would have been unnecessary. But of course, oral reports and interpretations of any event give rise to conflicting opinions. Also, at this meeting it is said that the seeds were sown of the two major divisions that today are known as the opposing Mahayana and Theravada Schools of the founder's 'way to salvation' – as if there could be two ways to anything real, except to the local supermarket.

Similarly, divergent opinions and interpretations followed the death of Jesus. Christianity became the personal faith and exposition of St Paul, based not so much on the teachings of Jesus, but on Paul's vision on the road to Damascus and his religiously-inspired building on his version of the Jesus legend.

And like Jesus the man, Gautama the man, within a century or so of his death, had been raised by reputation into a super-human Being – a status both he and Jesus would have derided and rejected outright. The realisation of God, Self or nirvana is not available to super-beings, only to extraordinary ordinary human beings.

A closer look at the definition of religion at the beginning of this essay may show us the areas in which the religions fail. Also, why their priests and ministers are accepted and inducted on the basis of educated learning and memorising of scriptures, and not on the day-by-day living of the true religious life. And why the administered religions appeal to a vast majority of the world's population who don't have the time, self-discipline, inclination, or inspiration to live the same real religious life.

With no one living the true religious life, who's to say what it is? The Muslims would disagree with the Christians who would disagree with the Buddhists who would disagree with the Jews who would disagree with the Hindus who would disagree with the Calithumpians, if such a religion existed. If they all did agree there'd be no need for any of them.

The extraordinary thing, however, is that without the fanatical zeal of believers, the atrociously invasive enthusiasms of missionaries, the casual and intermittent faith of followers, and the downright ignorance and pretence of the clerics of all religions that have ever influenced humanity, the common man and woman will agree on what is good and what is right. Not a so-called golden rule but a natural way of life.

Has God Lost Control?

As organised religion itself is divided into many beliefs, it is a self-evident truth that their well-intentioned efforts will result in division and conflict. To see this and their contribution to the good, or otherwise, of humanity as a whole, all we have to do is look at *the world as a whole* over which together they reign supreme. What do we see?

Muslim Palestinians and Israeli Jews locked in years of mortal combat. In Afghanistan the Christian West bombing and unseating an oppressive Islamic tribal government which, without demonstrating who's right, shows us the excessive zeal and futility of two beliefs supposedly acknowledging the one God. In India and Pakistan we see Muslims and Hindus continuously killing each other in border clashes and terrorist acts, and threatening all-out war; in Northern Ireland, we see Protestants and Catholics indiscriminately bombing and killing each other, and in Sri Lanka, minority Hindu Tamils fighting the majority Buddhist government to establish a Tamil homeland.

An obvious question arises out of this terrible continuous slaughter and tension between the world's many different religious groups. Has the one God, the one and only power behind existence, lost control?

Of course not. God has not lost control. The problem is that man is not responsible. Man, as a race of believers, thinks, or believes, he has free will. He demonstrates this belief every day in the conflicts of his home, work and relationships, and particularly where opposing warring religious beliefs are concerned. He trumpets loudly – on both sides – that he fights in God's name and that God is with him. And reassured by his stupidity and confidence in his wilful self-righteous decisions, he kills and maims people the world over.

The truth is that God, the power behind everything, is the core essence of man – his reality. But the projection of man as a separate physical body containing an independent psychological system comprising a mental and emotional self, which is held together by a reflective thinking mind constantly processing external data, is a long, long way 'out' from his inner essence.

However, as God is in charge that is how it's supposed to be, simply because *that's how it is*. From the seemingly ludicrous juxtaposition of unreality and reality comes the divine Will of becoming, evolution or movement. Not that the reality ever moves. But its sheer presence sets all actual things in motion.

Why? Because all things – galaxies, suns, planets, people and microbes – in essence are lesser formal aspects of the reality, and their constant imperceptible inner mutations and changes of position are due to the irresistible divine power drawing 'them' back whence they came. Thus, it can be said, that the force of gravity which holds the universe together and pulls all objects back towards the centre, is an actual reflection of the power of reality that in time overcomes all separation.

But meanwhile, man must have his wilful way. He must be free – and is free – to use his free will as he sees it. Inevitably his free will leads him into various forms of pain and suffering. And if ever his free will leads him into a happier or more contented mood, it's not long before his free will once again plunges him back into discontent and frustration. This is because man is imperceptibly always kept moving towards reality.

Only when he realises that his so-called free will is the cause of all his unhappiness – including his fear of death – is it possible for him to surrender without interruption to the one Will which will then control his life for good.

102

Spiritual Intuition

All that I've written of truth in this book has two sources. One source is empiric observation, empiric meaning direct experience now, derived from having lived – but without regard now for rational assumptions, religious belief or scientific theory. In other words empiric means 'my' or 'your' own experience now, free of any reference to experience in the memory. The author's own experience is derived from nearly eight decades of living. The second source is spiritual visions and spiritual intuition.

My many visions I've touched on. Although real in their origin behind the faculties of normal experience, all visions have to come up through the psyche. And the psyche, especially where it meets sensory existence and the personal mind, is the most unreliable and unpredictable of mediums. Spiritual intuition on the other hand is utterly reliable. Unless spiritual intuition is associated with a vision, the vision will appear to confirm *what you already believe.* Examples are the many reported religious visions such as those of Christians who have seen Jesus or the Virgin Mary; of Hindus who have seen Krishna; of Buddhists who see the meditating Buddha(s) and of Muslims who, in the absence of any concept of Allah, may see the Archangel Gabriel (who in a vision is said to have dictated some of the Koran to Mohammed).

The doubtful thing about visions is that they involve time. Although the origin of the source of the vision is not questionable, the vision itself and its apparent meaning is questionable; questionable because all visions are the product – an end result – of time. Time is the problematical element that distorts all impulses of truth.

Time-distortion even applies to sense-perception and to all of our self-conscious assumptions and conclusions. In the Hindu and Buddhist religions the distortion of time is described as maya. But unfortunately for the people maya is not defined so simply, if at all, in ordinary meaningful terms.

Time of course means distance. And distance means separation – so all visions involve separation from the source. The most
important vision in my life, when the Lord immanent spoke to
me through the image of Ann, was no exception in that sense. It
may have happened within me, as of course it did, but like all
visions, it was still apart from me, so it was in time.

Even in those early days I knew that no historical figure, or
indeed any image, could represent God. I had no belief about
God and so the Lord 'appeared' to me as I knew God to be – as
'nothing'; nothing, absolutely free of attributes, and nothing that
could ever be described. Even so, with immediate recognition I
exclaimed, 'It is the Lord.' And the Lord replied, 'Of course it is
I, there is no Ann.' Which, as I've pointed out, means that no one
in essence exists: it is the Lord, only.

That statement of the Lord is an example of spiritual intuition
accompanying a vision and revealing the most profound truth in
everybody's life: within the image of the body, and beneath all
the personal notions and feelings, is the Lord, free of time and
attributes.

Spiritual intuition is immediate because it doesn't involve time.
It is direct knowledge, *now!* And at its purest there are no accompanying visions, all of which are eventually left behind. Spiritual
intuition is a continuous, uninterrupted flow of instantaneous
knowledge – always present immediately the moment requires.
It involves no reasoning or thinking. The master of spiritual
intuition has cleared his inner space so that communication from
the reality is unhindered by psychic or time distortion.

Normal intuition which many people experience at different
times is also immediate. It too, is direct knowledge which seems
to arrive out of nowhere; suddenly something is known or
cognised with unusual certainty. But is it true? Yes, in its origin.
But mostly no – due to psychic or time distortion – unless the
mirror of inner space has been cleansed and purified by
complete surrender to the one Source of all knowledge.

As described previously, spiritual intuition develops gradually
in the unconscious with the accrual of self-knowledge. As self-
knowledge varies in everybody so it seems that people,

particularly spiritual teachers, express varying degrees of truth. But it's not the truth that varies, it's the degree of purification of the teacher's mind.

Even so, because every event at its deepest level is part of the Great Design which serves all, the truth communicated by each teacher is unconsciously tailored to suit the self-knowledge of those drawn to him or her. This results in many teachers and many teachings – each providing something for everyone, and with the depth of self-knowledge determining who listens to whom. Even the most vaguely sourced and imaginative of teachings serves its audience until the Great Will of reality draws those who are ready to a slightly more real teaching.

The more real a teacher's truth, the greater is the self-knowledge amongst the audience. Some people drawn to a teaching necessarily slide back into an easier and less-demanding one – because they were ready for a time, but not quite ready enough. Others attend out of curiosity but inevitably drift away, while others simply stay and serve out of love of the truth and love of the reflection of the teacher's realised presence.

Due to the pressing need in many people to belong and believe, and not to have to know, followers tend to form like-minded communities around the teacher or teaching, with only a small percentage of actual serious practitioners. This applies particularly to dead teachers and is noticeable among the established and organised religions that depend on mostly fictional and absurdly mythologised accounts of the founding master's life and teachings. The result is meaningless ceremonies, doctrines and dogmas containing as much intelligent self-knowledge as a recital of the alphabet.

As soon as any man or woman realises the ultimate truth, such as happens in God-realisation, they can no longer be a Christian, a Muslim or a Buddhist – a point that the Buddha is said to have made, but hardly surprising if he was God or Self-realised.

And so goes on the amazingly slow and unconscious intelligent direction of everyone's life, drawn by the irresistible magnet of the divine idea of reality, which may never be realised – not in this lifetime, anyway.

103
Fact and Truth

No one alive, which means anyone with a brain, can speak of reality. But then I for one don't know that I've got a brain. That's because I don't accept as truth anything I've been told, or anything I presume to know, unless it is in my own experience – my empiric knowledge, now, this moment. And I don't know now at this moment that I have a brain.

It comes down to separating truth from fact. A fact is a fact because it can be proved repeatedly to the satisfaction of the externalised mind. If the fact can't be repeated, or doesn't repeat itself, the mind dismisses it as irrelevant or imagination. Truth, on the other hand, can't be repeated by volitional action or experiment. Truth is only in the moment and beyond human manipulation. The mind, however, regards the fact as the truth, and trying in vain to pursue the truth through the fact, cannot find the truth.

It's an obvious fact that every body has a brain because when the skull is cut open the brain can be seen; and if the brain is dead it can be weighed, measured and studied to the satisfaction of any rational or scientific mind. Moreover, anybody under a medical closed-circuit TV camera can see a projected image of their brain on the monitor screen.

All that is fact. But it's not the truth of the brain because as soon as the electricity is turned off, or the person gets up, the image of the brain vanishes. It's only a fact again when the process is repeated. Even if the image is retained as a negative on a static piece of film, it can't be said that the image represents the condition of the brain now, this moment. To find that out the process must be repeated.

Truth is nothing like that. Truth is immediate, continuous, knowledge, whereas every fact comes down to being not-so-reliable disjointed information. If you knew the fact 'then', you can't be sure it's the fact 'now', because in the world of fact and information everything is moving and changing unforeseeably.

Also, the truth only reveals itself in the purified intellect of the subject, not in the observing mind of another body. Another body-mind can give a reasoned factual interpretation of events and conditions, but not with any certainty, particularly regarding life and death. The reason is that an observing mind, without a purified intellect behind it, will regard living as life, and death as the end of life, whereas the truth is that living is living death and death is life.

Truth 'increases' but does not change. What was truth yesterday is still truth today; and on that unshakeable ground or knowledge, inner revelation continues to expand into greater truth and knowledge.

The fact relates to external sense-perception accompanied by the mind's unreliable interpretations, thoughts and conclusions. But the purified intellect, which is the power of the truth, reveals inner realities. These indeed relate to existence inasmuch as you have read my descriptions of the *scheme* of existence – both concrete and abstract – behind the human mind's usual purview.

The 'real' truth in human affairs addresses the most vital and meaningful subjects in everybody's living life – love, life, truth, death and God. The rational, scientific and human mind of facts, assumptions and theories fails miserably to contribute one iota of truth in these all-important matters.

104
'Here'

You'll recall that the book is titled, *From Here to Reality*. Up to this point I've described the 'Here' part. And just to remind you, that means I've described the whole divine scheme of Here, where you and I are, in finite existence. I've also demonstrated that most radical idea of existence: that existence is not only the finite visible side which our senses and mind confirm, but is also the other abstract side comprising the whole immense cycle of life after the death of the physical body.

If we agree, as logic demands, that you and I are Here now in visible existence, it has to mean that you and I are also Here now in invisible existence since there cannot be only one meaningful side to a whole. With most of the consciousness fixated on the finite side, I have to admit that that leaves the abstract side pretty hazy, and even very doubtful from the usual finite viewpoint.

It's all a matter of 'getting the idea'. Getting the idea does not mean understanding what is said. It means having the knowledge that a statement is true in your own experience and not according to what you've read or been told. This is self-knowledge. And the depth of self-knowledge determines the power of vision to truthfully register the invisible side of existence. (Truthfully means in truth, and not just psychically.)

The spiritual logic of this is that self-knowledge, or knowledge of self, finally amounts to knowledge of the whole – both sides – of existence. *This in turn means that the whole of existence is the whole of both sides of yourself.* (Does anybody seriously contend that they don't have two sides?)

And further, according to the logic, the whole of yourself – visible and invisible – is what you really are *not.*

Your body may die at any moment. That does not mean that your innate intelligence goes anywhere. The intelligence is simply released from having to support the physical anchor of the body in the concrete side of existence. The greater part of your intelligence is always in the abstract. It's a bit like you having the freedom of the whole house while having to keep an eye on the toddler in the nursery. Depending on your concern for the child, you can't really enjoy the unrestricted freedom of the house.

So while your physical body still labours away in tedious time, the greater part of your intelligence (nine-tenths of it would be a fair estimate) is in the far swifter time of the invisible. It is that, in the first instance, which draws you on. In that place you know better.

All that I've written of in the many essays and pages so far is about Here – the sum total of existence, concrete and abstract. As such the book is a gradual descriptive descent into the human psyche, with one aim – to help you, the reader, know yourself better. Inasmuch as the book outlines and addresses much of 'all there is' in the great mystery of being human – it is a continuous exercise in self-knowledge.

Is reality self-knowledge? It seems to me that reality is utterly beyond human existence and therefore beyond self-knowledge. But is it? Or does 'sufficient' self-knowledge simply provide another perspective of self? And who's to say whether what that perspective reveals is reality? But then who's to say that reality is not your self?

I for one suspect that 'your self' is pretty close to the truth – but not close enough. To me, reality finally is what you and I and every thing is. But as such, can it be called 'self' or 'Self', both of which imply a certain centred perspective? I suspect that ultimately self is Self and Self is self. And it seems to me that the much-prized realisation of Self or enlightenment has never given us a realistic and living description of reality.

Anyway, I'm going to give it a shot. So please read on.

105

Logic, the Key

The only way I know to attempt to reveal reality in words, is to begin logically. Logic, you'll recall, is putting first thing first, and beginning at the beginning.

To the rational or scientific mind – which we all have – beginning at the beginning usually means going back into the past. The theoretical scientist does this by presuming a beginning of the universe billions of years ago. The religionists start with the carrot of the future, with heaven or God, or nirvana and enlightenment, all dependent on following a past teaching or way.

Future is another word for becoming, and past is another word for not now. As logic applies only to *now*, past and future are meaningless to the logic of reality.

The fact remains that no one who's 'become' Self, God or enlightened has yet been able to describe reality logically. Every attempt has involved a rational explanation instead of the logical fact. Even after the 'deepest' God-realisation, attempts to communicate the knowledge have always addressed the understanding of the rational mind of the people. But understanding is the mind's limit and satisfying it perpetuates rational ignorance.

So where to begin?

It is unarguable that you and I are earthlings. Earthling means that you and I live in a place, or on a planet, called Earth. We don't really know it's a planet. But we do know, whatever it is called or whatever it is, that our bodies are the product of eating earth food, breathing earth air, drinking earth water and living in the ambience of the earth. We also know that our physical senses, which enable us to apprehend our bodies in relation to the earth, are products of the earth.

Further, everything we use comes out of the earth or is of the earth. Everything that we discover or invent is also of the earth, inasmuch as it is all the product of our senses, our experience of living on earth, and our earth mind, which then invests everything with significance or meaning appropriate to our understanding.

Then there are the extensions of the human body and mind in the form of telescopes and microscopes, and the vehicles to carry the earth body, culminating in spaceships, spacesuits and space stations.

Everything so far mentioned is of the earth body. Then there's the sun, the other planets and galaxies as seen through the earth body and its mechanical and electronic extensions. None of these cosmic bodies can exist, first, without an earth body to perceive them, and second, without an earth mind to award them, or assume, their significance.

Remove the earth body and *everything* vanishes.

But wait a minute. Am I assuming something here?

106

The Hypostasis (actuality) of the World

To us sensory creatures the earth is the only reality. But why don't we see the reality? Clearly, if we were seeing the *reality* of the earth, we who see it would be real too. But as it is, we 'know' instinctively that we're not really real because the physical body we perceive the earth with, dies. And of course that which dies cannot be really real.

So what stops us from seeing the reality, and being the reality?

As this is a real exercise in self-knowledge, I'm not going to answer the question immediately. By now you probably know the answer, anyway. But knowing serves no purpose when it comes down to reality because knowing without self-knowledge is what's getting in the way. That being the case, the solution is for you to follow all that I say in your own (empiric) experience, without referring to what you know.

The way we live our daily lives affirms that we're completely focused on what is unreal. Each of us is vitally and actively concerned with our work, leisure, relationships, health, love-life, money, and so on. And others – some more, some less – apply themselves to the notion that trying to live a life devoted to a pre-scribed religious idea is the way to reality. We engage in all those concerns and activities despite the fact that our perception depends entirely on the physical senses and reasoning mind which are mortal and die with the body.

Are we, as a race of human beings, so universally mistaken as to be so wrong? Or could it be that we are *naturally* equipped and meant to be seeing a greater reality in the objects revealed by our mortal senses? And again, if that is true, what is stopping us?

The inevitable question then is: is there an integrity – a direct reality – behind the instrumentality of our mortal and imperma-nent physical senses? This is the most difficult and debated question on earth.

In reality however it's not difficult, and certainly can't be debated. The reason is that knowledge of the direct reality depends on the degree of self-knowledge. As self-knowledge has many degrees, some people 'see' more of the reality than others; while the common folk of humanity, who live wholly in the world of their senses, have no interest in any abiding reality. In fact, if suddenly exposed to even a reflection of it, they would (as sometimes happens) immediately assume they were going mad. (As everything has to evolve here, the Will's way of gradually facing people with a taste of reality was to induce experimentation with mind-altering drugs.)

The truth is that there *is* a greater reality and it's in every object we see with the senses.

So, what is stopping us? And the answer is the world. The world prevents humanity from seeing the earth as it really is.

The World Begins

The world has been developing in the human psyche since man first started to enter his environment. Before that he was pure spirit, completely unified with the divine idea behind the projection of life on earth. Then, moved by the inscrutable Will, a replica of the divine idea of the earth was projected into the psyche and along with it a *replica* of pure intelligence, or formless man. Pure intelligence, or formless man, is formless because it occupies the deepest level of the psyche 'closest' to impossible-to-describe spirit. Thus the intelligence that man essentially is, although only a replica of the indescribable reality, is akin to that radiant origin.

As all things in the psyche move towards manifestation, the projected replicas of man and the earth escalated up through the psyche, becoming more and more formed, formal and distinguishable. At some point in the pure psyche the intelligence of man perceived the separate replica of the earth. This was a delight. So delighted and entranced was he by the rapidly oscillating and reforming beauty, that gradually, under the impulse of the Will, he began to 'enter' the scintillating pageant.

As he did so, he and the pageant-scene began to break up into separate forms or units. These had very little definition to begin with. But as the Will continued to move everything towards manifestation, and the density of the levels of the psyche increased, man and his environment became more solid. Yet, despite his manifestation as a substantive psychic body amidst the equally psychic substantive environment, he had no problem. His wonderful intelligence still retained the knowledge of his and the earth's sublime origins. He enjoyed both worlds. When the image of his body faded and disappeared (in what he would later call death) he was unaffected and simply 'waited' for another to form for his intelligent enjoyment.

But somewhere within all this man began to form a separative, reflective, thinking and then reasoning mind – an obscure shadow representation of his former intelligence. The mind consisted of mental *reactions* to the environment, whereas beforehand man was simply a *response* to the wonder within allowing him to enjoy the environment. His mental reactions in the form of judgments, deductions and reasoning, created a psychic field of mental agitation. This disturbed his equilibrium and intelligent balance between the two worlds. Unable to resist the attraction of his own thinking, his now degraded intelligence tottered over into the disturbance and he lost the inner vision.

Unbeknown to man during all this, his many thoughts and *lines of thinking* were forming an inner mental grid of psychic mind-stuff – the foundation of his mind. The grid was destitute of any knowledge of the reality behind it. And the more he thought and reasoned along the set lines, the more fixed and rigid the lines and his thinking became; and so did his environment.

This wasn't too bad to start with. Through spaces in the grid, and in moments of stillness, his intelligence could more or less access the enlightening self-knowledge of his divine origins and immortality. But then man began *identifying* with the agitated and disturbing mental world he'd unconsciously created; trying to make sense of his creation, and having to defend himself against it, made him warmly and then heatedly emotional. Fired by humanity's continual emotional outbursts, this clammy psychic stuff stuck to the grid like gooey tar and eventually covered it entirely.

Today the mental grid and its thick covering of emotion is like a lens cap on a camera that allows no light in and no light out. It sits ever-so-neatly over man's inner eye of pure intelligence rendering him virtually blind – so that no direct light of reality shines into him, or is reflected from the physical senses. All he sees is his own distorted and distorting world.

Blind to Reality

What can man do?

First, he can do nothing to overpower the world while he still believes in it and is a slave to it. In short, while he busies himself with knowing everything else but himself. While the reality of man and the earth never ceases shining inwardly, his faith and attachment to his world is greater than his desire for reality. Against the pull of the world, the reality has very little effect on the majority of humans. This is all by the design of the Will and it points to a very drawn-out process equivalent to the imperceptible passage of evolutionary time. (From this arises the notion that all people will eventually become enlightened.)

But sometimes, when an individual's faith in the world is traumatically and permanently destroyed, God or Self-realisation occurs. Such realisations are random and unpredictable. They don't depend on austerities, meditation or following any of the innumerable spiritual ways devised by man in his ignorance of reality. But it has to be said that the whole of the living life from the moment of birth to death *is the only* spiritual path.

Although the deepest God or Self-realisation clears the existential inner space, the 'content' of the realisation is still purely a reflection. This and the truth that such realisations are *ultimately* incomplete, is demonstrated by the fact that none is universal – not given to all men and women. In the integrity of reality no man or woman is special or an exception.

So why doesn't everybody have the direct knowledge of reality?

Because everything we perceive through our physical senses, and every thought and conclusion arrived at in the mind, comes through the heavy, hard and distorting cap of man's self-made world – his world of attachment to beliefs and expectations.

107
The External Reality

Dissolution of the cap of the world covering the eye of pure intelligence allows the light of pure intelligence to shine through and reflect off the purified intellect. The earth of the senses is then seen as it is. This has two seeming aspects, or profundities: the outer-inner and the inner-inner.

The Outer-inner

The outer phenomenal actuality is seen as a whole – even the space. Nothing is particularised because the dividing self has been made transparent. In the light of pure intelligence it has no separative power. Without the separating of objects, nothing is seen to be special. All is intrinsic to the whole.

Even so, every man or woman is initially a sensory creature. The externalising senses are an unavoidable imperative except in dreamless sleep, unconsciousness and dreaming. Everyone waking up from sleep or unconsciousness finds themselves in the sensory phenomenon. The removal of the cap of the world makes no difference. The sensory imperative is the same for everyone – except that purified intelligence provides an immediate knowledge of non-separation.

However, as no one in truth is special, everyone on waking has the *opportunity* to see and be in that extraordinary state. For a split second there is no differentiation. The room and its objects are one whole. There's no separation because there's no separative cognition – no re-cognition – no screen of self, yet. But then a thought occurs. Sometimes the thought after waking from enforced unconsciousness is, 'Where am I?' In that instant of thought the sensory memory kicks in. The troublesome mind is now in action; you re-cognise or recall where you are. And not only that, all your remembered troubles descend on you.

Pure intelligence has no remembered troubles, no troubles. Only what demands action is addressed. Troubles are known to be self-made, the result of attachment to objects or conditions. Attachment has vanished with the screen of the troublesome self. Even so, the essential memory remains. But no longer is there attachment to the memory which causes aimless thinking, worry and daydreaming. The memory is used for specific purposes only as determined by the practical demands of living. There is no thinking back or thinking over things.

Purified intelligence arises from a source in the psyche far deeper than sensory perception. And it is not restricted in power to 'travel up' through the various levels of the psyche and exist at the sensory level. There the intelligence remains centred in the present or presence within while communicating and living in a global society whose focus is on everything but the present and the presence.

The Inner-inner

The inner-inner aspect, or profundity, of purified intelligence is rarer and deeper than the other. The difference is due to Grace or the inscrutable divine Will and is not the result of any individualised purity. The presence of the inner-inner profundity gives an immediate spiritual vision and intuitional knowledge of the reality of the earth.

The earth and everything on it is *within* as a brilliant shimmering ethereal whole without dimension or spatial separation. Nothing moves as we know movement. But there is ceaseless involution. The entire ethereality is disappearing endlessly into itself while at the same time reappearing in increasing scintillating beauty. There's no pause or interruption. It is a complete and continuous harmonious 'becoming' without end or beginning.

In physical time the continuous ethereal involution is represented by the erosion, passing, death and disintegration of all things, and the endless simultaneous reappearance of form and matter. But in its own right the ethereality is the sustaining and motivating power behind all phenomenal movement and change without any variation in its essence. The apparent motion of involution is due to the living physicality of the observer.

The earth in all its intrinsic splendour is here but with no differentiation of oceans, clouds, land-masses or the innumerable forms of nature. It is the essence, the source, of all that is beautiful on earth, and of man and woman's fundamental impulse to love, be loved and be absorbed. It is the earth – and amazingly, it is what we are.

But can it be named earth any more than we can be named man or woman? In a differentiated sense, yes, inasmuch as it is the reality of the perceived earth and us. Essentially, however, it is simply life on earth, or more simply, life.

Intelligence

Life and intelligence are inseparable. So where is the intelligence?

The intelligence is seeing the vision. There'd be no vision and no life without it. The intelligence is observing the ethereality from 'outside', showing that it is not part of what is being seen. It just makes the vision of life possible. Although one with life on earth the intelligence clearly is not life. Its source has to be elsewhere.

The intelligence in everybody is the same essential intelligence (just as the life in everybody is the one life). But the intelligence has to be purified to see the inner-inner reality. When purified the intelligence remains indescribable because it can no longer be called 'I'.

The vision described is spiritual vision. Not psychic. Or perhaps it's as close as the psyche gets to spirit. Spiritual vision, nevertheless, does not present an image as in psychic visions. Spiritual vision combines with spiritual intuition to become pure knowledge. Like pure intelligence, pure knowledge has no form; it is direct and enables the vision and its significance to be described without the distortion of interpretations. Spiritual vision is immediate, occurring now in the moment of seeing. Its uniqueness, compared with thought, is that it may be *re-seen* as it is at any moment. It cannot be remembered. It must be re-seen.

The reason is that inner-inner spiritual vision is always of the aspect of reality being addressed. The reality is always there. If, for instance, the purified intelligence focused on the source of pure intelligence mentioned above, the vision and knowledge of it would be there. It's possible that somewhere in this book the source has been described or referred to. If so, the author can't remember where. So he'll have to leave it to you the reader to find – either in these pages or preferably within your own reality.

108
Reality

Any reality we intuit or speak of while alive has to be relative – relative to our sense-perceptive brain. Clearly, reality can't be modified or secondary to anything. However, since the mystical life in its many aspects seems in the moment to affirm (or indicate) an unconditioned reality, we human beings endeavour to keep trying to describe it.

And who's to say we're wrong? Maybe the brain, the senses and the body are simply reality temporarily manifesting in form. Maybe at any moment when the human form is nearing dissolution, as in the terminal illness of a loved one, reality shows itself in the innocent sweetness shining in the form. Perhaps to the one who dies the shining is their enduring reality? Anyway, it seems to me that the shining is potential in everyone and is in fact each individual's immortal reality.

But the question persists, what is the reality? Can it be explained logically so that the entire premise of existence is accounted for?

To me everyone's reality is their self-knowledge – self-knowledge gathered over many, many living lives; in other words, real knowledge of living and the world in their innumerable dual aspects, together with the climacterics of life and death. For 'many living lives' implies being born and dying many times.

Each manifested individual or body is clearly sustained and animated by life. When life withdraws the body dies. But life is not individual. Life is in every living thing and as such is universal, yet completely subtle and beyond registration by the mind. I can know I am alive but knowledge of the life in me escapes me; similarly the self-knowledge in everyone is inaccessible by the mind.

The reason is that the self-knowledge accrued from living life to living life is preserved in the life of the individual. And it is the self-knowledge that distinguishes the life, which otherwise is all-pervading and undistinguished. 'My life' in each birth is my self-knowledge. That self-knowledge is the reality that directs each living life according to the great purpose behind the mystery of human existence.

This is not reincarnation; it is recurrence in form – the recurrence of 'my self-knowledge' as my reality, my shining or light in each birth. Each living life adds to the depth of self-knowledge. 'By my knowledge will you recognise me – the degree of your own reality.'

Everyone has far more self-knowledge than they may display in this living life. Only that which is necessary for coping and dealing with existing circumstances is generally active.

I am not attempting to define the indefinable, since the mystery of God is always indefinable. I merely attempt within the scheme of things to make more clear the amazing and wonderful venture without end that each one of us is engaged in notwithstanding the difficulties and traumas that must be passed through. Each living life is our contribution in self-knowledge to the inscrutable purpose of the whole.

Thank you for listening.

Bibliographic Notes

Full bibliographic details of Barry Long's books in English and in translation are available at www.barrylongbooks.com.

Works by Barry Long cited in this book

MAKING LOVE
Published as a book and a two-CD set, this is the central statement of Barry Long's teaching on love between man and woman. He explains why so many couples cannot reach the true fulfilment of lovemaking and offers a revolutionary solution – sexual love the divine way. Here is his step-by-step lesson in what to do and what not to do [see p. 85].

THE ORIGINS OF MAN AND THE UNIVERSE
Barry Long's master-work, containing gnostic revelations about the structure of the human psyche, the Seven Levels of Mind, terrestrial evolution and the *Myth That Came to Life* [see pp. 136, 235, 251, 328].

MY LIFE OF LOVE AND TRUTH
Barry Long's spiritual autobiography [see pp. 147, 197, 249].

START MEDITATING NOW
Available as an MP3 download from barrylong.org [see p. 42].

SONGS OF LIFE
Available as an MP3 download from barrylong.org [see p. 214].

EPIC SPIRITUAL POEMS
Available as an MP3 download from barrylong.org [see p. 141].

WHERE THE SPIRIT SPEAKS TO ITS OWN
Collected poems with Barry Long's commentary, subtitled "The Passion of Spiritual Awakening." Contains the complete version of the epic poem, "Man the Thinking Piece of Sand" quoted in the text [see p. 151].

Other books by Barry Long

STILLNESS IS THE WAY
Based on an intensive meditation class taught by Barry Long in 1984.

ONLY FEAR DIES
The causes and effects of unhappiness and how to be rid of them.

A PRAYER FOR LIFE
The cause and cure of terrorism, war and human suffering.

TO WOMAN IN LOVE
Answers questions about love, relationships and the spiritual life.

TO MAN IN TRUTH
How to be true to life and love while facing the stress of the world.

RAISING CHILDREN IN LOVE, JUSTICE AND TRUTH
Detailed advice for parents, children and young people.

MEDITATION – A FOUNDATION COURSE
A book of ten lessons – the practical and effective bestseller.

KNOWING YOURSELF
Discovering the true by discarding the false.

WISDOM AND WHERE TO FIND IT
Early talks from the period just after Barry Long's mystic death.

THE WAY IN
A book of self-discovery – collected writings from the 1980s.

Audio books read by Barry Long

Start Meditating Now
A Journey in Consciousness
Seeing Through Death
Making Love
How to Live Joyously

All Barry Long titles are published in the English language by Barry Long Books, an imprint of The Barry Long Foundation.

The Foundation holds an archive of audio and video recordings of Barry Long's talks 1986–2002. For current details of the available recordings see www.barrylong.org.

THE BARRY LONG FOUNDATION INTERNATIONAL
PO Box 838, Billinudgel, NSW 2483, Australia
www.barrylong.org
Email: contact@barrylong.org